Waterfront Workers

The Working Class in American History

Editorial Advisors

David Brody
Alice Kessler-Harris
David Montgomery
Sean Wilentz

*A list of books in the series
appears at the end of this book.*

Contents

Preface

The essays published here are intended to provide an introduction to current work on longshoremen. They are also intended to make a contribution to the debate on race and class in American labor history. I can speak for all the contributors in saying that we believe in the centrality of understanding the convergence of race and class in American labor history and that we are committed to continuing research on this vital subject.

We all gratefully acknowledge the assistance of the staff of the University of Illinois Press, in particular Patricia Hollahan, Emily Rogers, and Richard Wentworth, the director. In addition, we would like to thank Professors David Brundage and David Brody for reading earlier versions of the manuscript as well as the drafts of the chapters which are included here.

In addition, each contributor wishes to acknowledge particular assistance. Eric Arnesen would like to call attention to an earlier draft of his essay which was presented at the International Institute of Social History's Racism and the Labor Market Conference, held in Amsterdam in September 1991, and which appeared in the volume of conference papers, *Racism and the Labor Market: Historical Studies* (Bern: Peter Lang, 1995), edited by Marcel Van Der Linden and Jan Lucassen. In addition he would like to thank Katrin Schultheiss, Cal Winslow, Julia Greene, Bruce Nelson, Colin Davis, Dana Frank, Karen Shapiro, and Daniel Letwin for their comments on earlier drafts of the essay.

Colin Davis is thankful for support from Faculty Development Grants of the University of Alabama at Birmingham and the Irish Cultural Institute. He also thanks Bruce Nelson and Eric Arnesen for providing invaluable comments on the essay.

Howard Kimeldorf presents his chapter as part of a larger project that incorporates insights from colleagues and friends too numerous to mention here. For this particular study, he is most grateful to the contributors to this volume, particularly Colin Davis, Bruce Nelson, and Cal Winslow for their helpful and constructive comments.

Bruce Nelson expresses his thanks and acknowledges his deep indebtedness to Nancy Quam-Wickham, Eugene Denis Vrana, and, above all, Antonio (Tony) Salcido. He also thanks Walter Williams (1918–95) and honors his memory.

I would like to thank all the contributors for what has been a collaborative project. In addition, I want to thank the organizers of two conferences, the Southwest Labor History Conference held in Santa Cruz in 1994 and the 1995 Mystic Seaport Conference, "Race, Ethnicity and Power in Maritime America," sponsored by the Connecticut Afro-American Historical Society and the New England American Studies Association, for encouraging research and debate on subjects considered here, in particular Jim Miller, David Brundage, and Dana Frank. I also want to thank the faculty and staff of the Northern College for Adult Residential Education, Wentworth Castle, Barnsley, and the University of York, both in England, for their essential support in keeping this project going from a distance. Finally thanks to Steve Early and Eric Hodderson for steady encouragement. My thanks must also go to Faith, Jessie, Samantha, Rosalie, and Matthew, who all share with me a thirst for history as well as the dream that racial injustice, which so afflicts our country's history, can still be overcome.

Introduction

Calvin Winslow

The history of longshoremen, writes E. J. Hobsbawm, is filled with "dramatic events and personalities," great triumphs as well as tragic defeats.[1] Almost everywhere, the ports, strategic intersections in the commerce of industrial capitalism, were the scenes of conflict. Waterfront workers persistently fought for trade union organization. They sought a means to challenge an industrial system which left them impoverished and powerless. They also fought to improve the conditions of the work, which was heavy and dangerous, as well as for a way to create a fair distribution of work in a highly competitive and chaotic industry. Against them were a host of employers, large and small: stevedores, small contractors, immigrant labor merchants, sharks and padrones, dock owners, as well as industrialists. By the beginning of the twentieth century, these employers were led by large shipping companies, including, increasingly, the great international shipping trusts. These trusts, the International Merchant Marine, Cunard Lines, and North German Lloyd, immensely powerful in themselves, were in turn allied with banks and railroads and sometimes the state itself.

On the piers, conditions were crude, and the longshoremen's work changed little from generation to generation. This was true throughout the industry. On the eve of World War I, for example, coal heaving was still done in hand baskets in Perth Amboy, on the Jersey side of the New York Harbor. There was not a single moving crane on the New York waterfront in 1914.[2] On the Gulf Coast, five-hundred-pound bales of cotton were hand-loaded into the holds of ships, by gangs of screwmen relying chiefly on physical strength and skill, aided by large metal jackscrews and wooden posts.[3] On Puget Sound, coarse lumber products, including whole logs, were piled on wharves and loaded into archaic steamers; this work was considered as rugged as any task performed by longshoremen.[4]

The shippers opposed the demands of these workers. Almost universally, they considered longshoremen, however experienced, unskilled workers, common laborers at best, who were abundant and easily replaceable. The waterfront neighborhoods abounded with them, and their ranks were continuously increased by others—men with strong backs: peasants and agricultural laborers from Ireland's West Country; migrants from Sicily and southern Italy; African Americans from Virginia, the Carolinas, and the Mississippi Delta; Poles and Swedes, loggers and sailors; ambitious newcomers as well as the victims of hard times and hard lives. Most employers considered it only natural to hire such men one day at a time, even a few hours at a time. They opposed permanent trade union organization and resisted any system which fixed hours and wages, except when this was clearly on their own terms. Consequently, while the history of trade unionism on the waterfront is long, victories were never easily won and were often fleeting.

Perhaps this helps account for the explosiveness of longshoremen and the fact that waterfront strikes could be gigantic, all-or-nothing affairs, and that small disputes might spread and paralyze entire ports and, on occasions, regions. This was the case in New Orleans in the years before World War I. It was also true on the West Coast, nearly half a century later. The "Big Strike" of 1934, the eighty-three-day San Francisco general strike, ended in triumph for longshoremen and began a crusade of insurgent unionism on the Pacific Coast.[5]

But other strikes, just as gigantic, were lost. The pattern almost everywhere was one of recurrent explosions, separated by long intervals of relative inactivity and apathy.[6] In New York, a series of such upheavals led to tragic endings. The first of three huge waterfront strikes, the "Big Strike" of longshoremen in 1887, led by the Knights of Labor, tied up New York Harbor for a month, only to end in devastating defeat, leaving longshoremen demoralized and with no union at all. The longshoremen struck again in 1907—for ten cents an hour: thirty thousand longshoremen joined a strike which began with a May Day celebration and lasted until mid-June. And in 1919 New York longshoremen struck yet again, in a dispute which at one point involved one hundred and fifty thousand men and women, the largest longshore strike ever, only to lose again, in a defeat which not only allowed the shippers a free hand but also opened the door for racketeers, widespread crime, and a degree of trade union corruption perhaps unparalleled.[7]

Such drama, with such contradictory results, was not confined to the international ports, nor was it restricted to the traditional forms and issues of industrial conflict. In more modest settings, longshoremen also established themselves as class-conscious, militant workers, imaginative and often fearless in the face of staggering odds. On Michigan's Upper Peninsula in the 1890s, for example, Irish iron ore trimmers fought "wars" with shippers and Irish strikebreakers and more than once displayed their strength and solidarity with armed marches through the streets of Marquette and Escanaba, much to the amazement of local citizens of all classes.[8] The first black trade unions were formed by black longshoremen, and in Charleston the Longshoremen's Protective Union Association was referred to as "the most powerful organization of the colored laboring class in South Carolina."[9] In the 1880s and 1890s, the organizations of black dockers in New Orleans were well known throughout the South, yet, even in such smaller ports as Mobile, Galveston, and Hampton Roads, black longshoremen established themselves as the aristocrats of southern black labor and in so doing challenged the basic tenets of the segregated South.[10] In 1920, New York longshoremen supported opponents of British rule in Ireland. Irish women, nationalists, organized a strike and boycott in solidarity with the imprisoned nationalist mayor of Cork, Terence MacSwiney. They gained the support of the 250 African American longshoremen in Chelsea. These longshoremen were in turn supported by Marcus Garvey and the United Negro Improvement Association in what was altogether an unusual and unexpected display of solidarity.[11] The year 1919 was all but apocalyptic on the waterfront, with strikes from Boston to Seattle, including four major disputes in New York Harbor alone.

Solidarity and internationalism are themes in longshore history. The occupation carried with it an identity which was powerful and possibly universal. "We believed fervently in international organization," recalled the London dockers' leader, Tom Mann, in the aftermath of the 1889 strike. Mann and the British dockers sent organizers to Boston, New York, and Philadelphia in the 1890s to rekindle trade unionism and forge links across the Atlantic.[12] In Seattle, in October 1919, longshoremen impressed fellow workers by discovering rifles labeled "sewing machines" bound for Siberia, Admiral Kolchak, and the civil war in Russia. They not only exposed this deceit but then refused to load the rifles in a display of internationalism, which worried, to say the least, the upper classes already concerned about the intentions of Seattle's workers.[13] San Francisco longshoremen, organized in the International Longshoremen's and Warehousemen's Union (ILWU), were led by an Australian, Harry Bridges. After their victory in 1934, they proclaimed themselves "Lords of the Docks," immodestly announcing, "we are the most militant and organized body of men the world has ever seen."[14] But others might have said the same. Longshoremen everywhere played an important part in the development of the labor movement. As Hobsbawm suggests, longshoremen were "powerful" workers; they carried "strong traditions of militancy" and were taken "extremely seriously" by the employers and the authorities alike.[15]

There were limitations to this power, however, and despite their ability to disrupt economies, longshoremen were not often favored by the odds. Repeatedly, for example, they fought the shippers alone. While they worked alongside seamen, teamsters, and railroad workers, only rarely were alliances organized, and few of these were lasting. Agreements were for the most part settled with employers separately. International cooperation was transitory. In 1907, James Connolly, the Irish socialist organizing for the Industrial Workers of the World (IWW) in New York, complained that the New York longshoremen had been betrayed even by seamen belonging to some of Europe's most progressive unions.[16] The International Longshoremen's Association (ILA) leadership strongly opposed sympathy strikes and actively fought to prevent them. One result of this, in the autumn of 1936, was a rank-and-file seamen's and longshoremen's general strike which tied up ports and lake harbors across the country. This rebellion, according to Louis Adamic, was directed as much against the leadership of the AFL maritime unions "as against the employers who supported (and had actively helped to corrupt) that leadership."[17] Nevertheless, the evidence of cooperation among longshoremen from port to port is limited, even in such strike waves. The outlook of longshoremen was just as often local as national, let alone international, and solidarity was mostly portwide at best. The sheer variety of the longshore experience along the American coastline was an imposing obstacle to organizers, and this fact alone does much to explain the difficulties faced by both the ILA and the ILWU—the latter did often

© 1998 by the Board of Trustees of
the University of Illinois

Manufactured in the United States of America

1 2 3 4 5 C P 5 4 3 2 1

This book is printed on acid-free paper.

Library of Congress Cataloging-in-Publication Data
Waterfront workers : new perspectives on race and class / edited
by Calvin Winslow.
p.   cm. — (The working class in American history)
Includes bibliographical references and index.
ISBN 0-252-02392-7 (acid-free paper). —
ISBN 0-252-06691-x (pbk. : acid-free paper)
1. Stevedores—United States—History. 2. Afro-American steve-
dores—United States—History. 3. Trade-unions—Stevedores—
United States—History. 4. Strikes and lockouts—Stevedores—
United States—History. I. Winslow, Calvin. II. Series.
HD8039.L82U733   1998
331.88'11387544'0973—dc21   97-33754
CIP

Waterfront Workers

New Perspectives on Race and Class

Edited by Calvin Winslow

University of Illinois Press

Urbana and Chicago

support solidarity—in building and holding together national unions of waterfront workers.

The dockers' ability to strike was restricted by higher authorities, including the state, which in the name of the public interest, including national defense, often combined with the shippers to defeat the longshoremen. It used the power of the courts and the injunction and, if necessary, the police, and in 1919 even the army. In the aftermath of World War I, the FBI kept all longshore leaders under surveillance, even the conservative ILA international president, T. V. O'Connor, who at that very time was colluding with shippers and conservative trade unionists to destroy the IWW's marine unions on Puget Sound.[18] After World War II, turmoil on the New York waterfront again prompted government intervention, this time presidential. In 1948, President Truman used provisions of the recently passed Taft-Hartley Act to obtain a federal injunction restricting strikes in the harbor. In 1959, President Eisenhower used the act again, in response to a strike that brought the East Coast and Gulf ports to a standstill.[19] Despite this, in the sixties, the government counted on the collaboration of union leaders on both coasts to ensure the steady flow of military goods and personnel into Vietnam. Again in 1971, the Taft-Hartley act was used in the strike of the West Coast longshoremen, this time invoked by President Nixon. This did not deter insurgent longshoremen, however, from conducting the longest longshore strike in United States history.[20]

Charles Barnes, the industrial reformer who wrote the classic study *The Longshoremen*, emphasized the fact that waterfront work was intense and dangerous. At the same time, he wrote: "It is probable that there is no other heavy physical work which is accompanied with so much overtime and such stretches of toil without interruption."[21] Dennis Delaney, a New York longshoremen, told congressional investigators that "After working day and night, longshoremen are ordered back again under a penalty. 'Don't come any more if you don't come back.'"[22] Timothy Carroll, a Liverpool docker who migrated to New York "to make his fortune," discovered "Chinese labor" instead and was often forced to carry 280-pound sacks of flour for periods as long as fourteen hours.[23] The term "Chinese labor" referred to harsh conditions of work, but it was also an example of protest expressed in the racial and imperial language of the times.

In addition to enduring oppressive toil, longshoremen were casual laborers, for whom the method of hiring was the daily shape-up in circumstances of intense competition. This system formed the outlook of the longshoremen. Traditional accounts of longshoremen quite rightly emphasized these conditions, particularly hiring practices, in the waterfront system of industrial relations, often with an eye to reform.[24] Certainly, there was cause for concern. In 1930, an anonymous writer, shocked by the hiring system on the New York waterfront, reached back to Henry Mayhew for help describing the "shape-up" in New York. In *London Labour and the London Poor*, published in 1861, Mayhew, the well-known Victorian investigator, had described hiring at the gates to the London docks: it was a "sight to sadden the most callous, to see thousands of men struggling for only a day's hire; the scuffle being made the fiercer by the knowledge that hundreds out of the number there assembled must be left to idle the day in want."[25] In the 1920s, this system still prevailed in New York. On Columbia Street in Red Hook, Brooklyn's Italian quarter, thousands of men would assemble at daybreak, overflowing into side streets, and await word of arriving ships, then rush to the docks to shape again. There were always police on duty to maintain order. But sometimes they were not sufficient, and foremen would use clubs and fire hoses to clear the gates.[26]

The employers, at times pressed by civil authorities and outside reformers, began the process of reorganization and rationalization of hiring practices, though only when the disorder of the industry seemed out of control. By the eve of World War I, American opponents of "the system"—casual work and the shape-up—could point to numerous northern European ports as examples of the success of rationalization in terms of industrial efficiency.[27] In Portland, Los Angeles, and Seattle, West Coast shippers, as part of the open-shop campaign, abolished "the system" in the early 1920s, but, again, after a long period of conflict and the defeat of the local unions. In Seattle, the first American port decasualized, this amounted to a "counterrevolution on the docks" and put an end to the 1919 contract which mandated hiring preference for union members from a list controlled by the ILA. In 1920, longshoremen struck to defend this agreement, but O'Connor, the union's international president, refused to sanction the strike and revoked the Seattle local's charter, and the longshoremen were defeated. The shippers took exclusive control of hiring, instituted a company union, made hundreds of workers ineligible for work on the docks, and maintained anti-union policies until the revival of unionism in the 1930s.[28] On the East Coast, the ILA defended "the system" and used it in collaboration with the employers, as a perverse form of closed shop; it asked only that union members be given preference, promising in return to deliver these to the employers, whatever the circumstances. ILA "President for Life" Joe Ryan steadfastly supported casual hiring and the shape-up, even after World War II.[29] Although there is evidence that in New Orleans employment practices were "less competitive and less ritualized" than in New York, this was the product of union power and ended in the twenties.[30] By then, there were "more rumors . . . of the abuse of the hiring power by the foremen than at any other port in the United States."[31] The shippers who favored "the system" argued that the nature of the industry demanded it. Profits depended on fast turnarounds, but the sea, the tides, and the traffic made exact planning impossible. Still, "The ship must sail on time," so the shippers compensated by taking full advantage of casual labor and extreme competition in overcrowded labor markets.[32]

In New York, in 1915, there were three longshoremen for every job. On a "normal day" on the Chelsea waterfront, twenty-five hundred men might be hired, but five thousand or more would shape-up.[33] In New Orleans nearly all the goods from the lower Mississippi passed over the city's wharves. A city guide in 1885 reported that nearly two million bales of cotton passed through the city annually, "requiring an army of men, and furnish[ing] occupation for nearly two-thirds of the population." In 1930, there was "no limit to the supply of labor in the port."[34] That same year, the number of longshoremen in the United States was estimated to be 120,000, with the largest number in New York—more than 50,000. New Orleans followed with 10,000 workers. The ports of Boston, Philadelphia, and Baltimore had considerable numbers of longshoremen, as did Hampton Roads, the Gulf Ports, and the Pacific Coast ports already mentioned. On the Great Lakes, where the ILA originated, there were thousands more, and there were also longshoremen in river port towns, as well as in the smaller ocean ports. There were hundreds of ILA locals, ranging from those with a handful of members to those that were thousands of members strong.[35]

The power of longshoremen, then, was not simply strategic. It was also a product of a "system" in which competition had to be overcome because survival depended on cooperation and a sense of common identity. The most experienced as well as the least skilled dockers depended on others—in perilous settings their lives literally depended upon this cooperation. Longshoremen worked in gangs, and while employers might well see them as individual "human machines," in practice longshoremen were unique. They were required, in David Montgomery's words, "to push or pull enormous weights, aided only by the most elementary inclines, pulleys, winches, hooks, and screws and above all by their own teamwork."[36] This conditioned the longshoreman's identity and consciousness and created a common outlook which could extend even into the crowded waterfront neighborhoods which also depended for survival on the labor of longshoremen. It helps explain the common classification—longshoreman—a term used almost exclusively for a vast array of men, of whom the most skilled, riggers for example, were simply the advanced guard of an army of laborers, loaders, shovelers, pushers, and general helpers. This classification included even the "shenangos"—marginal men at the bottom of the occupational hierarchy, whose strength might in fact be quite small and who were indeed unskilled. Still, these men, whatever their race or ethnicity, were all "longshoremen." This can only be understood in terms of the unique working conditions of longshoremen, and above all the shared experience of "the system"—an experience which carried on in the consciousness of these workers even after it was abolished, a memory still shaping their identity.

How did longshoremen respond to such circumstances? Not always as reformers, as union leaders preferred. Some longshoremen attempted to compensate with petty crime and pilferage, arguing these were the necessary and just perquisites of the occupation. Still others voiced their complaints in the language of revolution, and on the West Coast shiploads of lumber from the ports of Puget Sound and the Columbia River bound for booming southern California often carried the literature of the IWW. On these docks, radical seamen and loggers mingled with longshoremen, a highly inflammable mix. Perhaps more than most groups of workers, longshoremen have been the subjects of moralizing and myth. Predictably, they were often held in contempt by their employers. More interestingly, however, they frequently failed to live up to the expectations of sympathizers and supporters. Social workers saw them as drinkers and brawlers who neglected their families and whose behaviors bordered on criminality. Industrial reformers were bewildered by their reluctance to challenge the shape-up and casual labor. Socialists were frustrated by the longshoremen's suspicious exclusiveness and parochialism, and by their conservatism, as well as by a bigotry which sometimes seemed pervasive in their culture and communities.

But they did respond, and in ways that made sense, given their experience. Consider, for example, the issue of the shape-up and casual labor. The cruelty of this system was self-apparent, but the longshoremen's response was not. Why were longshoremen reluctant to embrace rationalization and modernization? The answer becomes apparent when we attempt to understand the issue from their point of view. They endured casualism not because they were shortsighted or ignorant but because they may have considered their employers' alternatives equally threatening. The longshoremen feared restriction because they feared unemployment. Their work was irregular, often seasonal, and even the most steadily employed experienced long periods without work. When reform appeared to mean restricting access to work and threatened unemployment, not only for an individual docker but for members of his family, friends, and neighbors, self-preservation often seemed the issue. It was in this context that longshoremen, adopting a somewhat perplexing yet authentic form of solidarity, preferred "the system," however reluctantly. But the choice was not really up to them, and the fatalism of the longshoremen, which so often dismayed observers, was as much realism as apathy.[37] When the alternative involved workers' control over hiring, for example, through a union hiring hall, longshoremen lost their reluctance. This was one of the great achievements of the ILWU's "men of '34." But when the union was the ILA, the prospect became complicated. Experience indicated that ILA control might offer only an alternate avenue to manipulation, compounding favoritism with additional kickbacks and corruption.

The essays in this volume all begin with longshoremen themselves. They explore varying experiences and responses to conditions of work and conflicts on the waterfront. In particular, they focus on race and on the complex relationships involved in the intersection of race, class, and ethnicity. Few issues have been more important on the waterfront. Almost everywhere the waterfront was cosmopolitan. There were Irish dockers from Chelsea to Ashtabula to Tacoma, but workers of many races, ethnicities, and nationalities congregated on and around the docks. African Americans, Poles, Scandinavians, Germans, and Italians joined the Irish on New York's docks. Eastern Europeans worked alongside Irish and blacks in Philadelphia, and, farther south, African Americans were the majority, for example, on the Baltimore waterfront in the 1930s, where they numbered 60 percent of the workforce. In the southern ports, work was divided between blacks and whites, while on the Pacific Coast, waterfront workers were mostly white. Chinese were excluded, and African Americans were relatively scarce until World War II. Still, there were often sailors on the docks, and these men came from many lands. Seasonally, laborers of all sorts found their ways to the ports—so the workforce was heterogeneous everywhere, and, predictably, there was always competition, providing possibilities to divide and rule.

But above all it was race which divided the longshoremen, with consequences which were obvious, particularly in times of conflict with the employers. Solidarity was at best partial, and always conditioned by prejudice. Across the United States, the "color line" separated black and white longshoremen into separate, unequal, and often hostile camps. As early as the 1840s the New York Irish were attempting to drive black workers off the docks. This culminated in the racial violence of the draft riots of 1863. Gangs of white workingmen took advantage of the riots to introduce a "whites-only" rule on the waterfront. Committees of the "Longshoremen's Association" patrolled the piers in the daylight hours, insisting that "the colored people must and shall be driven to other parts of industry, and that the work upon the docks . . . shall be attended to solely by and absolutely by members of the 'Longshoremen's Association' and such white laborers as they see fit to permit upon the premises." After sundown, these "committees" were replaced by parties of men and boys, including longshoremen, who were responsible for a number of the riot's most grisly killings.[38] Docks, occupations, local unions, even whole industries were segregated, a circumstance that frequently resulted in the total exclusion of African Americans. As these essays show, the trade unions often sanctioned this division and participated in the institutionalization of a racial hierarchy everywhere. In ports such as New York, this was complicated by the fact that Italians were also considered nonwhite and organized into separate local unions. On the docks of Portland, Oregon, even after the strikes of 1934, longshoremen who were members of the ILWU practiced industrial apartheid. The national leaders of the ILA boasted of black vice presidents, scores of black delegates at its conventions, and thousands of black members, yet in practice its locals were segregated North and South.[39]

Solidarity demanded coming to terms with prejudice as well as with the institutions of segregation, and these essays also consider efforts to overcome racial and ethnic division. But they go beyond simply reporting the proclamations of the unions and the statements of their leaders. They consider, for better or worse, the beliefs and especially the actions of the longshoremen themselves. It is in this sense that the essays in this volume might also be called "histories from the bottom up." The experience of the longshoremen was never consistent nor universal, and neither was it predictable. The longshoremen, like "Christ's poor," were not always pretty, to borrow E. P. Thompson's admonition in *The Making of the English Working Class*.[40] Nevertheless, the results of these investigations significantly add to our understanding of race and class on the waterfront.

Racial and ethnic animosity was pervasive but never predetermined, and patterns of behavior and organization varied enormously. E. Franklin Frazer, for example, investigating African American longshoremen in

New York in the years following World War I, found that they were unanimous in believing they were the victims of racial discrimination. They believed this was the result of the policies of the shippers, the practices of the ILA, and the prejudices of the other workers, above all the Irish longshoremen. Yet, with equal unanimity, they supported the ILA and were deeply suspicious of Frazier, lest his study be used against the union. They were also careful to qualify their characterizations of other workers. Black longshoremen reported that the Italians showed "less antipathy" toward them than others and as a result were the first to accept blacks. But, they believed, the Italians were "assimilating . . . the prejudices of the white men, in order apparently to insure their own standing." The blacks found the "greatest antagonism" to be "on the part of the Irish," but warned that "during hard times . . . common misfortune softens the prejudice even of the Irish."[41] Black longshoremen often supported the ILA even when it was challenged by more radical unions, as when the ILWU campaigned in the South in the late 1930s. But they were far from oblivious to discrimination within their own union. A Brooklyn longshoreman explained, "We are in the union today . . . because the white man had to take us in for his own protection. Outside the organization the Negro could scab on the white man. Inside he can't. In return for this we get a share of the work, the protection of the union contract and organizational support."[42] Black longshoremen consistently supported trade unionism, yet they did so in circumstances which they did not control and which greatly restricted their choices.

When the IWW challenged the segregated unions of the ILA on the East and Gulf Coasts, they promised one union for all workers. The sensationalist report of the Department of the Navy, published in December 1918, found IWW members in almost every port in the United States, including throughout the South. Surely this was a great exaggeration. But in circumstances which were adverse in extreme, the IWW accomplished more than is commonly known, though they rarely won the support of more than a small proportion of longshoremen.[43] This was not the case in Philadelphia, however. Howard Kimeldorf's essay, "Radical Possibilities? The Rise and Fall of Wobbly Unionism on the Philadelphia Docks," explores the unique experience of the Philadelphia longshoremen who, led by an African American longshoreman, Benjamin Fletcher, organized the port for the IWW's Marine Transport Workers Union, Local 8. They generated a remarkable group of indigenous black leaders, and, to almost everyone's amazement, survived as the union of Philadelphia dockers for nearly a decade.

Class conflict conditioned race consciousness, and in the strikes of 1907 and 1919 in New York Harbor, there were movements to overcome racial and ethnic discord.[44] In the 1907 strike, black longshoremen were the first out. In 1919, black locals of the ILA joined Italian and Irish locals in a harborwide wildcat strike in defiance of the union's leaders and used the opportunity to challenge racial discrimination in both the union and on the docks. My own essay, "'Men of the Lumber Camps Come to Town': New York Longshoremen in the Strike of 1907," explores the perplexities of race and ethnic relations. The strike, led by Italian immigrants, was supported by all nationalities on the waterfront, including the growing numbers of African Americans. They played an important role in the crucial first days of the strike, and then joined in the movement for an industrial union on the New York waterfront. Colin Davis's essay, "All I Got's a Hook: New York Longshoremen and the 1948 Dock Strike," continues the New York story in the aftermath of World War II, when rank-and-file longshoremen, now faced with an entrenched and reactionary union leadership, responded with a wildcat strike movement, the success of which depended once again on uniting workers across the color line.

The 1907 strike in New Orleans strengthened an interracial alliance which allowed longshoremen to resist employers, as well as state and local authorities, even though, as Eric Arnesen noted in *Waterfront Workers of New Orleans*, this "violated the sentiment of the community."[45] His essay here, "Biracial Waterfront Unionism in an Age of Segregation," extends his analysis to other southern ports. He argues that throughout the South, longshoremen attempted to establish unity, even though organized in separate local unions. They developed a form of biracial unionism which, while "imperfect," represented an "unparalleled strategy." It reflected the South's prevailing ideology, but also promoted the possibility of black and white unity against the common enemy, the shippers. Such movements were exceptions in the longshoremen's story, yet, as these chapters show, they appear recurrently, expressions on the waterfront of a tradition of interracial trade unionism never dominant in American society but always present.

Today, as Bruce Nelson argues, the analysis of racial division is a concern of greatest importance to historians. Nelson examined the origins of the ILWU in *Workers on the Waterfront: Seamen, Longshoremen and Unionism in the 1930s*. Now he looks again at the union in his essay, "The 'Lords of the Docks' Reconsidered: Race Relations among West Coast Longshoremen, 1933–61." The ILWU also made promises to black longshoremen: "Our Union represents a New Deal for Negroes."[46] But, as

Nelson shows, this promise was not always kept. San Francisco longshore-men, for example, did sometimes promote interracial unionism, as well as the cause of equal rights. As recently as the 1980s, there were reports of business agents singling out ships bound for South Africa for "special treatment."[47] Yet, in fact, union policy was at best highly inconsistent. In Los Angeles Local 13, the focus of Nelson's investigation, there was wide-spread support for the exclusion of African Americans from the docks, despite the stated policies of the Communist president of the union, Harry Bridges. Bridges, rather than challenge racist practices, made peace with the local, no doubt with the purpose of preserving the union on the Pacific Coast, as he did with the white longshoremen in Portland, Oregon.

Racial division seems a constant in the history of American workers. Yet, this should not lead us to neglect struggles for black and white unity, however much they may seem to have been lost causes and their adher-ents victims of history. Indeed, there still may be much to learn from the experiences of longshoremen concerning the issues of race relations, positive as well as negative. There were few settings with a longer and richer history of black, white, and multiethnic interactions than the wa-terfront. Taken together, these essays show a field of remarkable diversity and vitality and they add significant original materials to our understand-ing of race and ethnicity in working-class history.

In the past thirty years, waterfront work has been entirely transformed. Mechanization, foremost containerization, the process in which cargo is prepacked in large containers which can then be loaded directly by crane from trucks into the holds of ships, has decimated the ranks of longshore-men, replacing them, for the most part, with crane operators and truck drivers. The 1960 Mechanization and Modernization Agreement between the ILWU and the Pacific Maritime Association now seems an ironic justification of the longshoremen's earlier fears. This agreement sus-pended ILWU work rules, allowing for a vastly reduced workforce on the docks and clearing the path for containerization. In return the union received a multimillion dollar trust fund to be used for retirement pen-sions and no-lay-off guarantees for registered workers. The ILA reached similar agreements with East and Gulf Coast shippers, in particular the Guaranteed Annual Income Program which began in 1966. The technolo-gies now in place are virtually identical. They are also typical of the or-ganizational and technological transformations which have greatly re-duced industrial occupations throughout the world.[48]

Today, containerized cargo travels across the continent on computer-guided, satellite-tracked "intermodal" "rail bridges." These new systems have revived both railroads and ports such as Elizabeth, New Jersey, now a vast container depot. The volume and speed of these systems is astonishing, so rapid that freight deposited by rail on the huge container docks of Elizabeth can be out to sea on the Atlantic literally within hours—bound for ports in Europe, Africa, and South America.

The workers on the docks are still called longshoremen, but they are a far cry from the men who traditionally worked in gangs on ships and wharves. Stereotypes persist, and there are men who fit the images in Marlon Brando's classic film, *On the Waterfront*—brawling, barrel-chested men with bulging biceps, thick waistlines, and colorful language. There are probably a few more blacks and Latinos working on docks which were once all white. There are also a small number of women longshoremen. But these workers, overwhelmingly, are truck drivers and crane operators who do rather solitary work. They live and work far from the waterfront neighborhoods of the past. The mean streets where the seamen and the longshoremen fought the great battles of the past are gone. The gangs, a determining source of the unique identity and rough solidarity of the longshoremen, are also gone. Longshoremen do repetitive, often rather simple tasks, driving trucks across vast container lots or working in the cranes which tower over the docks. Surely there are few examples of an industry so transformed by technology, rationalization, and reorganization. In 1950, fifty thousand longshoremen worked in New York harbor. In 1996, perhaps two thousand were dispatched in a day, mostly to New Jersey. These new dock workers continue to be of interest, however. They occupy, after all, a strategic, highly sensitive position in the world's commerce, a link in the new multinational chain which now promises its customers not just transportation, but fast, on-time delivery.[49]

There remains, of course, much to be done on the history of longshoremen, and labor historians especially must begin to go beyond the docks themselves and into the waterfront neighborhoods, no easy task, as these were often considered as tight-knit and exclusive as the longshoremen themselves. At the same time, there are still periods needing work, as well as important towns and regions to be examined, in particular the ports of Puget Sound, where waterfront unionism was perhaps most radical, and the Great Lakes, where the conservative ILA was founded and built the base from which it became the leading longshoremen's union in the nation. Moreover, the controversies referred to, the debates engaged in, and the questions asked in these essays remain for the most part unsettled, but all this, of course, is beyond the scope of this volume.

Notes

1. E. J. Hobsbawm, "National Unions on the Waterside," in *Labouring Men* (New York: Anchor Books, 1967), p. 241.

2. Ibid., p. 244; Charles Barnes, *The Longshoremen* (New York: Survey Associates, 1915), p. 39; *Commission on Industrial Relations*, vol. 3 (Washington, D.C., 1916) (hereafter *CIR*, 3), p. 2067.

3. Eric Arnesen, *Waterfront Workers of New Orleans: Race, Class and Politics, 1863–1923* (Urbana: University of Illinois Press, 1994), p. 42.

4. See Ronald Magden and A. D. Martinson, *The Working Waterfront: The Story of Tacoma's Ships and Men* (Tacoma: ILWU Local 23, 1982).

5. Bruce Nelson, *Workers on the Waterfront: Seamen, Longshoremen, and Unionism in the 1930s* (Urbana: University of Illinois Press, 1988), pp. 127–55.

6. For interesting comparisons with Liverpool, see Eric Taplin, *The Dockers' Union: A Study of the National Union of Dock Labourers, 1889–1922* (Leicester, Eng.: Leicester University Press, 1985), pp. 23–45. Also, Ken Coates and Tony Topham, *The History of the Transport and General Workers Union*, vol. 1 (London: Basil Blackwell, 1991), pp. 347–52.

7. New York State, *Fifth Annual Report of the Bureau of the Statistics of Labor* (Albany, 1887), for the Knights of Labor strike. For the 1919 strike, see Calvin Winslow, "On the Waterfront: Black, Italian and Irish Longshoremen in the New York Harbor Strike of 1919," in *Protest and Survival: Essays for E. P. Thompson,* ed. John Rule and Robert Malcolmson (New York: New Press, 1993), pp. 355–93.

8. I want to thank John Beck for an account of Michigan iron ore trimmers in his unpublished manuscript, "The Irish Roots of Great Lakes Waterfront Violence" (ca. 1994).

9. Sterling Spero and Abram Harris, *The Black Worker: The Negro and the Labor Movement* (New York: Atheneum, 1931), p. 183. Also Arnesen, *Waterfront Workers of New Orleans,* p. 159.

10. Spero and Harris, *Black Worker,* pp. 182–84.

11. Thanks to Joe Doyle and David Brundage for information on this very interesting episode. See Joe Doyle, "Striking for Ireland on the New York Docks," in *The New York Irish,* ed. Ronald H. Bayor and Timothy J. Meagher (Baltimore: Johns Hopkins University Press, 1996), pp. 357–73. Brundage kindly allowed me to read his unpublished paper, "The 1920 New York Docker's Boycott: Class, Gender, Race and Irish-American Nationalism," (1992).

12. Tom Mann, *Tom Mann's Memoirs* (London: MacGibbon and Kee, 1967), p. 106. Also, "The Position of Dockers and Sailors in 1897 and the International Federation of Ship, Dock and River Workers" (1897), Tom Mann Collection, Coventry City Libraries.

13. Harvey O'Conner, *Revolution in Seattle* (New York: Monthly Review, 1964), pp. 158–59.

14. Nelson, *Workers on the Waterfront,* p. 269.

15. Hobsbawm, "National Unions on the Waterside," p. 242.

16. IWW, *Industrial Union Bulletin,* Feb. 1, 1907.

17. "Investigative Case Files of the Bureau of Investigation," 1908–22, R.G. 65, M 1085, O.G. 48655, National Archives, Washington, D.C. Louis Adamic, *My America* (New York: Harper, 1938), p. 375.

18. "Investigative Case Files of the Bureau of Investigation."

19. Colin Davis, "'All I Got's a Hook': New York Longshoremen and the 1948 Dock Strike," pp. 131–54. Daniel Guerin, *100 Years of Labor in the USA* (London: Ink Links, 1979), p. 205.

20. Charles Larrowe, *Harry Bridges: The Rise and Fall of Radical Labor in the U.S.* (New York: Lawrence Hill, 1972), p. 360.

21. Barnes, *Longshoremen*, p. 130.

22. *CIR*, 3, p. 2170.

23. Ibid., 3, p. 2104.

24. See Barnes, *Longshoremen*; Charles Larrowe, *Shape-Up and Hiring Hall: A Comparison of Hiring Methods and Labor Relations on the New York and Seattle Waterfronts* (Berkeley: University of California Press, 1955); Maud Russell, *Men along the Shore* (New York: Brussel and Brussel, Inc., 1966); Vernon H. Jensen, *Hiring of Dock Workers and Employment Practices in the Ports of New York, Liverpool, London, Rotterdam and Marseilles* (Cambridge: Harvard University Press, 1964), and *Strife on the Waterfront: The Port of New York since 1945* (Ithaca: Cornell University Press, 1974).

25. "Longshore Labor Conditions in the United States," *Monthly Labor Review,* parts 1 and 2 (Oct. and Nov. 1930), pt. 1, p. 4.

26. Rosario Ferrintino, "Italian Longshoremen," CUNY Oral History Project, Tamiment Library, New York. Also *CIR*, 3, p. 2117.

27. See "Longshore Labor Conditions," pt. 2, p. 25, and Mayor's Committee on Unemployment, "Report on Dock Employment in New York City" (Oct. 1916).

28. Dana Frank, *Purchasing Power: Consumer Organizing, Gender, and the Seattle Labor Movement, 1919–1929* (New York: Cambridge University Press, 1994), pp. 164–65. Larrowe, *Shape-Up and Hiring Hall*, pp. 91–94.

29. Mary Heaton Vorse, "The Pirates' Nest of New York," in *Rebel Pen*, ed. Dee Garrison (New York: Monthly Review, 1985), pp. 221–22.

30. Arnesen, *Waterfront Workers of New Orleans*, p. 41.

31. "Longshore Labor Conditions," pt. 2, p. 11.

32. Ernest Poole, "The Ship Must Sail on Time," *Everybody's Magazine*, 19 (Aug. 1908), 176–86.

33. *CIR*, 3, p. 2054.

34. Arnesen, *Waterfront Workers of New Orleans*, p. 36; "Longshore Labor Conditions," pt. 2, p. 11.

35. "Longshore Labor Conditions," pts. 1 and 2, pp. 1–20, 11–25.

36. David Montgomery, *The Fall of the House of Labor* (New York: Cambridge University Press, 1987), p. 97.

37. Hobsbawm, "National Unions on the Waterside," p. 247. Barnes suggested that "whether from selfish or altruistic motives they [the longshoremen] insist that the men squeezed out must be provided for" (*Longshoremen*, p. 74).

38. Quoted in Iver Bernstein, *The New York City Draft Riots* (New York: Oxford University Press, 1990), pp. 27–28.

39. Spero and Harris, *Black Worker,* p. 183.

40. E. P. Thompson, *The Making of the English Working Class* (New York: Vintage, 1966), p. 59.

41. E. Franklin Frazier, "The Negro Longshoremen" (1921) unpublished manuscript, pp. 27–29, Russell Sage Foundation, Columbia University Library, New York.

42. Spero and Abrams, *Black Worker,* pp. 199–200. See also Bruce Nelson's review of Gilbert Mers, *Working the Waterfront,* in *Labor History,* 31 (Spring 1990), 242.

43. Office of Naval Intelligence, "Investigation of the Marine Transport Workers and the Alleged Threatened Combination Between Them and the Bolsheviki and Sein Feiners," General Records of the Department of Labor, R.G. 174, 1907–42, 20/544 (box 89), National Archives, Washington, D.C.

44. Winslow, "On the Waterfront."

45. Arnesen, *Waterfront Workers of New Orleans,* p. 203.

46. Bruce Nelson, "The 'Lords of the Docks' Reconsidered: Race Relations among West Coast Longshoremen, 1933–61," p. 158.

47. David Wellman, *The Union Makes Us Strong: Radical Unionism on the San Francisco Waterfront* (New York: Cambridge University Press, 1995), p. 257.

48. Kim Moody, *An Injury to All: The Decline of American Unionism* (New York: Verso, 1988), p. 67. Also *New York Times,* June 22 and 23, 1983.

49. Kenneth C. Crowe, *Newsday,* Oct. 4, 1996, p. A55.

1   Biracial Waterfront Unionism in the Age of Segregation

Eric Arnesen

African American labor leader Thomas Woodland spoke passionately to the issue of race relations in Gulf Coast longshore unions at the biannual convention of the International Longshoremen's Association (ILA) in 1919. "Every Negro organization I have visited in the south, and I am closely connected with all the representatives, get[s] a square deal," he declared in response to a white official's invitation to black delegates to express any grievances they might have against white dock workers. African Americans in his home city of New Orleans, like those across the South, had suffered political disfranchisement, racial violence, and legalized segregation. The consolidation of Jim Crow that spelled subordination for black citizens and workers, however, apparently affected the waterfront less severely. "We in the Longshoremen's Association dwell together in harmony, in perfect peace, everything is calm and serene, white and colored work in harmony," concluded Alexander Paul, a black freight handler, civil rights activist, and union leader, in 1921.[1] Woodland and Paul were hardly alone in their positive evaluations, for numerous commentators in the early twentieth century singled out longshoremen's unions as exceptional labor organizations. The black weekly newspaper, the *New York Age,* for instance, praised the International Longshoremen's

Association, to which most southern longshore union locals belonged, for
its refusal to draw the color line and its extension to "the Negro unions
[of] a fair and square deal in long shore work."[2] One need not accept these
positive assessments at face value to recognize that southern longshoremen adopted racial practices that differed sharply from those of other
trade unionists and that violated some of the central tenets of the age of
segregation.

Southern dock workers confronted the issue of race in their ongoing
efforts to improve wages, win union recognition, and exercise some degree of control over the waterfront labor process in the late nineteenth
and early twentieth centuries. The small army of laborers which performed the arduous tasks of cargo loading and unloading in many southern ports was composed of both white and black men. In a racially divided labor force, blacks and whites could and did easily clash over access
to employment in a trade that privileged strength over skill. The task of
waterfront unionists was to neutralize the divisiveness that racial competition generated. In practice, this could be accomplished in several ways.
Whites could monopolize the best positions by excluding blacks altogether or by sharply restricting their access; black workers could cut their
own deals with employers by accepting lower wage rates; and blacks and
whites could arrive at informal understandings or formal institutional
arrangements to prevent debilitating struggles over access to work. Whatever the case, waterfront race relations were neither static over time nor
identical from port to port. The history of southern waterfront unionism in the Gilded Age and Progressive Era includes numerous examples
of racial exclusion, isolation, violence, collaboration, and even solidarity.

By the late nineteenth century, the labor movement on the docks of the
South was predicated on a simple organizational principle: biracial unionism. Without exception before the 1930s, wherever and whenever Gulf
longshore workers organized unions, they did so along racially separate
lines. By the second decade of the twentieth century, biracial union agreements of various kinds existed between black and white locals in New
Orleans, Galveston, Houston, Port Arthur, Mobile, Gulfport, Pensacola,
and Baltimore. Under biracial union structures, black workers belonged
to black locals, while white workers belonged to white locals. Those racially distinct locals coexisted, sometimes competing, sometimes collabo-
rating. At its best, biracial unionism involved the establishment of informal understandings and formal arrangements among unions across the
racial (and sometimes occupational) divide, on the basis of a degree of
racial parity; the ILA at times oversaw an equal division of work between

blacks and whites. At its worst, biracial unionism isolated better-paid white workers from lower-paid black ones, simultaneously sanctioning a racially segmented labor force and reinforcing African Americans' weaker position in the labor market.

By the early twentieth century, the ILA had emerged as a unifying force whose goal was to overcome occupational and racial divisions. Toward that end, it assumed the role of mediator between races and for the unions, carefully negotiating the resolution of group conflicts and promoting interracial collaboration in many ports of the American South. The southern ILA built upon preexisting patterns of biracial unionism and sought to create biracial arrangements where they did not yet exist. "The black man has got to play fair with the white man, and the white man has got to play fair with the black man," lectured ILA president T. V. O'Connor to an interracial assembly of union delegates at the founding meeting of the ILA's Gulf District Branch in 1911. "We are not going to attempt to take up the question of social equality, but we can, if we achieve the proper organization, bring about industrial equality." The following year, he announced (inaccurately) that "racial prejudice has been almost entirely overcome among the workers themselves." In 1919, George H. Slater, the white president of the Texas Federation of Labor, sang the ILA's praises in similar terms: "The ILA has met and disposed of some of the most vital issues of any organization in the country. It met industrial, economic and race questions, and disposed of all of them with a neatness and dispatch which has been the envy of other branches of organized labor." The ILA's track record was not, in fact, as clear cut as either O'Connor and Slater, on the one hand, or New Orleans black leaders Woodland or Paul, on the other, suggested. If the southern ILA aggressively fought for industrial equality on many occasions, at other times it defended a racially inequitable status quo. Yet whatever its limitations, the organization actively embraced black workers as members, and many black workers in turn actively embraced the ILA.[3]

This essay, which explores the early evolution of biracial unionism in a number of southern port cities, addresses several related sets of questions. First, what were the sources of biracial unionism? How and why did southern dock workers navigate the rough waters of segregation's rising tide to forge a movement that ran counter to the legalized segregation and scientific racism that characterized the white South's racial thought and practice? Second, what impact did biracial unionism have on waterfront race relations in the era of Jim Crow? Specifically, how did black workers fare under biracial unionism? If black ILA representatives Thomas Woodland and Alexander Paul offered an overwhelmingly positive perspective on the New Orleans experience, black activists in other southern ports sometimes advanced more critical assessments. This leads to the final issue: How do we account for the variety of forms that biracial unionism assumed? And why did black workers do better in some ports than in others?

These questions, ultimately, lend themselves to no simple answers. Biracial institutional arrangements were the products of the interaction among port-specific, regional, and national forces as well as local traditions and activism. The variety of biracial union structures, their multiple sources, and the ILA's uneven track record on the issue of racial equality in the workplace all suggest that race and labor relations remained highly fluid in the Jim Crow era. This essay offers an examination and assessment of race and labor relations on the waterfronts of the South in an attempt to understand the contradictory history of biracial unionism.

* * *

However exceptional the ILA was in the early twentieth-century labor movement, there was nothing inherent in the character of waterfront work that promoted interracial, interethnic, or intertrade collaboration. Rather, fragmentation along racial, ethnic, and occupational lines had long marked relations between various categories of longshore labor. In the nineteenth and early twentieth centuries, American waterfronts were often the site of sharp ethnic and racial conflict, as dominant groups sought to exclude by violence "competitors" of a different (or even the same) ethnicity or race. In periods of industrial conflict, union violence against strikebreakers, of whatever nationality or color, was commonplace. In dock strikes in Virginia's Hampton Roads district in 1885 and 1923, for example, fighting broke out between black strikers and black strikebreakers; in the Seattle dock strike of 1916, targets of white attacks included not only black and Japanese workers but white strikebreakers as well. But rare was the instance in which employers' introduction of African Americans—during strikes, economic downturns, or even during prosperous times—into a previously all-white labor force did not occasion sharp objections or temporary walkouts or precipitate a violent white response. A list of flashpoints of white hostility would include Irish longshoremen's savage attack against blacks shortly before the infamous New York City draft riots in 1863 and against New Orleans blacks in the waterfront riots of 1894–95, as well as more modest levels of white violence against black strikebreakers in Cleveland in 1887, San Francisco in

1916, New York in 1890, 1919, and 1920, and Hoboken, New Jersey, in 1919.[4] Whites on the waterfront understood that the largely unskilled character of their work allowed employers to manipulate the labor force's racial composition with ease, as a means of undermining workers' influence. Relying upon a solidarity defined by race, ethnicity, and occupation, dominant groups of white dock workers raised sharp barriers to newcomers of any kind.

Ideological commitment to interracial working-class solidarity did not figure strongly in the emergence of biracial unionism in the South. Only the Industrial Workers of the World aggressively championed such solidarity, on the grounds that the working class was composed of both whites and blacks, that employers used racial divisions to undermine workers' strength, and that class divisions were more fundamental than racial ones. "Labor organized on race lines will drown," the IWW's *Industrial Worker* declared. "Only organized on class lines will it swim." But among longshoremen, the IWW's influence extended only to the single port of Philadelphia in the 1910s and early 1920s.[5] Its efforts to win converts on the docks of Baltimore and Norfolk, as well as New Orleans, were met by longshoremen's indifference and the active resistance of ILA officials.

Pragmatism, more than ideology, motivated the southern supporters of biracial unionism. Sterling Spero and Abram Harris, pioneer African American labor historians, argued that demography prompted white trade unionists to establish biracial agreements with blacks. Longshoremen constituted "one of the largest industrial groups in the Negro community of nearly every shipping center," they wrote in 1930. The very "importance of the Negro's place in their industry has made it impossible for the longshoremen to ignore him in their organizations. He probably plays a more important role in their movement than he does in any other labor union. . . . Race prejudice and interracial competition have by no means been abolished, but the white and black workers have effected a working arrangement which harmonizes their differences sufficiently to enable them to work together in a single organization." When the presence of large numbers of black workers made a policy of exclusion unfeasible, "economic necessity," in a more recent historian's words, "led to the practice of dividing work between . . . locals on a fifty-fifty basis."[6] Whatever the specific configuration of race and occupational relations, the very fact of racial competition (or its potential) hung over Gulf longshore workers, leading the ILA to adopt policies toward black workers that differed sharply from those of other southern American Federation of Labor (AFL) unions.[7]

Pragmatism and demography were indeed important in generating the impulse toward biracial unionism in the South. But by themselves, they do not explain either its dynamics or the variety of forms that it assumed. Three additional factors must be taken into account. First, the structures of waterfront employment could encourage or discourage biracial collaboration. How workers acquired their jobs—a process which was influenced by the number, size, and power of employers and the character of the products being shipped—mattered. In some cases, a port's employment structure made biracial collaboration imperative if unions were to maintain any degree of power or control; in other cases, it sheltered black and white workers from one another, reducing both competition and collaboration. Second, the extent of black self-organization and blacks' level of organizational strength determined how white workers— and the ILA—treated African Americans. Strong black unions were in a position to demand a degree of "industrial equality," while weak black unions were not. And third, the history of a port's racial division of labor influenced the shape of its biracial structures. Prior racial segmentation could be institutionalized by the unionization process, while unionization itself might, in some circumstances, provide the context for challenging that segmentation.[8] One factor that appears to have had little effect on the strength or weakness of the biracial impulse was the attitude of white workers: there is little evidence that white workers in one port were more or less racist in their overall outlook than white workers in another.[9] Unlike recent studies which identify white racial identity as the most important subject in histories of race and labor, this essay instead suggests that workers' institutions and practices can only be understood through careful examination of political economy, the characteristics of labor markets, and the activism of both blacks and whites in their particular historical contexts. Rather than infer workers' racial practices and perspectives from the broad sweep of culture and ideology, our readings of culture and ideology should be more firmly grounded in scholarly attention to institutions—political, economic, and associational.[10] In the sections that follow, the examples of New Orleans, Galveston, Mobile, and Baltimore serve to demonstrate the variety of biracial union patterns, the factors shaping them, and their impact upon race and labor relations.

* * *

By all criteria, New Orleans dock workers between 1880 and the early 1920s created the most powerful biracial labor movement in the nation. The largest city in the Deep South, New Orleans was primarily a commercial center, dependent upon the transportation of agricultural staples, of which cotton was the most important. The complex division of labor that set apart multiple waterfront trades included black Mississippi river roustabouts, black and white cotton screwmen, longshoremen, and cotton yardmen, black cotton teamsters and loaders, and black round freight teamsters. The city's biracial union system first took shape in the years immediately following Reconstruction's collapse in Louisiana and the ending of the 1870s depression. A wave of unionization swept the riverfront between 1879 and the early 1880s, affecting workers in a wide array of crafts on and near the docks. Two locals, one representing black workers, the other whites, appeared in the longshore, cotton screwing, and cotton yard work sectors (that is, in trades where both blacks and whites labored). During the 1880s, black and white longshoremen and cotton yardmen divided available work equally, observed the same wage rates, and negotiated with employers as a single unit. In addition, a Cotton Men's Executive Council bound together most dock workers in a single federation, linking them in a complex network that nurtured extensive collaboration and even genuine solidarity. But the interracial alliance of Gilded Age New Orleans did not survive the depression of the 1890s. Violent attacks by white screwmen—the one group that had not agreed to an equal division of work—and longshoremen upon blacks in 1894 and 1895 effectively destroyed what remained of the biracial alliance. The entire edifice of union power disintegrated, as employers successfully used racial tensions to lower wage rates dramatically, repeal union work rules, and manage their affairs with a relatively free hand.[11]

With the return of commercial prosperity at the end of the decade, whites in the labor movement pursued two strategies with regard to black labor. White craft unionists formed a Central Trades and Labor Council in 1899 that excluded blacks from their ranks. (Barred from the new alliance's deliberations, blacks demanded and won from the AFL the right to form their own Central Labor Union.)[12] The experience on the waterfront stood in sharp contrast. On the city's docks, longshore unions rebuilt their interracial alliance. Black and white locals of longshoremen and eventually cotton screwmen agreed to abide by the same wage rates and work rules, conduct joint negotiations with employers, and share all work equally. The formation of the Dock and Cotton Council in October 1901 allied eight unions of black and white cotton screwmen, black and white longshoremen, black teamsters and loaders, black and white cotton yardmen, and black coal wheelers. After a series of fierce battles with employers from 1901 to 1908, the Cotton Council emerged supreme, winning employer acceptance of the biracial system, raising wages, imposing the closed shop, and shifting a substantial degree of managerial power into workers' hands. From the early twentieth century until the Cotton Council's demise in 1923, blacks and whites in key trades shared all existing work (sometimes working in integrated, or "amalgamated," crews) and jointly ratified all contract proposals. At the leadership level, black delegates served on negotiating committees with whites, while the screwmen's and longshoremen's joint executive committees, composed equally of black and white delegates, conducted the organizations' affairs, oversaw trials of members accused of violating union rules, and represented their associations in public. In essence, they had more or less successfully eliminated crippling racial competition for jobs and institutionalized intertrade, intratrade, and interracial collaboration.

How was it that New Orleans longshore laborers managed to violate many of the basic tenets of the age of segregation at the workplace? Four factors help to account for reconstitution of this interracial alliance. First, dock union leaders recognized the difference that the alliance made with regard to conditions and wage rates. Just as the rise of waterfront union power in the 1880s depended in large part upon intertrade and interracial alliances, the fall of waterfront union power in the 1890s resulted from the collapse of those alliances. In the twentieth century, dock leaders, black and white, repeatedly acknowledged that the riots of 1894–95 had led to the deterioration of all longshore laborers' working conditions; to labor, the lessons of division were plain enough. Second, the largely unskilled nature of the work made this recovery of the legacy of interracial cooperation imperative. While familiarity with the techniques of loading, unloading, coaling, or rolling and carting cotton or round freight gave old hands important advantages over green hands, these workers could, in theory, be easily replaced. Only control of the labor supply and solidarity across trade and racial lines could reduce this possibility. That meant that alliances between unions and, most importantly, between black and white unions, were essential to reducing competition between different groups for jobs.

This functional imperative—to enter into interracial and intertrade alliances or remain weak, vulnerable, and divided—assumed a greater importance given the third factor—the particular structure of employment relations on the docks. The majority of New Orleans levee laborers worked in the competitive contracting sector, characterized by a multiplicity of employers, many of whom hired gangs of workers to complete discrete tasks, such as unloading a particular ship or carrying a particular consignment of goods. This meant that a contracting stevedore or steamship agent, for example, could hire a black gang one day, and a white gang the next. And this meant that he could (and did) use the threat of racial competition to keep a given group of workers in line. The domination of the port's employment structure by a large number of labor contractors built regular competition for work into the employment structure itself. Last, it was not merely the number of black workers, as Spero and Harris suggested, but the existence of large and strong black unions (particularly the longshoremen) that forced unskilled whites to negotiate equitable deals or ignore their black counterparts at their peril.[13] When white screwmen and longshoremen repudiated the interracial alliance in 1894–95, they not only failed to displace blacks but made conditions for all workers substantially worse. Unlike whites in certain skilled trades, dock workers could not impose a racially exclusionary solution even when that was what they desired. Black longshore labor's availability, ability, and determination to work, coupled with employers' incentive to retain a racially divided labor force, made that an impossibility. The only alternative to division and powerlessness lay in intertrade and biracial collaboration.

The forging of an alliance between New Orleans cotton screwmen in the opening years of the new century provides evidence to support this argument. At the top of the port's occupational hierarchy, white screwmen were the "aristocrats of the levee," whose indispensable strength and skill in packing cotton bales tightly and carefully in ships' holds enabled them to command the highest wages and promulgate the strongest union work rules. Unlike white longshoremen and yardmen, nineteenth-century white screwmen had rejected an equal division of work in favor of a restrictive quota system that permitted black screwmen only twenty gangs a day. This restriction angered some black screwmen, who welcomed offers by steamship agents to work at reduced wages and without certain work rules during the depression of the 1890s. Unwilling to address the long-standing grievances of their black co-workers, white screwmen, joined by white longshoremen, refused to work with blacks or for any employer of black labor; in 1894–95, they violently attacked black workers on the levee. The casualties of the riots included not just several murdered black levee workers but any semblance of union control on the docks as well.[14]

Although the lifting of the depression at the end of the 1890s enabled waterfront workers to regain some ground lost during the previous years, conditions proved unstable in the new century. During the nineteenth century, screwmen performed the essential work of compressing as many bales of cotton as possible into the holds of steamships by means of huge jackscrews and wooden beams; the careful stowing of cotton could mean the difference between profit and loss for the shipping agents. But by the start of the twentieth century, the economic pressures generated by new shipping technologies, larger vessel size, and increased competition meant that speed, not skill, was central to profitability. For some firms, screwmen were an expensive, often unnecessary group of workmen. In their quest for lower costs, New Orleans steamship agents turned their attention to the organization of the waterfront labor process and to the role of the cotton screwmen in particular. After the turn of the century, the four major shipping lines that controlled the overwhelming bulk of the port's cotton inaugurated a new "shoot the chute" system of loading, designed to maximize speed and minimize skill. Screwmen complained that this dangerous process undermined their power and control over the performance of their work and "annihilated all regard for the number of bales to be stored."[15]

Successful resistance to the "shoot the chute" system required coming to grips with the enduring problem of racial competition. Although relations between the black and white screwmen's unions had remained tense since the riots of 1894–95, the process of healing deep divisions began in April 1902 when the two unions devised a uniform wage scale.[16] In the following autumn, white screwmen went farther, agreeing to an unprecedented "amalgamation" with the black screwmen. Motivated by a desire to eliminate the "shoot the chute" system and reduce the amount of work performed daily, white workers reasoned accurately that success lay in reducing all possible divisions between black and white workers and preventing a revival of a split labor market on the docks. Black screwmen had their own reasons for approving such an alliance with whites. A. J. Ellis, the black union's delegate to the Dock and Cotton Council, explained in a public letter in April 1903 that members were "tired of being used as an instrument to starve our brother workmen, the white men . . . who have the same right to live that we have. We stood for it for eight years; got nothing for it but abuse, and depreciation of manhood. We did not get together to stop work and sit down in ships and draw money that was not earned. But we did . . . [so in order to] stop men from forcing us to starve other men and ourselves as well."[17]

In the fall of 1902, the two associations pledged both to act jointly with regard to all demands and to share equally all available work. A new half-and-half compact provided for the integration of work crews: each crew of four would consist of two blacks and two whites, with either a white or black foreman, to prevent the stevedores and agents from playing one race off against the other (a frequent union complaint).[18] The unions now demanded that stevedores and shipping agents employ only half-and-half gangs and distribute them equally in every hatch; that union workers would take orders only from the walking foreman after beginning work; and that screwmen would recognize no foreman's authority unless he was a member of either the black or white workers' union.[19]

Implementing the new biracial accord brought the unions into sharp conflict with their employers, who rightly feared that the new alliance would shift the locus of managerial control toward labor and would result in a decrease in the amount of work performed. The equal division clause and other union work rules were at the heart of a series of strikes and lockouts from the shipping season in the fall of 1902 to the fall of 1903. When the conflicts ended, the screwmen, with the substantial backing of the other levee unions in the Dock and Cotton Council, had won.[20] Not only did the victory cement the new collaborative relationship between black and white screwmen but it enabled them to resist employer efforts to intensify the waterfront labor process, and instead to wrest control of the labor supply and process from the agents and stevedores. The transformation in waterfront power relations found clear expression in the observations of one stevedore in 1908. William J. Kearney, stevedore for the Harrison line, argued that he "had absolutely no control over his men; that the foreman of a gang was simply a figurehead and that a conference committee, consisting of twelve whites and twelve negroes, had the absolute say as to what sort of work the men should do." By 1907, employers strongly resented the fact that dock workers had put the steamship agents in "such a position . . . so as to be almost controlled by the laborers." One member of a Port Investigation Commission expressed incredulity: "These niggers and whites rule the whole roost."[21] There was little question that cotton screwmen had regained their position as aristocrats of the levee.

Central to the unions' acquisition of a far greater degree of control over the labor process was their highly pragmatic subordination of racial divisions to the goal of biracial collaboration. Longshoremen and screwmen defended their alliance in strictly practical terms, as a means to end abusive treatment, stop racial competition for jobs, and reassert control over the labor process. Workers repeatedly commented on the improvements in working conditions that biracial collaboration had made possible. Before the screwmen's amalgamation, black union leader E. S. Swann testified in 1908, it was "a case of slavery," with foremen pitting black and white gangs against each other. "We saw that we were being used as a cat's-paw in the labor situation," testified black longshore leader Alonzo Ellis. "The steamship agents were making us the enemy of the white laborer, and at the same time robbing us of our earnings. . . . We didn't seek social equality with the whites. We just didn't want to keep up the strife and bitterness on the levee. We wanted peace. We started into the business as a question of meat and bread, and we did not want to be wedged between the white screwmen and the steamship agents, for we knew that if it ever did come to a pinch the white man would stand by his own color and we would get the worst of it."[22]

T. P. Woodland, a black screwman and ILA vice president, similarly commended the biracial arrangement in 1914: "The conditions in my craft are second to none. . . . If there are two gangs to be hired there is one white and one colored gang. . . . This method of working does not mean that there is social equality, but it does mean industrial equality."[23] The effect of the amalgamation convinced even white opponents that collaboration was preferable to competition. "I put up the most vigorous fight of my life in opposing amalgamation of our local with the colored men," Thomas A. Harrison, white screwmen's union delegate and former state commissioner of labor recalled before delegates at the ILA's 1913 convention. "I am pleased to say today that the fight was of no avail and today I realize that my fight was a mistake." Harrison further boasted that his union's contract was "the best contract existing anywhere, because it is the only contract which permits us to say just how much cotton we will stow in one day and when we have done that we do no more."[24] The reasons for his change of heart were clear: cotton screwmen and longshoremen—the largest and most powerful groups of dock workers—had succeeded in shifting a considerable degree of managerial authority away from employers into their own hands. And it was the alliance of convenience which put an end to racial competition on the docks that had allowed the screwmen to reassert and extend their control over the labor market and the conditions of their work.

Not all waterfront workers fared as well as the screwmen and longshoremen. From the 1880s through the 1920s and beyond, dock workers employed in the freight yards of New Orleans's railroads occupied a domain defined by geographical separation from other dock workers, substantially lower wages, and harsher working conditions. Freight handlers were generally longer term employees of the railroads; that is, they did not compete daily for jobs. But they confronted economically powerful, resourceful, and determined railroad companies. With vast financial resources unavailable to smaller steamship operators or stevedores, railroad corporations were in a strong position to resist attempts by employees to secure benefits won by the rest of the port's cotton laborers. When freight handlers of the Illinois Central or the Southern Pacific struck, the rail companies simply erected huge fences, employed armed guards, and imported hundreds of strikebreakers on their rail lines. Separate unions of black and white handlers did form periodically in the nineteenth century and permanently in the early twentieth century, but they won few of the benefits and rights exercised by dock workers in the more competitive contracting sector.[25]

Although the interracialism of the Dock and Cotton Council was impressive compared to the racially exclusionary tendencies of the city's white craft union federation, it had clear limits. Indeed, the council's white union members were hardly immune to the ideology of white supremacy. Despite the application of the principle of the equal division to the election of council officers, the distribution of available work, and the composition of the joint conference committees, there were limits beyond which some white workers were not willing to venture. If blacks served as vice presidents and secretaries of the Dock and Cotton Council, whites always dominated the federation's presidency. While there is no evidence that black workers protested this practice, they did object to another, perhaps more important restriction. The overwhelming number of foremen were white, and white longshoremen refused to extend the half-and-half compact to the division of foremen's positions. This inequality provoked considerable conflict within the black union in 1904 and 1907. Vowing to "make a firm stand for equality in everything," black longshoremen demanded an equal share of foremen's positions. White longshoremen remained adamant—"We'll have no nigger bossing us" as foreman, declared one enraged white worker in 1907. In the larger interest of maintaining the alliance, black unionists backed down. The withdrawal of their controversial proposition reestablished the racial status quo on the docks and secured a tenuous peace between the two unions; it was nonetheless a defeat for the black unionists.[26]

The failure to extend the principle of the equal division of work to the foreman's position affected neither the interracial alliance nor the application of the half-and-half compact. Only weeks following the resolution of the controversy over foremen, the waterfront was again the scene of tremendous conflict. A renewed assault by waterfront employers upon the cotton screwmen in October 1907 appeared to dock workers to be "only the forerunner of a war of destruction upon all the other labor unions" on the riverfront. When the Dock and Cotton Council ordered a general strike, over eight thousand workers struck every shipping agent and stevedore who had not signed the screwmen's tariff. Three weeks later, a compromise plan calling for arbitration brought the strike to a temporary end.[27] But the arbitration committee never met. Businessmen chosen by the agents and stevedores objected to two black representatives on the committee. "The committee will have many important things to look into," one prominent businessmen on the committee declared, "and I, for one, can't see how a negro belongs on it." With his carefully crafted solution to the general strike endangered, Democratic machine mayor Martin Behrman explained that the "sentiment of the community" was against "having colored men figure so prominently in public matters." He asked black union members "to sacrifice their representation temporarily, in order that the peace, tranquillity and prosperity of New Orleans might be restored." Personally addressing the Dock and Cotton Council, Behrman implored members to recall the black delegates and instruct the black screwmen to choose whites to represent them.[28] Significantly, the council held fast to the principal of equal division. In the discussion that followed, radical journalist and participant Oscar Ameringer recalled, "every white speaker declared himself in opposition to the withdrawal" of the black delegates, and the council almost unanimously defeated the motion for reconsideration.[29]

Although whites dominated the presidency of the Cotton Council, refused to extend the principle of equal division to the foreman's position, eschewed any hint of "social equality," and failed to support black workers' struggles against segregation and disfranchisement, black union leaders and the black press recognized the experiment in interracial collaboration as unprecedented, and praised it constantly. Even Booker T. Washington, a staunch opponent of the white labor movement, singled out the Dock and Cotton Council for guarded praise in his 1913 assessment.[30] The "sentiment of the community" notwithstanding, New Orleans waterfront workers maintained their powerful interracial alliance into the 1920s, when it fell victim to the open shop drive of the New Orleans Steamship Association.

* * *

Galveston, New Orleans's strongest commercial rival in the South, developed a pattern of biracial unionism that resembled New Orleans's in some ways but differed from it in others.[31] The Texas port experienced fewer large-scale labor conflicts than New Orleans and its biracial unionism generated less cooperation between blacks and whites. One southern white newspaper put the matter succinctly: "negro laborers are not so well organized as those in New Orleans and on that account the whites can not make their demands too forcibly on account of a fear that the negroes will work against them." Or, as another journalist put it, "There is small love lost between the two races."[32]

Not just "small love lost" but the structure of Galveston's employment relations contributed to union fragmentation and the weakness of interracial collaboration. As in New Orleans, two different systems prevailed. Under the first, railroad companies and affiliated coastwise steamship lines employed large numbers of regular freight handlers, either all white or all black, to load and unload their cars and ships. Since most workers in these railroad/coastwise enclaves were regular hands of one race or the other, there was, for the most part, little overt competition between blacks and whites. Moreover, like their New Orleans counterparts, what unions that did emerge in this sector exercised little power against their very powerful employers.[33] By the start of the 1910s, the nonunion Harrison, Leyland and Mallory steamship lines, as well as the Head and Booth lines, employed only black workers in Galveston, while the huge Southern Pacific hired only whites.[34] Under the second system of employment relations, stevedoring firms filled contracts for labor by employing and discharging gangs when needed. It was in this type of sector that racial competition—or competition between unions—could be intense, often making biracial union agreements imperative if unions were to maintain any degree of control over employment and work rules. This is where Galveston's structure of employment relations differed sharply from that of New Orleans. In New Orleans, the competitive contracting sector employed vastly larger numbers of longshoremen and screwmen along the city's publicly owned wharves; it was in this sector that union power and the biracial system proved strongest in the twentieth century. In Galveston, the situation was reversed: the railroad (and the coastwise shipping) sector employed the majority of dock workers, the competitive contracting sector hired far fewer. Not surprisingly, given the built-in absence of racial competition on a day-to-day basis, the biracial system proved much weaker in Galveston than it did in New Orleans.[35]

Still, there is some evidence to suggest that black and white workers in Galveston at least passively supported each other from the late nineteenth century through the 1910s. This had not always been the case. In 1885, black laborers "captured" the Mallory wharves when managers hired them to replace white strikers who had affiliated with the Knights of Labor. "While the employment of the colored labor on the [Mallory] wharf is the main issue" in a short-lived general strike of Galveston's white Knights, the city's press reported, "some strikers claim that it is a movement of organized labor against unorganized labor and a protection of white labor as against a substitution of colored labor in this city." While both blacks and whites eventually accepted in principle a plan to divide equally all work on those docks (alternating ships or alternating weeks), Mallory officials rejected the offer, retaining their black, nonunion labor force.[36]

Once established, the racial composition of a dock labor force in the railroad/coastwise sector remained remarkably constant. Although isolated from one another, blacks and whites strove to preserve the racial status quo, in effect respecting each others' domination of particular docks. Even labor conflict could not upset the balance. Take, for example, an 1898 strike by some five hundred black workers of the Mallory company for union recognition. The walkout by the newly formed black longshoremen's union received the endorsement of the city's Legislative Labor Council and a vow from white longshoremen to reject offers from the Mallory company to work as scabs. The *Southwestern Christian Advocate,* a black New Orleans weekly often hostile to organized white labor, issued a celebratory, if premature, assessment. The labor situation in Galveston, it argued, "indicates what it would be the country over if the Negro and white laborers were related throughout the North and South as they are in Galveston. The white laborer of that city discovered through a sad experience some time ago that the only way to control the situation there was to control the Negro labor. To do this, he saw they had to become brethren, and this they proceeded to do. . . . [The black worker] and white brother stood together, are standing still yet." Such support from whites was hardly enough to allow black strikers to defeat the company. With the full backing of the city's mayor and under the protection of local police, deputized private citizens, and the Houston Light Artillery, the steamship company easily withstood the three-week strike by its black workers, destroying, at least temporarily, the young black union.[37]

Almost a decade later, in 1907, black workers extended their support to some 1,100 white Southern Pacific strikers. Two black dock unions (numbering 500 and 250 members) unanimously rejected company offers to replace striking whites with blacks. A committee from the black Lone Star Cotton Jammers' Association—a union which combined black screwmen and longshoremen—promised the white strikers that its organization would help to keep all outside labor, black and white, away from the Southern Pacific docks. Members of the black organizations showed their loyalty to the strikers, observed the *Houston Post,* by giving "assistance to the [strikers'] committee in every way that is asked," by seeing to it that "none of the local colored men are even attempting to take the strikers' places," thus demonstrating their "loyalty to the cause of unionism."[38] Like the black Mallory strikers nine years before, the white Southern Pacific unionists went down to defeat. In the following months, Galveston dock workers created a Dock and Marine Council, modeled on the New Orleans Dock and Cotton Council, as a forum for coordinating longshore union activities. The weakness of biracial unionism (and union-ism in general) in Galveston meant that the council exercised little power. But as the 1898 and 1907 strikes demonstrated, neither unionized blacks nor whites were willing to scab on the other group in moments of labor conflict. Such behavior reduced the pool of local strikebreakers, forcing both the Mallory and Southern Pacific lines to import black strikebreak-ers from Houston.

Even in the smaller, more competitive contracting sector, movement toward interracial collaboration or biracial agreements was rather slow and halting. Galveston's cotton screwmen, like those in New Orleans, constituted an elite group of levee workers. During the late nineteenth century, the Screwmen's Benevolent Association (SBA) was Galveston's strongest and oldest labor organization. Successfully protecting its mem-bers, the SBA held itself aloof from other labor associations, on and off the docks.[39] In 1869, it barred its members from working for any firm that employed any "persons of Color," upon penalty of expulsion. Excluded from the white screwmen's union, a small number of black screwmen formed a rival Cotton Jammers' Association in 1879 and secured a per-manent foothold on the Morgan steamship wharves, at wages well below those of the whites, during an 1883 strike.[40] This competition from black workers proved to be the exception, rather than the rule, and whites con-tinued to dominate the screwmen's trade through the end of the century. Although they entered into a series of agreements with African Ameri-cans by the mid-1890s, establishing common wage scales and agreeing not to strikebreak against one another, whites rejected the New Orleans plan of an equal division of work until 1912. As J. H. Fricke, president of the white Screwmen's Benevolent Association and a cotton screwmen since 1884, explained in 1908: "You know we do not associate with those fellows. It aint like they do in New Orleans. We don't associate with them at all."[41]

That changed dramatically in 1912. Under pressure from technologi-cal changes (the introduction of the high-density cotton press) that threatened the screwmen's dominance, white screwmen finally adopted the New Orleans formula. The 1912 "Memorandum of Agreement" between white Local 317 and black Local 329 mandated that employers hire "half white and half colored men" and distribute them equally in each hatch; the memorandum further empowered a conference committee of five members from each association to administer the unions' agreement—"to try fairly and impartially members of either Association for any violations of the conference rules."[42] A decade after New Orleans screwmen had formed a powerful biracial compact, Galveston's elite levee workers appeared to be following the same path.

But the New Orleans formula failed to take hold in Galveston. In April 1913, white screwmen repudiated the "amalgamation contract" (set to expire in September 1913) by signing contracts with four large stevedoring firms providing for the employment of only members of the white ILA Local 317. "Oil and water will not mix," explained the president of the white screwmen's union, "and we are not going to try to force it." The white local's objections were more complicated. First, the white screwmen alleged that black Local 329 had grown too rapidly over the course of the amalgamation contract (numbering two hundred at the time of amalgamation, it was 450 by the summer of 1913); the black local was "taking men in right and left," so as to have the "same number of gangs as Local No. 317," whites complained.[43] This proved problematic, in part because of the existence of the Lone Star Association, an independent, non-ILA black local on the Galveston waterfront formed in 1898. Under the original amalgamation agreement between 317 and 329, the black ILA screwmen had promised to absorb the independent men into their ranks—where they would be subject to the joint rules—or to drive them "out of town." Despite some effort, the black ILA local failed to accomplish this task; while some Lone Star men affiliated with it, the majority remained in the independent union outside of the ILA's jurisdiction. The Lone Star black screwmen explained their reluctance to join in any biracial compact: "the white men may stand with you about one season and then blow up."[44]

Turning for assistance to the International Longshoremen's Association—the "highest tribunal to adjust a grievance"—black screwmen in ILA Local 329 brought charges against the white local in July 1913. Black workers, who had proven themselves "to be among the best union men in Galveston," denounced the white local for treating them unjustly (and for violating a tentative agreement) by entering into five-year contracts with stevedores without even consulting the black local, thereby "depriving the members of Local No. 329 of participating in those contracts . . . or in any portion of the work." White screwmen "want all the work" for themselves, complained a black delegate, but "Local 329 won't stand for it." ILA officials sustained the black screwmen's charges. International president T. V. O'Connor intervened in the simmering dispute, traveling to Galveston to uphold the "amalgamation" contract and the pre-violation status quo. "It is my personal opinion that in the five years this agreement is made out for the stevedores are beating the workers out of thousands of dollars in wages. . . . [The stevedores] are at their old tricks using the white man against the black man today, and the black man against the white man tomorrow. You know, every man in the South knows, that the ship agent would not give a snap of their fingers if they could get those colored men to screw that cotton" for substantially lower wages. When the white screwmen refused the international's orders to cancel their new contract, O'Connor simply revoked their ILA charter.[45] This action meant that in the eyes of ILA men, the white screwmen were now nonunion workers. As a result, black union teamsters refused to truck cotton to their ships and longshoremen walked off any vessel on which the white screwmen worked. After a one-week stoppage, all longshore laborers returned to work pending a six-day truce which all parties hoped would produce some compromise settlement. It did not. When the truce expired without any agreement, ILA president O'Connor pulled out all longshoremen and teamsters not only in Galveston but in nearby Texas City and Port Bolivar as well; he also sent word to both New York and New Orleans ordering ILA men to refuse to unload any ship worked by the now nonrecognized white Local 317. The crisis finally ended when the white screwmen abandoned their contract, black Lone Star Cotton Jammers agreed to affiliate with the ILA (under a separate charter), and all locals accepted an equal division of work between all black and white screwmen. The "amalgamation contract," which mandated half-and-half gangs and joint hiring, was a casualty of the conflict. Embraced reluctantly by many of the parties, Galveston's new biracial system was but a weak reflection of New Orleans's.[46]

* * *

Biracial unionism took a substantially different shape in Mobile than it did in either New Orleans or Galveston. Located some thirty-three miles from the Gulf on the Mobile River, Mobile was Alabama's only real port, though it conducted a trade far smaller than its two other Gulf rivals. Its chief exports were lumber and timber (drawn from Alabama's yellow pine forests and east Mississippi's cypress forests) and, to a lesser extent, cotton. Mobile's patterns of commercial control resembled those in Galveston more than in New Orleans; virtually all of its four-to-five-mile wharf frontage was privately owned by railroad companies, including the Southern Railway, the Mobile and Ohio, the Mobile, Jackson and Kansas City, and the Louisville and Nashville, which serviced a number of powerful steamship lines (the Elder-Demster, Mallory, and Munson lines).[47]

A highly segmented employment structure shaped the character of dock work and waterfront union and race relations. Laboring in different sectors and loading and unloading different products, blacks and whites did not compete for jobs in the early twentieth century. Beginning at least in the 1880s, skilled white workers occupied the top of the port's occupational hierarchy, dominating the loading of timber (from lighters in the river onto ships) and the screwing of cotton. In 1881, they formed the powerful Workingmen's Timber Benevolent Association to serve social, mutual aid, and trade union functions for its roughly five hundred members. Black workers, in contrast, loaded lumber on the docks and performed all of the port's coastwise work, earning about half the wages (about 25 cents an hour in the early twentieth century) of the white timbermen and screwmen.[48]

Mobile's relative lack of labor turmoil—compared with that of New Orleans or even Galveston—was an indication of the economic bargaining position of that port's dock workers. Until World War I, white timbermen and screwmen performed their labor in the time-honored fashion. Unlike New Orleans screwmen, they faced no technological challenges or skill dilution, and employers remained highly dependent upon their services. Black dock workers, for their part, faced far harsher working conditions and lower wages. In 1903, over a thousand black longshoremen struck for several weeks to no avail. Within days, the railroads and steamship lines began importing outside black labor. The Mobile and Ohio Railroad, for example, imported some fifty section hands to unload Mallory line cargoes. The city's white unions offered little more than verbal support, and the strike quickly collapsed.[49] In its aftermath, conditions for black workers remained poor—wages for Mobile blacks were the "lowest . . . paid anywhere on the Gulf," ILA official Fricke reported—and their organizations remained weak. While "I expected to find the conditions [in Mobile] bad," explained an ILA official in mid-1913, "I was surprised to find as deplorable conditions as I did find."[50]

A decade after the failed black longshore strike, black and white Mobile dockers finally dealt with the question of interracial collaboration and the equal division of work. Testing the strength of the color line in the autumn of 1913, "all the members of the white 'longshoremen's union at Mobile quit work in order to enforce the demand of the 2,000 negro 'longshoremen for more pay," the *Nation* magazine noted, praising what it saw as "a new attitude" indicating "a growth in the feeling of solidarity among workingmen in the section where such feeling has hitherto been weakest."[51] That assessment vastly oversimplified a conflict that centered on overlapping jurisdictional and racial issues. In 1913, Mobile boasted two white locals, one handling timber and the other cotton work (together numbering roughly 318 men), and four small black locals (with at least 405 members). Conflicts over organization, union jurisdiction, and race broke out at the ILA's annual convention the previous year. White members of Local 369, established in 1881, had won wages and conditions "far superior to any local" in the city; their ILA charter granted them jurisdiction over the handling of timber and logs out of the water. Some stevedores, however, had offered work loading timber out of water onto barges to members of other locals, at a lower wage. The 1912 convention sustained 369's exclusive jurisdiction, but problems remained. At the following year's convention, Gulf Coast District chief Fricke argued that what Mobile blacks "needed most of all was organization, and if we did not get that we could not do much to better the conditions of the colored men of that port." ILA officials blamed the black locals' weakness on their fragmentary character and now insisted that they merge into a single unit. The locals resisted. At the same time, one of the small black unions demanded an equal division of work with white cotton and timber loaders, a move opposed by both the ILA and white Mobile unionists.[52] Fricke invoked the traditional segmentation of labor in defense of the racial and occupational status quo: "The work performed by these two white locals is work that has never been performed by the colored locals and I believe amalgamation at this time would absolutely destroy any and all conditions. The colored men of that port are not properly organized and are not sufficiently strong."[53]

The issues of jurisdiction and the equal division of work, which the ILA convention had failed to resolve, were at the center of the September 1913 strike on the Mobile waterfront. The four black locals struck on September 1 for a five-cent-an-hour wage increase; significantly, all but the largest added the explosive demand for an equal division of all timber and cotton work that had been hitherto monopolized by the white unions. Several major companies signed contracts with those three locals, perhaps sensing an opportunity to weaken further their unionized (if sometimes unrecognized) labor force. Mobile's white unions interpreted that move as an attack on their monopoly. An equal division of their work, white timbermen complained, would leave them without "enough work to support their families." Vowing to "fight our battle for our rights to the bitter end," the white locals, backed by the international, endorsed the demands of Local 389—the only black union that did *not* demand an equal division. Declaring the other three locals "outlaw"—that is, outside of the ILA and hence nonunion—ILA officials insisted that stevedoring firms repudiate their contracts and instead recognize the only legitimate black ILA union, Local 389. To enforce this ruling, white screwmen and timbermen, joined shortly by white boommen and raftsmen, struck. "The cause of the strike of the [white] longshoremen is not trouble between them and us," noted a statement signed by many of Mobile's contracting stevedores, "but is a family row between the white men and the negroes."[54]

In the end, an ILA threat to order all its Gulf workers to refuse to handle any cotton loaded by the non-ILA black unions proved sufficiently powerful to force a resolution to the crisis. By October 1, stevedores backed down and repudiated their contracts with the small black locals which, in turn, merged to form but two locals, one dealing with coastwise work, the other with deep water work. The black union men won a small wage increase; the white strikers returned to work; and the proposed equal division of labor fell victim to the settlement. In this conflict, the ILA upheld the traditional segmentation of labor and maintained the color line. Mobile's biracial union structure, then, ensured some interracial collaboration, but only on terms acceptable to the white unions.[55] Such a solution failed to satisfy black dock workers, much less improve their conditions. Less than three years later, black trade unionists pressed for a "better division of the work"—blacks had remained confined to lumber loading, while whites dominated timber and cotton—before the Gulf Coast District of the ILA, demanding, with no success, that "the same conditions should obtain [in Mobile] as in New Orleans, Galveston and other ports."[56]

The ILA constantly encouraged intertrade and interracial collaboration among its affiliates in individual ports and along the Gulf. A meeting of Galveston's numerous locals in 1916 held at the international's request, for example, aimed "to promote that harmony among the different locals of the I.L.A., . . . to get everybody together and adjust petty differences between them, if any exist, and let them come to a perfect understanding of the meaning of brotherhood and mutual dependence and support." Outside of New Orleans, biracial union structures in the twentieth century served less to promote interracial collaboration than to isolate black and white locals from one another, to reduce or eliminate the threat of an easy racial recomposition of the labor force (by maintaining preexisting occupational and racial hierarchies), and to keep members from strikebreaking against other unions during times of labor unrest. On the eve of the strike wave of 1919, ILA officials would describe relations between black and white members as distant at best. In that year, Galveston maintained sixteen ILA locals—seven white and nine black. "Each local is employed at its particular class of work, and each local is working for a particular firm of ship agents or contracting stevedores," remarked union official Fricke to the ILA's convention. "The line of demarcation of the work done by the white and colored locals is closely drawn, and under the present arrangement between the Galveston locals the members of one local will not interfere with the work coming under the jurisdiction of another." Another delegate explained on a similar note that the "white and colored men in Mobile do not work together."[57] Two years before, black Mobile delegates objected both to the existing division of labor and to whites' refusal to affiliate with blacks "when it comes to the point of working side by side."[58] Yet whatever the specific relations between racially separate longshore locals, the structure largely succeeded in reducing overt competition and encouraging some collaboration. In the years following World War I, ILA locals along the Gulf were put to their harshest test. While the biracial alliance held, the union movement itself did not. Strikes were conducted by black and white locals of New Orleans longshoremen in 1919, 1921, and 1923; New Orleans cotton screwmen in 1921 and 1923; Gulfport, Biloxi, Mobile, Pensacola, Galveston, and Houston longshoremen (and in some cases screwmen) in 1923.[59] In the aftermath of the war and postwar labor upheavals, the ILA barely emerged from the wreckage. Everywhere along the Gulf Coast (and in Newport News, Virginia, as well), proponents of the open shop carried the day, with disastrous results for union influence, wage rates, and in some cases, race relations. The federations of longshore unions had entered an age in which interracial and multitrade collaboration was simply insufficient to prevail against the better organized power of capital.[60]

* * *

The examples offered thus far have been drawn from the Gulf Coast, where native-born (or English-speaking immigrant) white and black workers forged a series of often uneasy alliances. But biracial unionism was not restricted to the Deep South. One last example—the case of the port of Baltimore on the mid-Atlantic coast—reveals an additional configuration of waterfront unionism and race relations. The Maryland city's political economy and the ethnic and racial diversity of its labor force made interracial and intertrade alliance the key to union success. At the same time, they constituted powerful barriers to the waterfront union movement's goal of unity and control. Baltimore's trade unionists on the docks learned that not only were interunion and biracial collaboration hard to maintain but they were not always sufficient, by themselves, to shift substantially the balance of power in labor's direction.

Although manufacturing was assuming an increasing importance in Baltimore's economy, commerce continued to dominate even after the turn of the century. Located on the Patapsco River some twelve miles from the Chesapeake Bay and under two hundred miles from the Atlantic Ocean, the city functioned as an important center for commerce and shipping. Three trunk railroads and numerous smaller rail lines served Baltimore, bringing it bituminous coal from western Maryland, Pennsylvania, and West Virginia, and foodstuffs from the region and the Midwest. By 1912, some nineteen transatlantic steamship lines, several coastwise shipping lines, and numerous tramp ships and firms serviced the Chesapeake Bay region. Baltimore exported copper, iron, raw and processed foodstuffs, chemicals, and cotton. The city's substantial trade with ports to its south earned it a reputation as the "metropolis of the South."[61]

"In its industrial development Baltimore is northern," Charles S. Johnson wrote in a study for the Urban League in 1923, but "in its social customs it is more southern than Virginia. . . . There are to be found strange mixtures of sentiments, methods and customs. This geographical position, it would seem, has tended to exaggerate differences and keep racial issues more prominently in the foreground."[62] Yet Maryland was itself a latecomer to a fully developed system of black subordination. As was the case in West Virginia, Maryland's black adult males exercised the franchise into the twentieth century, successfully resisting white efforts to deprive them of the vote, and playing an important, if secondary, role in the state's Republican party. Possessing the vote, however, "did not work in any substantive way to advance the position of the Negro nor did it protect him from certain harsh setbacks in his status," as Margaret Law Callcott has argued. Segregation, which had characterized public schools in the late nineteenth century, extended to transportation and public facilities by the turn of the century, and to housing by 1910. In the economic realm, most blacks performed unskilled labor along the city's waterfront, in its factories, and on construction sites, or worked in canning factories or in domestic service. "The nearer you get to the Mason and Dixon Line," one corporate executive told Charles Johnson in 1923, "the harder you find it to mix whites and Negroes on the job. . . . [I]n Baltimore the white workers demand separation in everything."[63] If a segregated work force was a fact of late nineteenth- and early twentieth-century life, the color line did not necessarily rule out occasional joint action between the black and white sectors of a segregated labor movement.

Baltimore's waterfront, like that of New Orleans, was not subordinate to an overly powerful railroad sector, as was the case in Mobile, Savannah, Pensacola, and, to a degree, Galveston. Instead, numerous transatlantic shipping firms, coastwise companies, railroads, and manufacturing establishments conducted their business along the docks. Although the multiplicity of employers and contractors rendered the port potentially susceptible to unionization, a number of factors mitigated against the emergence of a powerful dockside labor federation. First, Baltimore's shipping was dependent upon no single product; a tie-up in one sector might have no impact on trade in another, just as specific market conditions for the grain trade might have no effect on conditions for loading copper or lumber. In contrast, cotton dominated the export trade of New Orleans and Galveston. A strike of cotton handlers in the Crescent City's contracting sector might grind to a halt the entire waterfront labor process, drawing in all workers handling the product. This single product dependence, coupled with employment dynamics in the contracting sector, made New Orleans especially vulnerable to the solidarity of its workers. A commonality of interest between different waterfront sectors in Baltimore was never a given. Second, the port's labor force was composed largely of new immigrants, especially Poles, and blacks. While blacks were no newcomers to unions and new immigrants demonstrated no shortage of militancy, the barriers of language, race, and ethnicity were pronounced. Third, by the start of the century, Baltimore's employers had earned a strong anti-union reputation. "Baltimore has practically no labor troubles," boasted a 1912 municipal publication. "The city seems totally unaffected by those periodic gusts of labor agitation that sweep over one section of the country or another, unsettling conditions, causing industrial distress and financial loss."[64] Most of the city's employers had imposed open shop conditions on weak or nonexistent unions.

Not unionized, ethnically and racially divided, and laboring for strong employers exporting a variety of goods, Baltimore's dock workers confronted harsh working conditions. "The stevedores [in Baltimore, the term "stevedore" was interchangeable with "longshoreman"] of Baltimore are of many nationalities," Charles Girelius, a sympathetic if condescending observer, concluded in 1912. "They are of course crude and rough,—they have never had a chance to be anything else. They have had no rights that their employers were bound to respect, no opportunity to live decently." Wages had risen little from the late nineteenth century to 1912, with most dock hands earning between twenty and twenty-two cents an hour. The problem of low hourly wages was compounded by the irregularity of work. Dependent upon the arrival of ships, working in often-crowded labor markets, and guaranteed no steady employment, Baltimore's dock workers earned between $6 and $7 a week. Baltimore was "the poorest port in the world for stevedores," one union official declared with little exaggeration.[65]

Dock laborers launched two serious challenges to this state of affairs in the prewar era. In 1900 and in 1912, thousands of longshoremen struck for higher wages, double time for night work, union recognition and the closed shop, and access of union organizers to wharves, warehouses, and ships.[66] The two strikes unfolded in similar ways. Both union movements emerged virtually overnight, after some men had walked off the job. Strikers joined the ILA in 1900, and the National Transport Workers' Federation, affiliated with the International Seamen's Union, in 1912.[67] In each case, the organizations that formed attempted to link groups of workers divided by location, employer, and race. Community-based violence was common in each year, pitting strikers against nonstrikers, white strikers against black strikebreakers, black strikers against black strikebreakers, and black and white strikers against immigrant Italian strikebreakers. And lastly, both union movements failed. A brief examination of the two upheavals demonstrates that the obstacles to biracial unionism included not just racial tensions but a wide array of factors, ranging from the strength of shipping employers to the fragmentation of the labor force along occupational lines.

Baltimore's unions of stevedores emerged out of a series of short-lived and initially successful strikes in late May 1900 in Locust Point and Canton (geographically distinct regions of Baltimore's waterfront) over demands for higher wages, "humane" treatment by foremen, and, for one group of workers, a promise that "no colored men . . . be employed in the loading and discharging of vessels" (although the strikers would permit them to clean the holds of vessels). For their part, 125 black stevedores who loaded steel rails in Canton struck for a wage increase, exhibiting a "warlike disposition" (in the words of one journalist); grain shovelers at the Baltimore and Ohio (B&O) Railroad's Locust Point elevators also struck to equalize their wages with higher-paid workers at the Baltimore Elevator Company in Canton.[68] A more serious, and less successful, strike wave began on July 31 at Locust Point. Soon, when white Canton longshoremen struck over demands for a wage increase and union work rules,

Canton coal heavers (numbering roughly 1120 in Local Branch 195, Longshoremen's Union), black coal trimmers of Locust Point (numbering 140 in Local Branch 187), and grain trimmers quickly entered the fray in sympathy, bringing the total number of strikers to over two thousand.[69]

The 1912 strike began when fifteen hundred Locust Point stevedores walked out, demanding a five-cent-an-hour wage increase, formal union recognition, and access to wharves, warehouses, and ships for union representatives.[70] At that moment, dock workers formed three general longshore unions, one covering white Locust Point workers, another for white Fells Point workers, and a third for all blacks (numbering roughly one thousand). Strikers were joined in sympathy by gang foremen of the Johnstone Line, some forty stevedores of the Merchants and Miners' Transport Company, one hundred black Old Bay Line stevedores (who added their own demand for a small wage increase), six hundred black coal trimmers of the Rapid Coal Company, as well as coal trimmers of the B&O railroad, half of the B&O force at its Curtis Bay facilities, Baker-Whiteley Coal Company trimmers, three hundred lumber stevedores in the Back Basin, 250 banana stevedores, and the Baltimore Copper Smelting and Rolling Company's copper handlers.

Collaboration across racial and occupational lines was a prominent feature of both strikes. As Girelius put it in 1912, blacks and "Poles with little or no knowledge of English, crude and rough men of many other types and nationalities, all have been standing together as brothers, doggedly and pathetically demanding a chance to support families in decency—and recognition."[71] The 1900 alliance of ILA unions and the 1912 alliance of the National Transportation Workers Federation rested uneasily on agreements or understandings between distinct locals representing different groups of workers. For white longshoremen in Canton and Locust Point, geography and race formed the basis of their organizations; for black longshore workers in both sections of the city, race was the determining factor. Other groups of workers formed distinct locals on the basis of their place of employment: black coal trimmers, white coal heavers, grain trimmers, copper ore workers, lumber stevedores, and the like might belong to their own (recently formed) associations. (The one exception occurred in 1900, when the Locust Point white longshoremen's union apparently admitted into membership an unspecified number of black freight handlers from the Light Street and Pratt Street wharves.) Given the ethnic/national and linguistic diversity of their members, union leaders conducted their meetings—often attended by hundreds and occasionally exceeding a thousand—in English, Polish, and German.

Solidarity, while an impressive achievement, proved to be an inadequate weapon in the strikers' arsenal. Longshoremen confronted vastly more powerful employers, who imported hundreds of strikebreakers (mostly black, but including some native-born whites and immigrant Italians as well), secured sweeping court injunctions restricting the activities of union leaders (in 1912), and relied upon an army of private and public police to protect their newly recruited labor force. The 1900 strikers went down to defeat by early September, unable to hold out against the largest shipping agents' superior power to hire and protect strikebreakers. In 1912, the fate of each group hinged less on the power of the whole—that is, on the solidarity across occupational lines—than on immediate market conditions and the strength of their employers in specific trades. Lumber handlers and banana workers won their increase, as did laborers employed by the small contracting stevedoring firms; in contrast, copper stevedores lost their jobs, and many general longshoremen of the large transatlantic companies straggled back months later. Most workers, then, lost the strike, returning to work with no union recognition or contract.[72]

Neither labor activism nor biracial unionism disappeared with the loss of the 1912 strike. The ILA renewed its organizing efforts, and by 1914, Baltimore's newly formed small ILA locals joined together to form a waterfront council.[73] But unions remained ethnically fragmented and racially divided, their activities uncoordinated, their struggles only modestly successful. In 1916 and 1917, for example, individual gangs associated with particular piers, unions representing men working for particular employers, and unions of specific trades (grain trimmers, coal trimmers, general longshoremen) occasionally struck for small wage increases, an end to abusive treatment, and the closed shop; at times, black and Polish longshoremen would meet to discuss strategy. The Industrial Workers of the World, whose organizers arrived in Baltimore between 1915 and 1917, attracted a small number of black cargo handlers, and black Wobblies competed unsuccessfully with black and white ILA members for jurisdictional supremacy on the eve of the United States' entry into World War I.[74] Given the weakness of the port's union movement, black and white dock workers participated in few of the wartime and postwar upheavals that affected the longshore industry in New York, Virginia's Hampton Roads district, or the Gulf ports.[75]

* * *

Biracial unionism in the late nineteenth and early twentieth centuries assumed a variety of institutional forms. The nature of a port's employment structure and the related strength of black unions were crucial factors shaping the biracial systems that emerged along the waterfronts of the South. Both top ILA officials and white dock workers revealed that their positions on the question of "industrial equality" for black and white workers were more influenced by pragmatic considerations of power and stability than by principle. In New Orleans, black workers were a force to be reckoned with, and the strength of their unions compelled whites to enter into collaborative arrangements. In the large competitive contracting sector, that alliance reduced overt racial competition and enabled black and white longshore workers to exercise a tremendous amount of control over the performance and conditions of their work. In Galveston, black dock unions in the competitive contracting sector proved sufficiently strong to compete with whites; they could not be ignored without imperiling white workers' security and ILA stability. Thus, the ILA not only sustained that port's black screwmen in 1913 but actively mobilized against the white union which had repudiated the "amalgamation contract." But biracial unionism in Galveston was weakened by an employment structure dominated by railroads and allied steamship lines; the relative lack of racial competition for work reduced both interracial collaboration and competition. The railroad enclave generally proved too powerful for freight handlers of either race to exercise a degree of control comparable to that of workers in the competitive contracting sector. In Mobile, a strong railroad sector, racial segmentation of the labor force, and weak black unions combined to make biracial unionism a force that sustained rather than challenged racial inequality in the economic sphere. White workers and the ILA found that they could ignore weak black unions in the lowest-paid sector of Mobile's railroad-dominated waterfront. Invoking tradition and the need for stronger organization, the ILA in 1913 focused its energies not on breaking down the color line but on keeping it intact. Baltimore's complex patchwork of employment sectors, reflecting its reliance on the export and import of numerous products, weakened any alliance between different groups of waterfront workers. At the same time, the ethnic diversity of Baltimore's labor force that set it apart from its counterparts along the Gulf Coast did not prove to be an insurmountable obstacle to waterfront union organizing.

The development of biracial waterfront unionism in the South was varied and complex. Its shape was influenced heavily by the character of employment relations, the power of employers, the prior history of racial division or segmentation of labor, and the strength of black unions themselves. Biracial unionism was always a practical means to an end: the regulation or elimination of overt racial conflict over jobs and often the creation of a more effective labor alliance. It could promote interracial collaboration or inhibit racial competition; advance black access to employment or consign black labor to secondary positions; and ensure unprecedented degrees of black equality in local labor movements or lock blacks into an unequal alliance with more powerful whites.

Biracial unionism represented an imperfect but unprecedented strategy that reflected the strength of the white South's racial ideologies and practices while simultaneously violating many of its racial expectations and norms. That it was built upon racially separate union locals should not be surprising, given the near total pattern of segregation in the South during the Gilded Age and Progressive Era. To expect black or white workers to insist upon integration or to champion not just "industrial equality" but "social equality" as well is to impose unrealistic and ahistorical mid- and late twentieth-century political sensibilities on historical actors whose worldviews were profoundly different than our own; it is to deny the very real institutional and ideological constraints on those actors' lives, substituting contemporary political judgments for historical analysis.[76] In the context of the Jim Crow South, the ILA and the biracial unionism it championed both captured and defied the logic of white supremacy. The ILA's public stand in favor of the unity of southern waterfront workers across racial lines made it a rather unique and significant institution. Whatever its many limitations, it unquestionably broke new ground in the southern labor movement. Southern black longshore workers understood well its limitations, while simultaneously recognizing the real opportunities that biracial unionism offered them. Historians, too, would do well to appreciate the contradictory elements of biracial unionism's mixed legacy.

Notes

I would like to thank Katrin Schultheiss, Julie Greene, Bruce Nelson, Colin Davis, Cal Winslow, Dana Frank, Karin Shapiro, and Daniel Letwin for their comments on drafts of the essay. An earlier version was presented at the Racism and the Labour Market Conference, sponsored by the International Institute of Social History, held in Amsterdam in September 1991, and appeared in the proceedings of that conference as "'It aint like they do in New Orleans': Race Relations, Labor Markets, and Waterfront Labor Movements in the American South, 1880–1923," in *Racism and the Labour Market: Historical Studies,* ed. Marcel Van Der Linden and Jan Lucassen (Bern: Peter Lang AG, 1995).

1. International Longshoremen's Association, *Proceedings of the Twenty-fifth Convention, Galveston, Texas, July Fourteenth to Twenty-second, 1919,* 543; International

Longshoremen's Association, *Proceedings of the Twenty-sixth Convention. Buffalo, New York. July Eleventh to Eighteenth, 1921*, 305.

2. "New Orleans Longshoremen's Union Displeased with A.F.L.," *New York Age*, 30 July 1921.

3. *New Orleans Daily Picayune*, 13 Sept. 1911; James C. Maroney, "The International Longshoremen's Association in the Gulf States during the Progressive Era," *Southern Studies* 16 (Summer 1977), 225–32; "Longshoremen Convention Now in Session Here," *Galveston Union Review*, 18 July 1919; *Crisis* 3 (Nov. 1911), 9; W. E. B. Du Bois and Augustus Granville Dill, *The Negro American Artisan*, Atlanta University Publications, no. 17 (Atlanta: Atlanta University Press, 1912), 112; International Longshoremen's Association, *Proceedings of the Twentieth Convention. Port Huron, Mich. July 8 to 13, 1912* (Port Huron: Riverside Printing Company, 1912), 22.

4. *Seattle Daily Times*, 3, 16, 28 June, 3, 12 July 1916. Horace Cayton, Sr., believed that the Seattle longshore strike of April 1919 was "but a deep-seated plot to eliminate the colored members from the working force on the waterfront" (*Cayton's Weekly* [Seattle], 19 Apr. 1919). Also see Horace R. Cayton, *Long Old Road: An Autobiography* (1963; rpt. Seattle: University of Washington Press, 1970), 107; Jonathan Dembo, "The West Coast Teamsters' and Longshoremen's Unions in the Twentieth Century," *Journal of the West* 25 (Apr. 1986), 27–35. On Cleveland, see *Baltimore Morning Herald*, 15 June 1887; on San Francisco, see *Seattle Daily Times*, 19 June 1916, *San Francisco News*, 6 Oct. 1919; *Houston Informer*, 14 Feb. 1920; on Buffalo, New York, see Brenda K. Shelton, "The Grain Shovellers' Strike of 1899," *Labor History* 9 (Spring 1968), 218; on New York City, see *New Orleans Southwestern Christian Advocate*, 20 Mar. 1890; *Savannah Tribune*, 28 Aug. 1920; *New York Times*, 17 Aug., 3 Sept. 1920; *New York Telegraph*, 17 Aug. 1920; *New York Sun*, 10 Sept. 1920; *New York News*, 19 Aug. 1920; on New Jersey, *Jersey City Journal*, 16 Oct. 1919. In 1887, the only concession won by some two hundred white strikers on the National line pier in New York was the dismissal of black nonunion men who had replaced them. Two years later, 250 white longshoremen walked off the same pier when the company hired seventy-five blacks (*Baltimore Morning Herald*, 31 July 1887; *Atlanta Constitution*, 17 Dec. 1889). Also see Charles Lionel Franklin, *The Negro Labor Unionist of New York* (New York: Columbia University Press, 1936), 189–91. Black sociologist E. Franklin Frazier described in 1924 the history of black labor in the longshore trade as a "series of invasions, principally during strikes and periods of labor shortage" ("A Negro Industrial Group," *Howard Review* 1 [June 1924], 198). While his observation concerned the port of New York, it was descriptive of the experience of many ports in the United States.

5. *Industrial Worker*, 15 Aug. 1914, quoted in Philip Foner, "The IWW and Black Workers," *Journal of Negro History* 55 (Jan. 1970), 47. On the IWW and black workers, see Frederick A. Blossom, "Justice for the Negro: How He Can Get It," *One Big Union Monthly* 1 (Aug. 1919), 30–31; "I.W.W. Make a Strong Plea for Support of Negroes," *St. Louis Argus*, 22 Aug. 1919; "I.W.W.," *Crisis* 18 (June 1919), 60; Bernard A. Cook and James R. Watson, "The Sailors and Marine Transport Workers' 1913 Strike in New Orleans: The AFL and the IWW," *Southern Studies* 18 (Spring 1979), 111–22. For a glowing account of the interracial Marine Transport Workers Industrial Union, Local 8, in Philadelphia, see "Colored and White Workers Solving the Race Problem for Philadelphia," *Messenger* 3 (July 1921), 214–15. On Philadelphia, the IWW, and

black longshoremen, see William Seraile, "Ben Fletcher, I.W.W. Organizer," *Pennsylvania History* 46 (July 1979), 213–32; Lisa McGirr, "Black and White Longshoremen in the IWW: A History of the Philadelphia Marine Transport Workers Industrial Union Local 8," *Labor History* 36 (Summer 1995), 377–402; Howard Kimeldorf and Robert Penney, "'Excluded' by Choice: Dynamics of Interracial Unionism on the Philadelphia Waterfront 1910–1930," *International Labor and Working-Class History* 51 (Spring 1997), 50–71; "The Forum of Local 8," *Messenger* 3 (Aug. 1921), 234. Also see copies of "Fellow Worker" and bulletin of the "Marine Transport Workers Industrial Union" in Industrial Workers of the World Collection, box 70, folder 20, Archives of Labor and Urban Affairs, Wayne State University, Detroit; "Philadelphia's Sugar Strike," *Survey* 37 (17 Mar. 1917), 696–97; and correspondence from Fletcher in the Abram L. Harris Papers, Collection 43-1, Moorland-Spingarn Research Center, Howard University, Washington, D.C.

6. Sterling D. Spero and Abram L. Harris, *The Black Worker: The Negro and the Labor Movement* (1931; rpt. New York: Atheneum, 1969), 183; Maroney, "International Longshoremen's Association in the Gulf States," 225–32. Also see James C. Maroney, "Organized Labor in Texas, 1900–1929" (Ph.D. dissertation, University of Houston, 1975). The unusual position of blacks in the ILA was noted by numerous contemporary observers. See Charles S. Johnson, "Negro Workers and the Unions," *Survey* 60 (Apr. 15, 1928), 113; Department of Research and Investigations of the National Urban League, Ira DeA. Reid (director), *Negro Membership in American Labor Unions* (New York: Alexander Press, 1930), 48–49; "Labor Follows Industry South," *Opportunity* 6 (Dec. 1928), 379. "In cities near the Mason and Dixon Line and in the South Negroes were generally taken into the longshoremen's union. Their admission was no doubt influenced by the menace of their numerical strength" (Lorenzo J. Greene and Carter G. Woodson, *The Negro Wage Earner* [New York: Association for the Study of Negro Life and History, 1930], 308, 114). Also see Maud Russell, *Men along the Shore: The I.L.A. and Its History* (New York: Brussel & Brussel, 1966).

7. On the larger labor movement's racial policies, see Dana Frank, "Race Relations and the Seattle Labor Movement, 1915–1929," *Pacific Northwest Quarterly* 86 (Winter 1994/95), 35–44; Eric Arnesen, "'Like Banquo's Ghost, It Will Not Down': The Race Question and the American Railroad Brotherhoods, 1880–1920," *American Historical Review* 99 (Dec. 1994), 1601–33; Herbert R. Northrup, *Organized Labor and the Negro* (New York: Harper & Brothers, 1944); David R. Roediger, *The Wages of Whiteness: Race and the Making of the American Working Class* (New York: Verso, 1991).

8. A fourth and often crucial factor is state policy—how hostile or receptive to union organizing and, in particular, labor collaboration across racial lines were local or state politicians? This is an issue I explore in some detail in *Waterfront Workers of New Orleans: Race, Class, and Politics, 1863–1923* (1991; rpt. Urbana: University of Illinois Press, 1994); for reasons of space, I have chosen not to address it here.

9. An exception might be eastern and southern European immigrant longshoremen in Baltimore (discussed below), but there is no evidence here that distinct racial ideas played any role in the forms that biracial unionism assumed in this mid-Atlantic port.

10. Lest there be any misunderstanding, let me state clearly that white unionists articulated a racialist view of themselves and black workers; they drew sharp boundaries between themselves and blacks; and in many cases they ignored or campaigned against black interests outside of the workplace. Their identity of themselves as workers was itself racialized. I develop these points at great length in *Waterfront Workers of New Orleans* and "'Like Banquo's Ghost.'" But racial perspectives alone cannot account for the variety of racial practices and accommodations nor the historical evolution of those practices.

11. This discussion of the late nineteenth century is drawn from *Waterfront Workers of New Orleans*. Also see Arnesen, "Learning the Lessons of Solidarity: Race Relations and Work Rules on the New Orleans Waterfront," *Labor's Heritage* 1 (Jan. 1989), 26–45; David Paul Bennetts, "Black and White Workers: New Orleans 1880–1900" (Ph.D. dissertation, University of Illinois at Urbana-Champaign, 1972); Daniel Rosenberg, *New Orleans Dockworkers: Race, Labor, and Unionism 1892–1923* (New York: State University of New York Press, 1988); Spero and Harris, *Black Worker*, 184–85; George McNeill, *The Labor Movement: The Problem of Today* (New York, 1887), 167; Raymond Arthur Pearce, "The Rise and Decline of Labor in New Orleans" (M.A. thesis, Tulane University, 1938).

12. On segregation and disfranchisement in the city in general, see *Southwestern Christian Advocate*, 5 July 1895, 19 July, 1 Nov. 1900, 5, 26 June, 6 Nov. 1902, 26 Feb., 26 Mar., 23 Apr. 1903; A. R. Holcombe, "The Separate Street-Car Laws in New Orleans," *Outlook* 72 (20 Nov. 1902); William Ivy Hair, *Carnival of Fury: Robert Charles and the New Orleans Race Riot of 1900* (Baton Rouge: Louisiana State University Press, 1976). On the formation of the Central Trades and Labor Council, see *New Orleans Daily Picayune*, 14 Aug., 11 Sept. 1899; *New Orleans Times-Democrat*, 14 Aug., 11 Sept. 1899.

13. On the African American trade union tradition in this era, see Eric Arnesen, "'What's on the Black Worker's Mind?': African-American Labor and the Union Tradition on the Gulf Coast," *Gulf Coast Historical Review* 10 (Fall 1994), 7–30; Arnesen, "Following the Color Line of Labor: Black Workers and the Labor Movement before 1930," *Radical History Review* 55 (Winter 1993), 53–87; Peter Rachleff, *Black Labor in Richmond, 1865–1890* (1984; rpt. Urbana: University of Illinois Press, 1989).

14. On the 1894–95 riots, see John Smith Kendall, *History of New Orleans*, vol. 2 (New York, 1922), 515; British Foreign Office, "United States Report for the Year 1894 of the Trade of the Consular District of New Orleans," Diplomatic and Consular Reports on Trade and Finance, Annual Series, no. 1551 (London, May 1895), 15; C. Vann Woodward, *Origins of the New South 1877–1913* (1951; rpt. Baton Rouge: Louisiana State University Press, 1971), 267.

15. *New Orleans Daily Picayune*, 8 May 1903, 4 Nov. 1902, 19, 21 Apr. 1903, 23 Sept., 4, 22 Oct. 1902; *New Orleans Times-Democrat*, 10 May 1903; also see *New Orleans Daily Picayune*, 20 Mar. 1908; John Lovell, "Sail, Steam and Emergent Dockers' Unionism in Britain, 1850–1914," *International Review of Social History* 32 (1987), 237–40.

16. *New Orleans Daily Picayune*, 17 Apr. 1902; James Porter, "Report of Screwmen's Lockout, New Orleans," *Proceedings of the Twelfth Annual Convention of the International Longshoremen and Marine Transport Workers' Association, Bay City, Michigan, July 13–18, 1903*, 86.

17. *New Orleans Daily Picayune,* 4 Apr. 1903.

18. Porter, "Report of Screwmen's Lockout," 86; *New Orleans Times-Democrat,* 30 Oct. 1902, 12 Mar. 1908; *New Orleans Daily Picayune,* 22, 25, 26, 28, 30 Sept., 1, 4, 22, 27, 28, 30 Oct., 6 Nov. 1902, 12 Mar. 1908; Northrup, *Organized Labor and the Negro,* 149.

19. *New Orleans Daily Picayune,* 1, 5 Nov. 1902; *New Orleans Times-Democrat,* 1 Nov. 1902; "Special Meeting of the Board of Directors, Apr. 29, 1903," New Orleans Cotton Exchange Minute Books," 232, Special Collections, Tulane University, New Orleans.

20. *Report of the Bureau of Statistics of Labor for the State of Louisiana 1902–1903* (Baton Rouge: Advocate, 1904), 50; *New Orleans Daily Picayune,* 26 Sept., 3, 4, 6, 9, 13 Oct. 1903; *New Orleans Times-Democrat,* 1–4, 12–14, 21 Oct. 1903; *Labour Gazette* 11 (Nov. 1903), 305; *Union Advocate,* 19 Oct. 1903.

21. *New Orleans Daily Picayune,* 7 Sept. 1907, 28 Mar. 1908; *New Orleans Times-Democrat,* 28 Mar. 1908.

22. *New Orleans Times-Democrat,* 12 Mar. 1908.

23. International Longshoremen's Association, *Proceedings of the Twenty-second Convention . . . Milwaukee, Wis. July 13th to 18th inclusive, 1914* (Milwaukee, 1914), 11.

24. International Longshoremen's Association, *Proceedings of the Twenty-first Convention. . . . Boston, Mass., July 14th to 19th inclusive, 1913* (Port Huron: Riverside Printing Co., 1913), 173. Experience made some union leaders strong advocates of the New Orleans system. Harry Keegan, president of the white longshoremen, advised Texas delegates to the 1915 ILA convention: "We have had similar troubles to deal with in the port I come from. Why not handle it the same way? Organize your Dock and Marine Council; take in every craft that works along the docks. . . . I believe if the proper methods are pursued and the black men become organized they will be just as good unionists as anyone" (International Longshoremen's Association, *Proceedings of the Twenty-third Convention, San Francisco, CA, November 8, 1915,* 131).

25. On unsuccessful efforts of freight handlers to secure improvements, see Arnesen, *Waterfront Workers of New Orleans,* 99–103, 176–77, 202–3, 208–9.

26. *New Orleans Daily Picayune,* 25, 27 May, 3 June 1904, 28–31 Aug., 1 Sept. 1907; *New Orleans Daily News,* 29–31 Aug. 1907; *New Orleans Times-Democrat,* 28, 30 Aug. 1907; *Galveston Daily News,* 30 Aug. 1907; Pearce, "Rise and Decline of Labor," 63–64; George Carroll Miller, "A Study of the New Orleans Longshoremen's Unions from 1850 to 1962" (M.A. thesis, Louisiana State University and Agriculture and Mechanical College, 1962), 21. On the issue of social equality, see Daniel L. Letwin, "Interracial Unionism, Gender, and 'Social Equality' in the Alabama Coalfields, 1878–1908," *Journal of Southern History* 61 (Aug. 1995), 519–54; Nell Irvin Painter, "'Social Equality,' Miscegenation, Labor, and Power," in *The Evolution of Southern Culture,* ed. Numan V. Bartley (Athens: University of Georgia Press, 1988), 47–67.

27. *New Orleans Times-Democrat,* 24, 25 Oct. 1907; *New Orleans Daily News,* 23–26 Oct. 1907; *New Orleans Daily Picayune,* 24, 25 Oct. 1907. For a full account of the 1907 general strike, see Arnesen, *Waterfront Workers of New Orleans,* 196–203; Rosenberg, *New Orleans Dockworkers,* 115–41. Also see accounts by observers Oscar Ameringer (*If You Don't Weaken* [New York: Henry Holt and Company, 1940]) and Covington Hall ("La-

bor Struggles in the Deep South" [unpublished manuscript in Special Collections, Howard-Tilton Memorial Library, Tulane University, New Orleans]).

28. *New Orleans Daily Picayune*, 29, 30 Oct., 1–3 Nov. 1907; *L'Abeille de la Nouvelle Orleans*, 30 Oct. 1907; Ameringer, *If You Don't Weaken*, 215; Pearce, "Rise and Decline of Labor," 68–69.

29. Ameringer, *If You Don't Weaken*, 216–17; *New Orleans Daily News*, 1 Nov. 1907.

30. Booker T. Washington, "The Negro and the Labor Unions," *Atlantic Monthly* 111 (June 1913), 764. The *New York Age*, a black newspaper, observed in 1913 that "the best of feeling exists between the colored and white longshoremen . . . and a working agreement is in force between them which guarantees all a square deal" ("Longshoremen Draw No Line," *New York Age*, 14 Aug. 1913); W. E. B. Du Bois, ed., *The Negro Artisan: Report of a Social Study Made under the Direction of Atlanta University* (Atlanta: Atlanta University Press, 1902), 127–28.

31. On Galveston, see David G. McComb, *Galveston: A History* (Austin: University of Texas Press, 1986); Bradley Robert Rice, *Progressive Cities: The Commission Government Movement in America, 1901–1920* (Austin: University of Texas Press, 1977), 3–18; "Galveston, Texas. A Short History of the Port," *Longshoreman* 10 (Apr. 1919), 1; E. S. Holliday, "Port Facilities: The Port of Galveston," *Merchant Fleet News* 1 (Jan. 1928), 6–7.

32. *New Orleans Times-Democrat*, 12 Jan., 14 Mar. 1908; *New Orleans Daily Picayune*, 14 Mar. 1908.

33. This was true in New Orleans, Galveston, and Mobile. For an example of the tremendous power wielded by this sector, see James C. Maroney, "The Galveston Longshoremen's Strike of 1920," *East Texas Historical Journal* 16, no. 1 (1978), 34–38. The coastwise trade differed from the transatlantic trade in important ways. "Coastwise shipping is carried on by comparatively few regular lines" whose ships "cover a small number of ports," making "short and frequent voyages" with arrivals and departures "kept strictly within schedule time," wrote government investigator Boris Stern in 1930. Coastwise firms operated their own docks, performed their own stevedoring, offered more regular labor "from day to day [that is] less subject to the violent fluctuations which are the rule in 'deep-water' shipping." Coastwise longshoremen, then, had steadier work, but they received lower wages. Within the hierarchy of waterfront work, transatlantic, or "deep-sea" loading and unloading ranked above the coastwise trade (Stern, *Cargo Handling and Longshore Labor Conditions*, U.S. Bureau of Labor Statistics Bulletin no. 550 [Washington, D.C., 1932], 103–4).

34. *New Orleans Times-Democrat*, 11, 12 Jan. 1908.

35. The pattern of railroad domination of southern waterfronts proved to be the rule. The New Orleans Port Investigation Committee found Savannah "completely under control of the railroads." Local unions proved no match for the railroads. Savannah did "not know what serious labor trouble" was, the press noted, "and ever since the great wharf strike of fifteen years ago, when the backbone of unionism was broken, she has had peace on her levee." See *New Orleans Times-Democrat*, 5, 6 Feb. 1908; *New Orleans Daily Picayune*, 5, 10 Feb. 1908; testimony of Mr. Harris, ship broker, "Minutes of Investigation had in the city of Savannah, Georgia, as to Conditions pre-

vailing at the Port, February 4th and 5th, 1908," in Samuel L. Gilmore Papers, City Attorney, Minutes of Louisiana Port Investigation Commission, box 3, in Special Collections, Howard-Tilton Memorial Library, Tulane University, New Orleans; *Official Journal of the Proceedings of House of Representatives of the State of Louisiana at the First Regular Session of the Third General Assembly,* May 28, 1908. On Savannah dock workers, also see Mercer Griffin Evans, "The History of the Organized Labor Movement in Georgia" (Ph.D. dissertation, University of Chicago, 1929), 185–89; Mark V. Wetherington, "The Savannah Negro Laborers' Strike of 1891," in *Southern Workers and Their Unions, 1880–1975: Selected Papers, the Second Southern Labor History Conference, 1978,* ed. Merl E. Reed, Leslie S. Hough, and Gary M. Fink (Westport, Conn.: Greenwood Press, 1981), 4–21; *New Orleans Times-Democrat,* 10 Oct. 1903; *Atlanta Constitution,* 6, 10, 21 Oct., 14 Nov. 1903; *Savannah Tribune,* 15 Sept., 27 Oct. 1894, 31 Oct. 1903.

36. *Galveston Daily News,* 17–23, 28 Oct., 4–13 Nov. 1885.

37. On the 1898 strike, see *Galveston Daily News,* 31 Aug., 1–14, 23–28 Sept. 1898; *New Orleans Daily Picayune,* 31 Aug., 1–4, 6, 7, 9, 13, 14, 16, 18–28 Sept. 1898; *Southwestern Christian Advocate,* 8, 22 Sept. 1898. On ILA efforts to win over independent Galveston locals, see International Longshoremen's Association, *Proceedings of the Tenth Annual Convention, Toledo, Ohio, July 3–13, 1901,* 47–48; "President Keefe's Report of Visit to Pacific Coast and Gulf Ports," International Longshoremen's Association, *Proceedings of the Eleventh Annual Convention, 1902,* 25–27.

38. *New Orleans Daily Picayune,* 12, 13 Sept. 1907; *Houston Post,* 15 Sept. 1907. On the 1907 strike, see *Galveston Journal,* 20 Sept. 1907; *Galveston Daily News,* 6, 11–22 Sept. 1907; *Houston Post,* 12–21 Sept. 1907; *New Orleans Daily Picayune,* 12–15, 17–20 Sept. 1907; *New Orleans Times-Democrat,* 12–14, 17, 20 Sept. 1907. Several months later, unnamed white labor leaders explained to investigators from New Orleans that during the Southern Pacific strike, black dock workers had "showed a great deal of unionism" (*New Orleans Times-Democrat,* 12 Jan. 1908).

39. For example, when Galveston's Cotton Press Employees' Benevolent and Protective Association proposed the creation of a body of all cotton dock workers in 1883—an organization not unlike the New Orleans Cotton Men's Executive Council—the Screwmen's Benevolent Association's lack of interest doomed the plan. Although the white union did help establish a City Trade and Labor Assembly in that year, it withdrew from the assembly in 1885 because of its opposition to that body's advocacy of the creation of strike funds, endorsement of political candidates, and acceptance of black union delegates into its ranks. See James V. Reese, "The Evolution of an Early Texas Union: The Screwmen's Benevolent Association of Galveston, 1866–1891," *Southwestern Historical Quarterly* 75 (Oct. 1971), 175; Allen Clayton Taylor, "A History of the Screwmen's Benevolent Association from 1865 to 1924" (M.A. thesis, University of Texas, 1968), 71.

40. Reese, "Evolution of an Early Texas Union," 158–85; Taylor, "History of the Screwmen's Benevolent Association"; Ruth Allen, *Chapters in the History of Organized Labor in Texas* (Austin: University of Texas Press, 1941), 173; Virginia Neal Hinze, "Norris Wright Cuney" (M.A. thesis, Rice University, 1965); Lawrence D. Rice, *The Negro in Texas* (Baton Rouge: Louisiana State University Press, 1971), 189, Maud Cuney Hare, *Norris Wright Cuney: A Tribune of the Black People* (New York, 1913); Kenneth

Kann, "The Knights of Labor and the Southern Black Worker," *Labor History* 18 (Winter 1977), 56–57. Also see *Galveston Daily News,* 3–5 Apr. 1883, 17–23, 28 Oct., 4–6, 8–13 Nov. 1885. On early black union leaders and stevedores, see Merline Pitre, *Through Many Dangers, Toils and Snares: The Black Leadership of Texas 1868–1900* (Austin: Eakin Press, 1985), 170–71; Carl H. Moneyhon, "George T. Ruby and the Politics of Expediency in Texas," in *Southern Black Leaders of the Reconstruction Era,* ed. Howard N. Rabinowitz (Urbana: University of Illinois Press, 1982), 376–85; William Joseph Brophy, "The Black Texas, 1900–1950: A Quantitative History" (Ph.D. dissertation, Vanderbilt University, 1974), 157–62.

ILA president Keefe estimated that a total of 2,500 men worked on Galveston's docks in 1902: 900 unionized cotton screwmen (some 500 whites belonged to the Cotton Screwmen's Benevolent and Protective Association, 250–300 blacks to the Colored Screwmen's Association No. 2 and between 150–200 to Colored Screwmen's Association No. 3, the Excelsiors); some 500–700 nonunion blacks and approximately 200–300 white and additional black longshoremen. It is likely that most of the nonunion men worked for the city's main railroad and coastwise steamship lines. See "President Keefe's Report of Visit to Pacific Coast and Gulf Ports," International Longshoremen's Association, *Proceedings . . . 1902,* pp. 25–27.

41. Testimony of Fricke, "Minutes of Investigation Held in the City of Galveston, Texas, as to Conditions Prevailing at that Port, January 9th, 10th and 11th, 1908," p. 135, in box 3, Gilmore Papers.

42. "Memorandum of Agreement between Screwmen's Benevolent Association Local No. 317, I.L.A. and Cotton Screwmen and Longshoremen's Ass'n, Local No. 329, I.L.A. (colored) and Ship Agents and Stevedores of Galveston, Texas"; also listed as "Contract and Rules of Screwmen's Benevolent Association Local No. 317, I.L.A. and Cotton Screwmen and Longshoremen's Association Local No. 329, I.L.A. (colored), Rules of the Screwmen's Joint Conference Committee" (Galveston: Knapp Brothers, 1912), in the Southern Labor Archives, Georgia State University, Atlanta.

43. See testimony of Delegate Gray, Local 317, in International Longshoremen's Association, *Proceedings . . . 1913,* 98–99.

44. See testimony of Delegate Willis, International Longshoremen's Association, *Proceedings . . . 1913,* 100; *Galveston Labor Dispatch,* 22 Aug. 1913.

45. International Longshoremen's Association, *Proceedings . . . 1913,* 171. "If Locals 317 and 329 stick together as men and not be bought out by stevedores in Galveston, in less than three months Galveston will be the best union port we have," Willis concluded. "[C]ertain promises [had been] made to the colored men," O'Connor argued, "and I am strongly opposed to an action of this kind being taken."

46. On the conflict over the amalgamation contract in Galveston, see M. J. Gahagen, Secretary-Treasurer, Gulf Coast District, ILA, "Pertaining to Districts," *Longshoreman* 5 (Dec. 1913); Minutes of Local 310, Sept. 1913, International Longshoremen's Association (Screwmen's Benevolent Association), Local 310, 317, and 307 Collection, Special Collections, The University of Texas at Arlington; *Galveston Daily News,* 20, 23–28, 31 Aug., 2–5, 7–9, 15–18, 20, 21, 23 Sept. 1913; *Houston Post,* 3–7, 9, 16–21 Sept. 1913; *New Orleans Daily Picayune,* 4, 5, 16–18, 20 Sept. 1913; *Mobile Register,* 19 Sept. 1913.

47. Melton McLaurin and Michael Thomason, *Mobile: The Life and Times of a Great Southern City* (Woodland Hills, Calif.: Windsor Publications, 1981), 80–81; *New Orleans Times-Democrat*, 9 Feb. 1908; *Mobile Register*, 1 Sept. 1903; "Port Facilities: The Port of Mobile, Ala.," *Merchant Fleet News* 1 (Dec. 1927), 6; Ernest F. Ladd, "Mobile and the L.& N.," *L.&.N. Employes' Magazine*, Feb. 1928, 6–8; J. W. Jones, "The Port of Mobile," *L.&.N. Employes' Magazine*, Nov. 1930, 19–21; David Ernest Alsobrook, "Alabama's Port City: Mobile during the Progressive Era, 1896–1917" (Ph.D. dissertation, Auburn University, 1983).

48. On the Workingmen's Timber Benevolent Association, see *Mobile Daily Register*, 22 Mar. 1885, 23 Mar. 1886; on the racial division of labor, see "Report of the Statistician of L.A. No. 4180," *Alabama Sentinel*, 13 Dec. 1890; testimony of John B. Waterman, Manager for Elder-Demster Steamship Company in Mobile, in Minutes of Investigation Had in the City of Mobile, Ala., Saturday, February 8th, 1908, in Gilmore Papers. On blacks in Mobile, see "The Progress of the Negro Race in Mobile," *Mobile Register 100th Anniversary & 74th Annual Trade Review 1814–1914: The Gateway to Panama* (copy in Mobile Public Library); C. F. Johnson, "The Colored People of Mobile," *Mobile Register*, 1 Sept. 1900; "Negro Success in Mobile, Alabama," *Southwestern Christian Advocate*, 31 Aug. 1905. Mobile's screwmen received wages comparable to those of their New Orleans counterparts. Working in gangs of five, crew members received $5.00 a day, loading between ninety and one hundred bales per crew per day. Unlike New Orleans screwmen, however, Mobile screwmen could impose no daily limit on the amount of work performed.

49. The white Central Trades Union, at the strikers' request, asked stevedores and agents to meet with them to discuss the strike; employers declined. More importantly, but with equally dismal results, the white Workingmen's Timber and Cotton Benevolent Association voted to handle no cotton touched by nonunion men and called on Mobile's mayor to arbitrate. He refused. Following scattered harassment and violence by strikers against strikebreakers, city police arrested large numbers of black unionists, ensuring the hasty demise of their walkout (*Mobile Register*, 25, 27, 28 Oct., 3, 6, 7, 10–14 Nov. 1903; *New Orleans Daily Picayune*, 24, 25, 27, 29, 30 Oct., 3 Nov. 1903; *New Orleans Times-Democrat*, 25, 26 Oct. 1903). On the weak and divided character of Mobile's waterfront unions, see "Report of J. W. Thompson on Visit to Mobile, Ala., June 3, 1905," in International Longshoremen's Association, *Proceedings of the Fourteenth Annual Convention of the International Longshoremen, Marine and Transport Workers Association, Detroit, Mich., July 10th to 15th inclusive, 1905* (Detroit: Speaker Printing Company, 1905), 145–46.

50. International Longshoremen's Association, *Proceedings . . . 1913*, 178.

51. *Nation*, 7 May 1914. Drawing upon the *Nation* article, Greene and Woodson give an inaccurate portrait of the strike: "The power of the Negroes in these unions was demonstrated . . . when all the white longshoremen along the waterfront at Mobile quit work in order to enforce the demand of 2,000 Negro longshoremen for more pay" (Greene and Woodson, *Negro Wage Earner*, 114).

52. International Longshoremen's Association, *Proceedings . . . 1912*, 108, 131–32. Fricke continued his indictment: "The colored men of that port are not properly organized and are not sufficiently strong to ask conditions from any stevedore and our experience in the past under the four charters has been that when it came time

for contracts to be signed one local would always slip. I want to say further that under the present system if a member becomes a little dissatisfied in one local he joins another as they have only a small initiation fee" (International Longshoremen's Association, *Proceedings . . . 1913*, 178–79). Also see "Report of J. H. Fricke, President Gulf Coast District, to Third Annual Convention, Held in Gulfport, Miss.," *Longshoreman* 4 (July 1913). M. J. Gahagen, secretary-treasurer of the Gulf Coast District, explained the ILA officials' rationale in the newspaper of the international: "In compliance with the instructions of the Boston convention all the charters of (colored) locals performing the same class of work were canceled and Local 853 issued and installed instead. This will eventually overcome the ill-feeling which formerly existed between the members of these various locals. When the rank and file realize that this step was taken to benefit them, and their cause, they will surely assist in bringing about harmony for they well know the conditions which existed prior to this amalgamation. The stevedores were taking advantage of their weakness for greater profits from their labor but the colored men on this Coast are beginning to realize that as long as the employers are successful in keeping them from the organizations to which they should belong, and which are willing to assist in bettering their conditions, that the employers, and not themselves are the ones that are benefiting" (*Longshoreman* 5 [Dec. 1913], 1). Delegate Clemmons, of Local 356, Cotton, Timber, Lumber and General Cargo Loaders and Unloaders of Mobile, insisted that his union would "not give up timber on barges or cars, or give up their present charter unless we get one reading the same as our white brothers, and so far as amalgamation is concerned, we are willing to do that but let it be done in the right form. Now we are willing to take one ship and let them have one or we take on the same ship hatch one and two and they take three or four. . . . That is what we call amalgamating" (International Longshoremen's Association, *Proceedings . . . 1913*).

53. Testimony of J. H. Fricke, International Longshoremen's Association, *Proceedings . . . 1913*, 178–79.

54. *Mobile Register*, 3–7, 9, 12–17, 19–26, 28–30 Sept., 1, 2 Oct. 1913; *New Orleans Daily Picayune*, 4, 6, 9, 12, 13, 16, 18, 20, 21, 23, 25–27 Sept., 1 Oct. 1913; *Houston Post*, 4, 12 Sept. 1913; *Galveston Daily News*, 12 Sept. 1912; *Birmingham Age-Herald*, 12 Sept. 1913; *Nation*, 7 May 1914.

55. *Longshoreman* 5 (Nov. 1913); *Galveston Labor Dispatch*, 10 Oct. 1913. The ILA issued a new charter to Local 389, renumbering it Local 853.

56. *Houston Labor Journal*, June 16, 1917.

57. *Galveston Labor Dispatch*, 15 Jan. 1916; International Longshoremen's Association, *Proceedings . . . 1919*, 522, 533.

58. *Houston Labor Journal*, June 16, 1917.

59. Longshore workers in Houston implemented a biracial system shortly after that port opened in 1913. By 1916, black Local 872 and white Local 896 divided all work and foremen's positions equally "in order that any and all friction, or labor trouble be avoided." In that year, the Mallory Steamship company, long hostile to organized labor, "paying the lowest possible wage scale . . . and treating their employees in a most inhuman manner," discharged its white union workers, instead offering to employ members of the black local alongside black nonunion men. The black union rejected the deal, and the company locked out both the black and white unions. In

addition there is evidence that black and white union gangs worked side by side, at least for other firms, through the 1920s. See "Houston, Texas," *Longshoreman* 7 (Aug. 10, 1916), 2; "Report of J. H. Fricke," *Longshoreman* 7 (Sept. 10, 1916), 3; "A Brief History of I.L.A. Local 872," AR#8, Special Collections, University of Texas at Arlington. Ruth Allen notes that in the mid-teens the two locals entered into a ninety-nine-year agreement to divide all work equally (*Chapters in the History of Organized Labor in Texas,* 193–94). For a latter period, see Gilbert Mers, *Working the Waterfront: The Ups and Downs of a Rebel Longshoreman* (Austin: University of Texas Press, 1988).

60. On the postwar conflicts, see Arnesen, *Waterfront Workers of New Orleans,* 229–36, 244–49. Also see *Virginia-Pilot and the Norfolk Landmark,* 7–14, 15 Oct. 1923; *Gulfport and Biloxi Daily Herald,* 15, 17, 19, 20, 23 Oct. 1923; *Galveston Daily News,* 11, 16–21, 23, 24, 26 Oct. 1923; *Houston Post,* 30 Sept., 17 Oct. 1923; *Pensacola Journal,* 3 Oct. 1923; *Mobile Register,* 30 Sept., 1–5, 7 Oct. 1923.

61. On the economic history of Baltimore, see Eleanor Bruchey, "The Industrialization of Maryland 1860–1914," in *Maryland: A History 1632–1974,* ed. Richard Walsh and William Lloyd Fox (Baltimore: Maryland Historical Society, 1974), 408–31, 457–69; *Cost of Living in American Towns. Report of an Enquiry by the Board of Trade into Working Class Rents, Housing and Retail Prices, together with the Rates of Wages in Certain Occupations in the Principal Industrial Towns of the United States* (London, 1911), 72–86; Charles Hirschfeld, *Baltimore, 1870–1900: Studies in Social History* (Baltimore: Johns Hopkins Press, 1941), 32–83; Suzanne Ellery Greene Chapelle et al., *Maryland: A History of Its People* (Baltimore: Johns Hopkins University Press, 1986); Barbara Jeanne Fields, *Slavery and Freedom on the Middle Ground: Maryland during the Nineteenth Century* (New Haven: Yale University Press, 1985); *Sixth Annual Report of the Bureau of Industrial Statistics of Maryland* (Baltimore, 1897), 61, 74–75, 129–35; "The Port of Baltimore and Other Atlantic Ports," *Municipal Journal Baltimore* 7 (8 Aug. 1919), 1–2; G. H. Pouder, "Port Facilities: Port of Baltimore," *Merchant Fleet News* 1 (Mar. 1928), 12.

62. Charles S. Johnson, "Negroes at Work in Baltimore, Md.," *Opportunity* 1 (June 1923), 12.

63. On blacks in Baltimore, see Ira DeA. Reid, *The Negro Community of Baltimore: A Summary Report of a Social Study conducted for the Baltimore Urban League* (Baltimore, 1935); Margaret Law Callcott, *The Negro in Maryland Politics 1870–1912* (Baltimore: Johns Hopkins Press, 1969); Johnson, "Negroes at Work in Baltimore," 12–19; Charles S. Johnson, "The Negro in Baltimore Industries: A Study of the Industrial Situation in Baltimore Made by the Baltimore Inter-racial Committee," Study no. 1, Spring 1932 (typescript at Library of Congress); Jeffrey R. Brackett, *Notes on the Progress of the Colored People of Maryland since the War* (Baltimore, 1890); "The Baltimore Negro," *Southwestern Christian Advocate,* 4 May 1905; W. Ashbie Hawkins, "A Year of Segregation in Baltimore," *Crisis* 3 (Nov. 1911), 27–30; John R. Slattery, "Twenty Years' Growth of the Colored People in Baltimore, Md.," *Catholic World* 66 (Jan. 1898), 519–27; Karen Olson, "Old West Baltimore: Segregation, African-American Culture, and the Struggle for Equality," in *The Baltimore Book: New Views of Local History,* ed. Elizabeth Fee, Linda Shopes, and Linda Zeidman (Philadelphia: Temple University Press, 1991), 57–78. Also see issues of the *Afro-American Ledger* and its successor, the *Baltimore Afro-American.*

64. City of Baltimore, *The Baltimore Book: A Resume of the Commercial, Indus-trial and Financial Resources, Municipal Activities and General Development of the City of Baltimore* (Baltimore, 1912), 55. On Baltimore labor in the 1880s and 1890s, see R. T. Crane, "The Knights of Labor Movement in Baltimore," *John Hopkins University Circulars* 22 (Apr. 1903), 39; Peter H. Argersinger, "From Party Tickets to Secret Ballots: The Evolution of the Electoral Process in Maryland during the Gilded Age," *Maryland Historical Magazine* 82 (Fall 1987), 214–39; Roderick N. Ryon, "Baltimore Workers and Industrial Decision-Making, 1890–1917," *Journal of Southern History* 51 (Nov. 1985), 565–80. A valuable source of information on the Knights and the Federation of Labor locals in Baltimore in the late 1880s and early 1890s is the city's weekly labor newspaper, the *Critic*.

65. Charles G. Girelius, "A Baltimore Strike and What It Brought," *Survey* 28 (3 Aug. 1912); *Baltimore American,* 12 Apr. 1912; *Baltimore Sun*, 12, 13, 30 Apr. 1912; "Report of Secretary Joyce," *Longshoreman* 4 (Feb. 1913), 1; *Longshoreman* 5 (Mar. 1914), 2; *Baltimore Trades Unionist*, 10 Jan. 1914.

66. Details of the 1900 strikes are drawn from the *Baltimore Sun, Baltimore Morning Herald,* and the *Baltimore American* from April, May, July, August, and September; details of the 1912 strike are drawn from the *Baltimore Sun* and *Baltimore American.* Also see "The Stevedores' Various Strikes," in *Ninth Annual Report of the Bureau of Industrial Statistics of Maryland 1900* (Baltimore, 1901), 95–99; "Mr. Weber's Report Relative to the Baltimore Strike," International Longshoremen's Association, *Proceedings . . . 1901*, 14–15; "Strikes," *Twenty-first Annual Report of the Bureau of Statistics and Information of Maryland 1912* (Baltimore, 1913), 48–63.

67. For sketchy background to the Transport Workers' Federation, see Joseph P. Goldberg, *The Maritime Story: A Study in Labor-Management Relations* (Cambridge, Mass.: Harvard University Press, 1958), 33–41.

68. *Baltimore Sun*, 30 May, 2, 4, 6 June 1900; *Baltimore Morning Herald*, 30 May, 5 June 1900; *Ninth Annual Report . . . 1900*, 95.

69. The strike wave began when the Locust Point stevedoring firm of Patterson, Ramsay & Company utilized ships' sailors and cattlemen of the B&O railroad to load fifty cases of meat early one morning before union men assembled for work. In protest, union men refused to work for the firm until it had paid a fifty dollar fine levied by their union. The Locust Point men soon added the additional demand that only union labor be employed, which the company promptly refused. "It is a question whether we or the [union] stevedores shall operate our own business," one employer declared. "They cannot dictate whom we shall employ." Within a week, the firm had forged an alliance that included ten of the port's key foreign steamship lines. Vowing to employ no union members at all, steamship agents wasted little time in importing outside workers. White and especially black strikebreakers from Philadelphia, Norfolk, and points south were soon laboring under police guard along the docks. Agents were not always successful. Forty-three black and twelve white strikebreakers who arrived in Baltimore from Richmond on 8 August were "greatly amazed to find they were called upon to take the place of strikers"; the following day, between sixty-five and seventy Richmond blacks who claimed they were misled called on city officials to send them home. Acting mayor Gephart reached City Hall only to find

corridors filled with blacks. "Vague ideas of a race war or of a panic floated through his brain," the *Sun* reported. The men, however, were merely the defecting Richmond strikebreakers, who were stranded in Baltimore without money or employment (*Baltimore Sun*, 9, 10 Aug. 1900; *Baltimore American*, 10 Aug. 1900).

70. The state Bureau of Statistics and Information estimated that a total of 8,000 workers were involved in the strike at one time or another: 1,500 engaged in various trades along the waterfront went out in sympathy, along with some 2,000 workers of the Baltimore Copper Smelting and Rolling Company, 1,000 electrical workers, oilers, gas workers, and building trades workers as well (*Twenty-first Annual Report . . . 1912*, 61).

71. Girelius, "Baltimore Strike and What It Brought."

72. Some transatlantic steamship agents increased wages by 2.5 cents an hour as a concession to their individual workers. But the existence of a multiethnic and biracial alliance hardly eliminated tensions of an ethnic or racial character. In both strikes, union members, their families, and sympathizers confronted the hundreds of strikebreakers by turning to violence. And when strikebreakers were members of races or nationalities different from particular crowds, attacks could assume racist overtones. In 1900, for example, strikers and sympathizers participated in a series of assaults against black strikebreakers who rode the city's electric cars, hurling stones and sticks at their replacements. Daily small-scale riots pitted strikers numbering in the tens, hundreds, and at times one thousand against far smaller numbers of largely black strikebreakers. Upon several occasions, black strikebreakers fought back, firing hidden pistols at attacking mobs of men, women, teenagers, and children. Disavowing any union responsibility for the violence, white labor leaders protested the "importation of negro labor to take the place of tax-paying citizens," demanded that police give strikers the "same protection as they are offering to these negroes," and insisted that black strikebreakers be "as severely dealt with" as strikers "if they break the laws." The 1912 strike similarly involved repeated clashes, as strikers attacked strikebreakers on the docks, in the ships, on streetcars, and in the streets; strikebreakers often fought back, sometimes with guns. Large crowds of whites vented their wrath against strikebreakers, who were sometimes white but most often black. Upon occasion, white and black strikers jointly attacked black strikebreakers. At least once, black strikers attacked black strikebreakers: on 21 May 1912, black picketers wearing union buttons "advanced" or "rushed" toward a group of twelve black strikebreakers near the Baltimore Copper Smelting and Rolling Company plant in Canton; "somebody fired a shot and for several minutes stones and bricks flew in all directions." On 1 June, a gang of black strikers "swooped down on three Italian strikebreakers" eating their lunch near Canton's Pier 7. "Considering the fact that as many as 8,000 workmen, representing a dozen or more nationalities, were engaged in a three months' strike which invariably produces riot and disorder, it is remarkable to note that so little bloodshed occurred," concluded the state's commissioner of statistics and information (*Baltimore Sun*, 26, 27, 28 Apr., 1, 22 May 1912; *Baltimore American*, 22 May, 2 June 1912; *Twenty-first Annual Report . . . 1912*, p. 60; *Baltimore Labor Leader*, 6 July 1912).

73. A Savannah labor newspaper reported that according to ILA officials, "the colored workers are as enthusiastic to organize as the white workers" (*Savannah Labor*

Herald, 27 Feb., 20 Mar. 1914). Also see *Baltimore Trades-Unionist,* 10 Jan., 14, 21 Mar., 4 Apr. 1914; *Longshoremen* 4 (Sept. 1913), 2; 7 (Mar. 1916), 1; 7 (Apr. 1916), 2.

74. *Baltimore Trades-Unionist,* 27 Feb. 1915; *Baltimore Sun,* 10, 11 Jan., 25 Feb., 2, 3 May, 19 Aug. 1916, 19–21, 26–28 Feb., 12, 17, 25, 31 Mar. 1917; *Longshoreman* 7 (June 1916); 8 (Aug. 1917); *Baltimore Labor Leader,* 31 Jan. 1914, 27 Feb., 13 Mar. 1915, 9 Nov. 1918. According to Spero and Harris, by the late 1920s, Baltimore had five ILA locals—two mixed, one black, and two white. Ira Reid's 1935 study identified five ILA locals, with blacks being prominent in four (*Negro Community of Baltimore,* 13). Charles S. Johnson's 1932 study offered this summary of recent Baltimore waterfront history: "White and Negro longshoremen where they work together have a spirit of tolerance cooperation [*sic*] generally regarded as impossible in the city. There are some white members in the predominantly Negro union and some Negroes in the locals predominantly white. Some time ago it was suggested that in the distribution of work between white and Negro workers at the docks an agreement be tried similar to the one employed in New Orleans which required that whites and Negroes be carried on jobs in exactly equal numbers and that where men are laid off an equal number of whites and Negroes should go. This suggestion was overcome by opposition from both groups. The Negroes as frequently as the whites would get what they called 'a good thing' and objected to leaving it" (Johnson, "Negro in Baltimore Industries," 55). Spero and Harris argued that black dissatisfaction with white ILA members' attitudes led to their withdrawal after 1912 from two mixed locals, Number 826 and 829, and the formation of a new all black local (*Black Worker,* 192–93).

75. Boris Stern, in his comprehensive study, described labor conditions on Baltimore's docks at the end of the 1920s. Employers drew upon ILA members in the loading and discharging of foreign and intercoastal cargoes; work gangs (on a relatively permanent basis) shaped up twice daily, although much of the hiring was done in advance with specific gangs regularly employed by specific employers; the lack of a rotation system meant that certain gangs of workers earned substantially more than other gangs, and that those specializing in key cargoes—like tin plate, steel rails, and lumber—earned higher wages (*Cargo Handling and Longshore Labor Conditions,* 85–87).

76. David Roediger offers criticism of the white labor movement's "walling off of social and political equality from 'stomach equality'" in a recent essay. "As a strategy to organize all workers, the 'stomach but not social or political equality' stance was profoundly out of touch with the real world" ("What If Labor Were Not White and Male? Recentering Working-Class History and Reconstructing Debate on the Unions and Race," *International Labor and Working-Class History* 51 [Spring 1997], 87).

2   "Men of the Lumber Camps Come to Town": New York Longshoremen in the Strike of 1907

Calvin Winslow

On May 1, 1907, New York Harbor longshoremen went on strike, tying up the world's largest port for six weeks. The strike began in Brooklyn and spread to Manhattan's East and North (Hudson) River waterfronts, then to Hoboken and Staten Island. It ultimately involved tens of thousands of workers in a confrontation with the oligarchy of shippers, led by the Morgan Shipping Trust, as well as with the railroads, the civil authorities of New York and New Jersey, and armies of strikebreakers. These workers, according to Ernest Poole, "made only one demand . . . Give us higher pay!"[1] This demand, however, led to an extraordinary conflict, the outcome of which, for more than a month, was in the balance.

The 1907 strike ended in defeat. Nevertheless, it was a crucial episode in the history of waterfront workers in New York. Its significance, however, remains largely unexplored, and at best inadequately analyzed by historians.[2] First, therefore, it is necessary to establish the importance of this strike and the movement for industrial unionism which it generated. Second, the 1907 strike was a radical strike, and its history extends our knowledge of working-class radicalism in the period. Finally, the waterfront workforce in New York was remarkable in the degree to which it was divided along racial and ethnic lines. Irish, Italians, African Americans,

Germans, Scots and Englishmen, Slavs, and Scandinavians worked on the docks in significant numbers. These workers, who lived in segregated waterfront neighborhoods, competed for work in a highly overcrowded market, one which also reflected the racial and nativist hierarchy of the times. Nevertheless, the 1907 strike brought these workers together, albeit momentarily, in a unusual display of working-class solidarity and internationalism. In addition, therefore, the strike reveals important evidence concerning the relations between these workers in the years before World War I, in particular African Americans, Italians, and Irish, the three predominant groups on the waterfront. The purpose of this chapter is three-fold. It is to "rescue" an important historical episode and at the same time add to our knowledge of working-class radicalism, while also making a contribution to current discussions of race and class in the history of labor in the United States.

* * *

The 1907 longshoremen's strike was a great strike in an era of confrontation on the waterfronts of the world, an era when longshoremen, in the words of E. J. Hobsbawm, were known for their "raw power" and when their strikes were feared, "from Santos to San Francisco, from Sydney to Liverpool."[3] Moreover, the New York strike occurred in the midst of a period of rapid growth for the American industrial working class, a period marked by spectacular industrial disputes. It was part of the national upsurge in class consciousness and radical trade unionism prior to and during World War I, when, for example, the Industrial Workers of the World (IWW) raised the banner of "One Big Union" and the specter of revolutionary miners, field hands, and lumberjacks. In these years, the most basic conflicts, often concerning wages, could quickly become movements. Audacious strikes, frequently spontaneous and led by immigrants, were characterized by the use of direct action, working-class solidarity, and the demand for industrial unionism.

On the New York waterfront, there were three such strikes, each an explosive, harborwide confrontation. These occurred in 1887, in 1907, and in 1919; all three closed New York Harbor for a considerable period of time.[4] In between, there were periods of apathy and inactivity, and while trade unionism existed, it tended to be conservative, and its presence was minimal, restricted to local and sectional organizations. Most often, these reflected the craft forms of trade union organization of the American Federation of Labor (AFL), and, in New York, already a significant tendency toward petty gangsterism and corruption. One result was the inevitable accumulation of tension as profit-driven employers responded to the pressures of a highly competitive industry by squeezing workers and cutting labor costs.

In each period of conflict, however, the longshoremen overwhelmingly moved in the direction of industrial unionism, reflecting patterns in waterfront trade unionism internationally, as well as developments in industry in the United States.[5] The New York longshoremen in 1907 were virtually unorganized and almost all without trade union experience. They were immigrants and the children of immigrants, facing united, powerful employers, above all the shipping trust. Nevertheless, there were strong currents of radicalism on the waterfront, and these found expression during the course of the strike. This was seen first of all in the dramatic beginnings of the strike and in the mobilization of the ethnic contingents. Then it was evident in the tactics of the strikers as they fought to establish an industrial union, that is, a union of all whose work was loading and unloading ships in the harbor. In these years of conflict, industrial unionism was the preeminent demand of radical workers, and as this strike shows, it went far beyond the IWW and its supporters. This strike was an explosion up from the bottom of the waterfront working class, and even local craft unionists were caught up it. For a time, it seemed irresistible.

The New York longshoremen challenged not only the economic prerogatives of the shippers but also the patterns of work and organization on the waterfront, where localism prevailed and occupational, racial, and ethnic hierarchies were the rule. At the same time, they provided an illustration of the complexity of forging an industrial union in a highly fragmented workforce. The success of industrial unionism by definition involved overcoming occupational separation, but it was also determined by the degree to which racial and ethnic divisions, potentially fatal to workers in struggle, could be overcome. The importance of the 1907 longshoremen's strike is also found in what it reveals about the nature of this process. On the New York waterfront, racial and ethnic division was all too obvious in 1907. It certainly generated barriers to working-class unity. Yet in the course of this strike, racial and ethnic identities became a source not of weakness but of strength, for a moment transforming division into working-class solidarity. This should be a warning against rigid and deterministic analyses of racial and ethnic behaviors. On the New York waterfront, such relationships were intricate and shifting. They often simultaneously involved two or more ethnic groups, making the resulting behaviors far from predictable.

It is important to stress that this unity involved more than the simple substitution of class consciousness for racial, ethnic, and sectional consciousness. There was in fact a remarkable development of class consciousness among the various groups during the course of this strike. But this developed not just in the conflict between the longshoremen and the shippers but also within the various ethnic communities. The ethnic mobilizations were an expression of this. The strikers, after all, confronted not only employers and the police but also divided communities, including hostile labor contractors, the padrone, strikebreakers from every group, and ethnic trade unionists, clergy, and politicians, many of whom opposed the strike. The mobilization began within the separate groups of longshoremen and proceeded through them, producing a rank-and-file rebellion. In this strike, independent (that is, separate, racially and ethnically distinct) mobilization and organization, far from impeding solidarity, was an indispensable component in the movement for industrial unionism. Consequently, for longshoremen in 1907, racial and ethnic and class consciousness were intertwined and cannot be counterposed.

The 1907 longshoremen's strike, then, merits rescuing. It was an important strike, illustrating the potential power and radicalism of these workers, the degree of class consciousness among them, and the explosiveness of the ethnic populations along the waterfront. As strike-related violence spilled over from the docks into the working-class neighborhoods, other workers became involved, as well as family members, often women and children, sometimes whole communities in crowds which transcended not only occupational but also racial and ethnic frontiers.

* * *

New York Harbor in 1907 was a vast complex of piers, warehouses, railroad terminals, and neighborhoods, clustered on both sides of the Hudson River, on the Manhattan side of the East River, and all along the Brooklyn waterfront from Greenpoint to Bay Ridge. The Atlantic deepsea shippers were concentrated in Chelsea and Hoboken; the coastal trade prevailed on the East River and in South Brooklyn. There were coaling stations in Jersey City and the Bronx, lumberyards in Newtown Creek, and brickyards in Midtown.[6]

The industry of the harbor was both archaic and advanced. The dazzling new liners which arrived at the piers of the Cunard Line, and also those of North German Lloyd and the White Star Lines, were the symbols of modernity. These ships represented the highest levels of technology and the latest stages in the competition between the European steamship companies, a rivalry soon to be crowned with the *Titanic* itself. The piers, however, were old-fashioned, with improvements overdue and mechanization rare. The shippers might fight to have piers extended farther and farther into the river to accommodate ever-larger liners, but on the docks work was primitive.[7]

Working-class neighborhoods crowded the piers and warehouses, and these neighborhoods reflected the occupations of the longshoremen, as well as patterns of race and ethnicity. German longshoremen and their families lived in the tenements along the Hoboken docks. Chelsea in Manhattan was the Irish stronghold. The South Brooklyn district of Red Hook was Italian. There were large numbers of Polish longshoremen in Greenpoint. Still, these ethnic boundaries were not altogether rigid, and Charles Barnes, the foremost industrial investigator of the time, was accurate in describing the waterfront as "cosmopolitan."[8] The Irish were everywhere. Scandinavian longshoremen were scattered through the Italian streets of Red Hook. Italians were increasingly numerous in Hoboken. African Americans stubbornly fought for jobs and homes throughout the harbor. Thus, despite ethnic and racial segregation, the dockside neighborhoods were always in transition, far from stable, and only rarely homogeneous.

The workforce, therefore, was fluid, in an industry constantly in motion. The shippers made up for lack of innovation by taking advantage of a vast, fragmented army of workers, as well as the additional reserve, continuously swollen by immigration, of many thousands of unskilled workers in and around the waterfront. There were, according to investigators, three longshoremen for every job, not counting others who might seek employment on the docks.[9] In this context, job control unionism often appeared utopian.[10] The bargaining power of even the most skilled workers was highly limited, and the integrated nature of the industry made the prospect of organizing one dock at a time quite improbable. As of 1907, no employer had recognized either a union or a permanent rate of pay.[11] And while quite willing to favor some longshoremen over others, the shippers preferred to classify all longshoremen as unskilled. Of course, innumerable jobs could be performed adequately only after years of practical training; nevertheless, the shippers insisted that the very nature of the industry required casual employment. Consequently, all longshoremen were hired as casuals, one day at a time, and even the most skilled regularly experienced unemployment and were forced to search from pier to pier for work.[12] More than anything else, longshoremen feared this unemployment. It cut into their standard of living and left all, according to Barnes, "in a chronic state of unrest."[13] On their part, the employers, though frequently caught shorthanded, always had the possibility of manipulating the workforce to their own advantage.

Despite this, the longshoremen clung to casualism, even in the overcrowded labor market and ethnic complexity of New York.[14] However much this frustrated industrial reformers and union organizers, longshoremen had reason to fear proposals to rationalize and restrict employment, despite promises that the objective was to raise the standard of living in the water-front neighborhoods. Longshore work was heavy, grueling, and dangerous, and it often resulted in exhaustion, if not injury and death. Casual hiring allowed for the possibility of recuperation and offered opportunity for others, often relatives and neighbors. The strikers' single demand, higher wages, was an alternative path to improving their standard of living, as well as an example of what Hobsbawm called the longshoremen's preference for the "rough justice of casualism, even if it was only the justice of the lottery."[15] All longshoremen, the most skilled as well as the most transient, could support the demand for higher wages, and from there it was only a short step to demanding a uniform scale. As a result, self-preservation, for both the individual longshoreman and his community, produced solidarity, and this moved the strikers in the direction of industrial unionism. This direction, as well as the level of class consciousness, was strengthened by the scale of the 1907 strike and the intensity of the struggle. The longshoremen, in the face of staggering odds, fought to raise their rate of pay to forty cents an hour, sixty cents for overtime.[16]

* * *

The New York World devoted considerable attention to May Day events in 1907, reporting demonstrations by workers in New York and in cities and countries around the world. The May 1 edition of the World also noted that "all records for the number of immigrants arriving in the port in one day were broken yesterday when more than 15,000 [migrants] . . . got their first view of the city." The writer predicted one hundred and fifty thousand more would arrive within the month.[17] Two days later the New York Times reported fifteen thousand waiting on ships in the harbor to disembark and that the largest single group among them was comprised of migrants from Sicily and the south of Italy.[18]

New York's papers, however, failed to include accounts of Italian longshoremen, carrying red flags, marching in Brooklyn and Lower Manhattan.[19] These May Day marchers were demanding higher wages, and their numbers grew as longshoremen quit work and joined the demonstrations. There was widespread dissatisfaction with wages in the spring of 1907, and this created disputes in all parts of the harbor. With unemployment low and work plentiful, there were strikes and "all sorts of rumors of strikes," reported the Brooklyn Eagle, as longshoremen attempted to push up their wages, one dock at a time.[20] African American longshoremen on the Ward and Mallory Lines were already on strike on May Day, despite attempts to replace them with white strikebreakers. They demanded an increase in wages from twenty-five cents to thirty cents an hour for day work and forty-five cents for overtime and holidays.[21] Apparently the black workers were paid less than others, for when Italians walked out at the Bush Stores—warehouses in the Sunset Park district—they demanded forty cents an hour and sixty cents for overtime.[22] There is evidence of temporary settlements, under the pressure of moving ships, but none that employers were willing to raise rates consistently or permanently.

This pattern of strikes changed as a result of the May Day marches. In the first of these, a "body of Italians marched though the Atlantic Dock carrying flags," only to be driven from the Union Stores (warehouses) by armed superintendents.[23] Then, in Manhattan, several hundred striking Italian longshoremen from Brooklyn were reported in Battery Park, "a desperate looking lot," according to the *Eagle*. They carried red flags and the flags of various nations, and, "dividing their forces and cheering vociferously, one section attempted to march up West Street to clear out the longshoremen on the North River in a sympathetic strike."[24] Another group went "up along the East River front." More marchers were reported on May 2—hundreds of Italians marching "along the Clinton Street Wharf in Brooklyn demanding that work be stopped."[25] This was more than simply a strike, then; it also was a demonstration of immigrant laborers, as well as a May Day appeal for working-class solidarity. "There is a general impression along the waterfront," reported the *Eagle*, "that there will be serious trouble before this strike is settled."[26] Furthermore, "a peculiar feature" had already emerged, the reporter continued, "the Irishmen [are] joining issue with the Italians."[27]

The conflict soon became "the largest strike of any single trade ever in New York," announced Hearst's *Evening Journal*.[28] Within days the strike was ten thousand strong, and on May 6, four thousand Hoboken longshoremen struck in support of the New York longshoremen.[29] This constituted an unprecedented degree of solidarity, ultimately uniting an enormous mass of men, thirty thousand workers of all classifications, all nationalities, and all races, from every region in the huge port. These workers—Irish, Italians, African Americans, Poles, Swedes—mostly without trade union organization or experience, joined together right at the height of the massive wave of prewar immigration. This solidarity developed despite the use of thousands of strikebreakers, chiefly African Americans and Italians, recruited by the shippers. Strikebreaking became an industry in itself, as shippers collaborated with bankers, immigrant businessmen, and labor contractors, as well as a host of professional strikebreaking agencies, including that of the notorious Michael "Strikebreaker"

Farley, to replace the striking longshoremen and defeat the strike.[30] This led to continuous and escalating violence, beginning in a confrontation in Brooklyn between Italian strikebreakers and black longshoremen. In Manhattan, on the West Side, a strikebreaker, Joseph Bovano, a house-painter, was the strike's first casualty. He was killed as he and his son attempted to make their way home from work on the White Star Line piers. They were attacked by a crowd of Irish as they boarded a street car on Twenty-third Street and Eleventh Avenue.[31] In Brooklyn, the situation quickly became "so serious" that Captain Devaney of the Fourth Avenue Station ordered all saloons closed within three blocks of the piers.[32]

Coastal shippers continued to bargain with the longshoremen, but when the executives of thirty big companies met in the Anchor Lines building in Manhattan, they announced a policy of no concessions, a position they maintained until the end. On May 8, J. H. Thomas, the president of the International Merchant Marine, announced the employers' "solid front." "We are not experiencing great trouble so far. . . . We are getting plenty of men to do the work and expect the strike will soon be broken."[33] At the same time, the leaders of a small trade union, the Longshoremen's Union Protective Association (LUPA) emerged to speak for the strikers. "We strike for our families," LUPA president Patrick Connors, an obscure West Side trade unionist, told reporters. "They say we can live comfortably on our present wages. My answer is this. . . . Let them—the capitalists—go down in the holds of ships and work eighteen hours a day."[34] Connors also made the wage demand universal and, apparently, nonnegotiable; raise wages for all longshoremen to forty cents an hour, sixty cents for overtime, and eighty cents for holidays and Sundays. At the end of the second week of the strike, the *World* summarized: 30,000 on strike; Manhattan, 10,000; Brooklyn, 12,000; Hoboken, 6,000; Staten Island, 2,000; 1,000,000 tons of unmoved freight on the piers; business losses, $2,000,000; and strikebreakers arriving in the city at 1,000 a day.[35] Fully four weeks into the strike, the longshoremen and their union, LUPA, were, according to the well-informed writers of the *Brooklyn Eagle,* "in control of the situation."[36] The socialist *Daily People* was not alone when its June 4 issue predicted "Victory is at Hand!"[37]

* * *

The waterfront industry was divided into three main parts. First, in order of importance, was the foreign trade. Then, there was the coastal trade, that is, all the trade with other ports in the United States. Finally, there was the traffic within the port itself. The great majority of longshoremen, perhaps three-quarters in 1907, worked on the vessels which sailed to and from foreign ports, in particular on the ships of the great Atlantic lines.[38]

The foreign commerce was not only the largest but also the most varied. Anything and everything was transported on these ships. But despite revolutionary changes in dockside technology—technologies and organizational progress already in place in European ports—longshore work in New York Harbor in 1907 was rudimentary. In Liverpool and Hamburg, mechanical devices, such as traveling cranes and towers, were common. But in New York no such improvements had been made. Some German ships arrived equipped with traveling cranes on board, but American piers were poorly prepared to take advantage.[39]

Consequently, even though this work involved the world's largest ships, with enormous cargo capacity and sailing on strict schedules, including those carrying mail and passengers, the men worked as they had for decades. Supervision and drive were substituted for machinery, old methods were used alongside new. There were no uniform procedures, not even where the scale of work was greatest, on the Cunard and White Star piers in Chelsea and the Hamburg-American and North German Lloyd piers in Hoboken.

The longshoremen who worked these piers were classified as piermen, deckmen, and holdmen, and here the breakdown of the workforce by skill and status began. The piermen worked outside, on the piers, moving cargo, stacking materials, sometimes reloading them. The holdmen worked in the ship, "the most skilled" workers, according to Poole, doing "the most dangerous . . . work . . . taking the cargo as it came down from the crane and shifting it back in the hold—to trim the ship."[40] But the work of the deckmen, "riggers," was perhaps the most specialized. They rigged the ship in preparation for handling the cargo, running the winches that controlled falls and doing the signaling.

The deckmen, the holdmen, and the riggers worked in gangs, though this varied. Gangs were larger in Manhattan (eighteen to twenty-three men), smaller in Brooklyn (often only fourteen). Small gangs, according to the longshoremen, meant harder, more dangerous work. But mainly gang size was determined by whether the cargo was being loaded or unloaded. As many as 125 men might be employed to unload the five hatches of a large passenger liner. But, in a rush, two or three gangs might be hired on to work the same hatch, "inevitably," according to Barnes, causing accidents.[41]

At the head of the pier, in early morning shape-ups, longshoremen were forced to compete with each other for work. But on the job, the gangs had to work as a unit. They had to be able to establish intricate patterns of cooperation, rhythms of work without which the ships would never sail.

The nature of the work itself demanded that the men take responsibility for each other. Effectiveness and safety made this necessary, and a result was the common identity and capacity for solidarity this infused in longshoremen, in spite of all the forces that divided them.

All these workers were under the direction of foremen. There were head foremen, foremen for each pier gang, foremen who went up and down between deck and hold. The foremen drove the men, often without rest, until the work was done. Longshoremen reported routinely working sixteen, twenty, sometimes thirty hours and more in a stretch. One Chelsea longshoreman, according to Poole, "went on the job at four o'clock in the morning and worked the regular twenty-hour stretch with the gang. But when they quit at midnight, he stayed on and worked with the second gang . . . fourteen hours more."[42] Then the men would be laid off and have to wait two, three, four days for another job. Some chose recuperation, but poverty compelled others back to the next morning's shape-up.

Cargo was also brought to the piers on lighters, flat, uncovered boats propelled by tugs. From these lighters goods were transferred directly to the hold or loaded onto the piers. Longshoremen worked on the lighters, which were loaded with cargo and brought up to the side of the ship. The gangs on the lighters were sometimes regular piermen, but often "shenangoes," the most casual of longshoremen, employed directly by the captain of the lighter. They worked as though the lighter were a pier. Other longshoremen worked on barges bringing freight from New Jersey railroad terminals. Some rail cars were placed onto lighters and moved to the ships. Refrigerator cars were unloaded directly from floats to refrigerated holds in the ships. The huge Bush Terminals in South Brooklyn were linked directly to rail lines. All this, of course, put longshoremen in close contact with the seamen who worked the tugs, lighters, and barges, as well as railway workers. On the piers, longshoremen worked alongside teamsters.

There was more specialized work as well: sugar was loaded directly onto men's backs in bags weighing three hundred pounds and more. Oil was moved in cases. A gang of sixteen longshoremen was expected to stow ten thousand cases in an eight-hour day, thirteen hundred cases an hour, according to Barnes. Grain was brought to the ships in canal boats and transferred by floating elevators with conveyors of buckets, filled by men with shovels called grain trimmers. Working with coal was highly specialized. On the freight ships, though, longshoremen were expected to work whatever cargo was on board.

Work in the coastal industry was similar, but there was even less machinery as employers attempted to compensate for the shorter distances and irregular schedules by lowering operating costs. Some sections of the coastal trade were extremely irregular, in particular when the work was seasonal, involving such cargoes as lumber, grain, and cotton. The local harbor traffic consisted chiefly of building materials, as well as work loading and unloading canal boats.

Almost all the workers in this industry were considered longshoremen. There was an occupational hierarchy, though there was not always agreement on the order of ranking. Longshoremen were classified as general cargo handlers, coal men, oil handlers, grain trimmers, "banana fiends," and sugar handlers. The hourly rates of pay were similar, though this was never formalized. The quality of the work varied greatly, and this was significant. But the amount of work, the hours a man could work in a week, and the regularity of the work were crucial. Work was most regular on the transatlantic piers, and thus this work tended to be ranked highest.[43] On these docks, favored workers were classified by skill and by gang. The "good gangs" got more work than others, though in the last analysis the shippers determined which gangs were "good" and which were not. Trade union organization reflected this hierarchy, but race and ethnicity were equally important. In 1907, most union members were Irish regulars on the docks of the Atlantic shippers in Chelsea and their German counterparts in Hoboken. But the overwhelming majority of longshoremen, including the Irish, were not union members. Nevertheless, there was a tradition of workplace activism, as was shown by the rash of strikes in the spring of 1907.

Segregation by race and ethnicity was the rule on the waterfront in 1907, and this produced antagonism. "There was a time," a black longshoreman told investigator E. Franklin Frazier, "when a Negro could not walk down Atlantic Avenue," the arterial leading to the Red Hook waterfront.[44] But segregation was never total, and the resulting social relationships were not as simple as sometimes imagined.[45] Most observers commented on the racial and ethnic pattern of employment, but simultaneously noted its "cosmopolitan" character. According to Barnes, "the work of the ordinary longshoreman [took] him to so many different parts of the port" that there was a "continual interchange of individuals and nationalities in almost every locality."[46] This interchange, however, was conditioned by racial and ethnic ranking. Scandinavian workers, for example, seem to have enjoyed high status and were often found in skilled work such as rigging, even where the majority of workers were Irish.

African Americans, on the other hand, while found on the Chelsea docks, held only those jobs at the bottom of the hierarchy. Barnes described their status this way: "Back and forth, within and yet without, moves the Negro, still under the ban of his half freedom, doing as he may the simpler work of trucking on the pier."[47] But this was not at all the case on the piers of the Ward and Mallory Lines, shippers operating on both the Manhattan and Brooklyn sides of the East River. On these piers nearly the entire workforce was black. These black longshoremen worked as a result of company policy; they were kept on in all positions after strike-breaking in the 1890s. The contrast between these workers and those on the Chelsea piers was marked and can be seen in the strike reports. The *New York Times*, for example, presented positive accounts of black workers striking the Ward Line, recording that "the leaders of the strike . . . are Negroes" belonging to "Longshoremen's Union 14." The strikers' leader was "dressed in a fashionable Spring suit" and "appeared to be running matters generally."[48] One consequence of Jim Crow unionism, certainly unintended, was that black workers were able to establish a base and a tradition of organization.

The complexity of racial and ethnic relations was also seen in the course of the strike. The black longshoremen played a central role in the beginning of the strike. The Ward and Mallory longshoremen in Brooklyn were already on strike on May 1. The *Brooklyn Eagle*'s May 2 headline was "Italians and Negroes Out." Blacks were in the crowds that went from dock to dock spreading the strike. According to the *Eagle,* police and supervisors drove "Italian *and* colored strikers" off the Ward piers and away from Montague Street on the morning of May 1.[49] When the strikers crossed the bridge to Manhattan, the May Day demonstrations were begun in front of the Ward and Mallory piers, where they were joined by black strikers.[50]

African American longshoremen were few in 1907.[51] Their numbers were growing, however, and by the end of the war, there were more than five thousand black longshoremen working in the harbor, the largest concentration of black industrial workers in the United States.[52] "The history" of these longshoremen, wrote Frazier, "has been a series of invasions."[53] The Ward Line began hiring gangs of blacks in 1895 to break a local strike; the Mallory Line did the same in 1899. There were new invasions in 1907. In Hoboken, there seem to have been few blacks before the 1907 strike, and a strike report in the *Hoboken Observer* commented, "there are not more than thirty negro families in Hoboken." It added, however, that "the steamship companies have already imported several hundred [black strikebreakers] . . . and have six hundred more on the way from Baltimore and Philadelphia. It is feared that no matter how the strike turns out, a large percentage of these undesirable visitors will stay."[54]

These "invasions" help explain the contradictory position of African Americans in the industry. When black longshoremen worked as individuals on docks where whites predominated, they performed the menial tasks described by Barnes. But when they worked on predominantly black docks, they worked the entire range of jobs, skilled and nonskilled, and were sometimes supervised by black foremen. This was segregation, of course, but Frazier suggested that black longshoremen preferred "Black docks" (and all-black locals), while simultaneously opposing racial discrimination in hiring and in the unions.[55] These black longshoremen, it seems, were both class and race conscious. They supported all-black or majority black piers which allowed them access to work and gave them a voice and the opportunity to organize. They took advantage of this situation to expand their numbers on the waterfront and organize their own local unions. This policy made sense, given occupational segregation and the racism of white workers. But in 1907 it also enabled black longshoremen to join the Irish, Italians, and others in a classwide movement and to play a significant part in the strike. Blacks organized themselves as Local Union 6 and on May 12, according to Connors, eight hundred black strikers joined LUPA.[56]

The Italians also came in invasions, that is, as strikebreakers, though in far larger numbers. By 1907, they represented nearly a third of the workforce and were approximately equal in number to the Irish.[57] This complicated the issue of race and ethnicity, because Italian longshoremen were also considered nonwhite, and, according to observers like Barnes, "inferior workers" who, because of their "low standard of living" and their "inability to manage strikes," were responsible for the deterioration of the occupation.[58] When an *Eagle* writer reported that three gangs of "white men" had been hired to replace strikers on Brooklyn's East Central piers, he meant that Irish were replacing Italians.[59] Some hiring foremen apparently preferred blacks to Italians, alleging the former were stronger workers.[60] When Italians worked as individuals, they were treated in a way analogous to blacks. Italians might be used as piermen, sometimes holdmen, but rarely, according to Barnes, "on the deck."[61] The majority, however, worked with Italians on "Italian docks" or in occupations dominated by Italians. Coaling, for example, one of the least desirable jobs in the harbor, was done by special gangs, mostly Italian. On all-Italian piers, Italian longshoremen might be hired by Italian stevedores and supervised by Italian foremen. Italians from the Lower East Side worked throughout the harbor, but by 1907 the majority of Italian longshoremen lived near where they worked, in particular in the "Italian Quarter" of South

Brooklyn. They lived in "wretched tenements" along the waterfront, "not because they like to, but because they are too poor to go elsewhere."[62] One small house on President Street in Red Hook, for example, housed twenty-five longshoremen in 1910.[63]

Some shippers hired Italians instead of Irish because the former were considered "tractable" and less likely to unionize.[64] There was an Italian local of LUPA in 1906, but after a dispute with the Irish, it severed its ties. When the strike began, it was an independent union, all-Italian.[65] In the 1907 strike, the Italians were perhaps the most class conscious of the longshoremen; they too worked on segregated piers but used these as bases to develop workplace activism and trade unionism. This experience, as well as their lives in the United States, fused with the traditions of their homeland and made these Italian workers the backbone of the movement for industrial unionism.[66]

The formal leadership of the strike quickly passed to the Irish longshoremen of Chelsea and LUPA, but this did not diminish Italian participation. On May 14, the *New York World* reported, for example, that all eight thousand Italian coal heavers were out on strike and that they had been joined by the tidewater coal handlers, also Italians.[67] These workers brought coal to the coaling stations from Perth Amboy in barges; together with the coal heavers, they caused havoc even for those shippers who managed to load their ships, since without coal the ships could not sail. The Italian longshoremen also joined LUPA en masse, allying with the other longshoremen on class lines, despite bitter disputes within the Italian communities, chiefly concerning the massive use of Italian strikebreakers. These strikebreakers were often organized by Italian labor contractors and financed by Italian bankers who advertised their efforts in Italian papers, a fact which *Il Proletario,* the socialist Italian-American newspaper, angrily exposed.[68] In addition, in 1907 the padrone was still a factor on the waterfront. On May 9, the *Eagle* reported "padrones herding their Italian strikebreakers for use on the Brooklyn docks."[69]

The Irish were the traditional longshoremen, having established predominance before the Civil War. But by the end of the century, their position was threatened. Waterfront wages were stagnant, the standard of living was low, and efforts to unionize, both in the 1880s and 1890s, failed.[70] In addition, they were challenged by the arrival of large numbers of Italian workers. This undoubtedly fueled hostility; the anti-black racism of the Irish longshoremen was already legendary, dating from the 1850s. Still, the 1907 strike presents a more complicated picture. In 1907, the majority of Irish longshoremen followed the Italians out on strike and in the course of the strike united with blacks and members of other ethnic groups. They did this in advance of the Irish leaders of LUPA, and in spite of advice from the Catholic prelates. They also defied the Irish-American leaders in the New York City Central Federated Union and their allies in Tammany Hall.

By 1907, a small Irish American middle class had emerged from the immigrant communities and Irish were increasingly found in the ranks of the skilled workers, resulting in assimilation and, no doubt, some degree of prosperity.[71] But this was not always apparent in the neighborhoods of the longshoremen, which social workers still considered the poorest in the city. These Irish were viewed as a sort of underclass, who manufactured despair, perpetuated poverty, bred crime and disease, and added to the City's dangerous classes.[72] Some social workers believed longshoremen had immoderately large families and drank too much, and many reformers tied such excesses to casual labor. Some advocated restricting waterfront employment precisely to defend and elevate these Irish workers and their families.

But poverty, of course, was relative, and assimilation was almost always partial and highly uneven. In any event, Irish immigration continued in the 1880s and 1890s, crowding already poor neighborhoods with additional numbers of unskilled workers. The argument concerning assimilation and the decline of Irish radicalism should be seen in this context. Irish workers were not a homogeneous group in 1907, and their attitudes were no more predictable than their actions. James Connolly, the Irish socialist working in New Jersey at the time of the strike, was a keen and respected observer of American labor movements. He hoped, in the aftermath of the strike, to recruit longshoremen, including large numbers of Irish, to the revolutionary IWW.[73] Class consciousness continued to exist in the Irish longshoremen's neighborhoods, as well as the willingness to engage in militant direct action—a defining aspect of the radicalism of the decade.

Barnes divided the waterfront workers along "the great line of cleavage between the older and newer type of longshoreman," that is, between the old immigrants, Irish and Germans, and the new immigrants, chiefly Italians. But, interestingly, he placed "the younger Irishmen now going into work" whom he considered "a class inferior" across this line with the Italians and other newcomers.[74] Of course the meaning of "class" has a more fundamental importance, but the point is that the "old" versus "new" distinction does not work here. It is essential to differentiate not just among the racial and ethnic groups but also among the workers in these groups. The consciousness of the longshoremen was shaped by widely differing experiences, historical, cultural, and occupational. But these experiences were also determined by productive relations, the work itself, casual hiring, and the shape-up, all of which united longshoremen. While there may have been a *logic* to racial and ethnic antagonism and conflict on the waterfront, there was no *law* determining it.[75] Workers were divided, and class consciousness was at best partial and conditioned, but this did not preclude the possibility of overcoming division. An interesting feature of the 1907 conflict was the degree of division *within* the racial and ethnic communities along class lines. This division was heightened as a result both of the strike and the strength of the movement for industrial unionism within all the major groups.[76]

* * *

Though trade unionism existed on the New York/New Jersey waterfront in 1907, it was weak and fragmented. Reporters searched for leaders in the first days of the strike, but could find none, or so they claimed. There is little evidence, however, that they employed Italian-speaking reporters or made any attempt to question the Italian strikers. Nevertheless, trade unionism had a long, if troubled, history on the waterfront. There were significant strikes in 1874 and 1887, the latter the "Big Strike" led by the Knights of Labor.[77] Each ended in defeat. There was an attempt to organize the port in the 1890s, led and financed by Tom Mann, the British syndicalist and founder of the International Federation of Ship, Dock and River Workers. The federation sent Edward McHugh to organize the American Longshoremen's Union, most often referred to as the McHugh organization. McHugh was an Irish radical and follower of Henry George, who had been the general secretary of the National Union of Dock Laborers, based in Liverpool. McHugh came to New York in 1896 and by 1897, with the assistance of George, was the leader of an organization estimated at fifteen thousand members, including fifteen hundred Italian longshoremen.[78]

The American Longshoreman's Union was succeeded by the Longshoremen's Union Protective Association, a craft union based on the Irish Chelsea wharves. Barnes wrote the only account of this union, and his contempt for it has shaped most subsequent treatments.[79] He claimed to have reliable evidence that by the end of 1906, when the Italian locals had withdrawn after demanding and failing to get an Italian walking delegate, LUPA's membership was only about three thousand. The union seems to have been caught unprepared by the strike, though spokesmen later denied this, even claiming responsibility for initiating the strike.

Barnes's evaluation of LUPA in the strike was scathing: "Poor judge-ment on the part of the leaders, or their fanatical and even stubborn be-lief in the invincibility of the longshoremen have, almost without excep-tion, been the causes of failures."[80] This argument has been repeated, yet there is evidence to the contrary in contemporary accounts of the strike. Joseph Buchanan, a veteran of the railroad strikes of the 1880s and the labor writer for the *New York Evening Journal* in 1907, wrote the follow-ing at the end of the strike's first month: "The longshoremen's union is four times as strong in membership as it was at the beginning of the strike, four weeks ago. . . . In all my experience with strikes, I have never before known of such a large affair so well conducted."[81] The editors of the *Nation,* while critical of the strikers, offered support for Buchanan's as-sessments. They compared the longshoremen favorably to strikers in Paris and Turin and called attention to "certain features about the present dock-workers strike in New York which, in common with what we learn of the methods of conducting labor wars in other countries, indicate a marked progress in what almost deserves to be called a science of strike tactics and strategy."[82] *Il Proletario* praised Connors personally as the "captain of the battle . . . firm at his post."[83]

Barnes faulted LUPA and its leaders for their uncompromising support for the wage demands, but this Buchanan admired. There is evidence that the rank-and-file longshoremen admired it as well. The issue is worth ex-amining. There was immense pressure on Connors, as the union president, and on LUPA to retreat on the wage demands as a way to settle the strike. Ralph Easley, the chairman of the National Civic Federation, joined with the Tammany mayor, George McClellan, and leaders of the Central Feder-ated Union (AFL) to press for a conciliation commission. The Reverend Father Flannery of St. Veronique's Roman Catholic church in Christopher Street, claiming "the utmost sympathy for the men," urged the union to take part in a conference.[84] Samuel Gompers, the leader of the American Federation of Labor, called on the longshoremen to settle and sent his New York organizer, Herman Robinson, to mediate. James Archibald, an AFL leader and also a member of the National Civic Federation, went to the LUPA hall on Greenwich Street as the leader of a group of trade unionists promoting a settlement. "The whole trouble," he told reporters, "as I see it, is that the longshoremen are afraid their standing would be prejudiced if they consent to a conference. They have never been in a strike before. Had they been used to strikes it is probable that they would have asked for con-siderably more [money] than they hoped to get. Then, when it came to the point of arbitration, they could easily take less."[85] Edward Moffett, a spokesman for the Bricklayers and Masons, "was sure the trouble will be speedily patched up . . . if we can only get representatives . . . at one table." William Coakley, a spokesmen of the Lithographers, told reporters he was doing "missionary work" in favor of a conference.[86] Nevertheless, Connors refused to participate in a conference, stood by the wage demands, even declined Gompers' offer of mediation.

Why? There were important factors which Connors's critics failed to consider—or perhaps to understand. First, while many of the smaller shippers were willing to make temporary settlements with the longshoremen, there is no evidence whatsoever that the executives of the larger shipping companies ever considered raising wages, despite the fact that the strike cost them millions in business and profits. The shippers seem to have been quite clear from the outset that they could defeat the longshoremen. And with reason. In the 1890s, for example, the Atlantic shippers had combined to defeat both seamen and dockers in strikes in Liverpool.[87]

Second, this was no ordinary strike, certainly it was not the kind organized by the affiliates of the Central Federated Union. The strike was far from a simple walkout over ten cents an hour; it was an explosion of anger built up over years. It was also a rebellion against a system of work and a way of life—the shape-up, exhausting toil, days without work, life in crowded, disease-ridden tenements, and a level of competition for work that went well beyond the normal experience of "ethnic rivalry."

Connors and the union were criticized, it seems to me, for what was impossible, that is, for not negotiating an AFL-like settlement, benefiting some part of their supporters among the most regular and best-paid Irish longshoremen, at the expense of all the others. But the wage demand was both economic and symbolic, and surely the shipping executives recognized this. There was an "all or nothing" spirit among the strikers, a spirit very much at odds with the styles and strategies of the established trade unionists of the Central Federation of Labor. And there was tremendous pressure on Connors and the LUPA leadership from below, including from the rank-and-file Irish longshoremen, to win a major victory against the shippers. There is little reason to believe that Connors was in a position to negotiate a settlement of the strike in a conference. He did not lead the men out, nor did he choose the demands. How could he simply order them back? This was probably a situation unfamiliar to the condescending leaders of the New York labor movement. Connors's only real base was small and concentrated in Chelsea. The Brooklyn Italians and the longshoremen in Hoboken were in effect autonomous, as, one suspects, were considerable numbers of the Irish.

Moreover, on the piers and in the working-class neighborhoods, there developed what observers called a "war." There was violence almost from the beginning of the strike, most often between strikers, the police, and strikebreakers, both at the piers and on the water, where strikers fought to stop barges ferrying strikebreakers to and from the strikebound ships. The fighting spread to working-class neighborhoods adjacent to the docks and even to places well removed from the immediate conflict. Strikebreakers became the target of the strikers' anger, and, as the scale of strikebreaking was enormous, so the violence was widespread.

Some detail of this violence is necessary to illustrate the depth of feeling among the longshoremen, their families, and their supporters. In the Williamsburg section of Brooklyn, for example, longshoremen attempted to close down the waterfront with pickets. But this escalated into "savage rioting," according to the press, when, on May 7, two thousand sugar workers at the sugar trust's American Sugar Refining Company walked out in a wildcat strike. The company brought in Italian strikebreakers. The two strikes merged in the streets, and by the end of the day, the *New York World* reported "fifty wounded" in a "pitched battle" as longshoremen and refinery workers "rioted from daylight until dark."[88] "The strikers," the report continued, "were armed with monkey-wrenches, iron bars and big sticks and lay in wait in doorways" for the hundreds of strikebreakers. . . . *Ten thousand sympathizers with the strikers looked on.*"[89] At least one strikebreaker, Massena Giobanni, age twenty-eight, of East Houston Street in Manhattan, was killed. Among those arrested was Jacob Cohn, a barber, charged with making a "fiery speech" urging workers to fight for their rights, even if "violence was necessary."[90]

On May 11, in Manhattan, audacious strikers seized a ship and attacked the strikebreakers, again Italians, working on it. The strikers "rushed the gates" of the Thirty-fourth Street pier, "when foremen opened them to bring in freight in the morning" and stormed the big liner *Campagnia.* The police and armed supervisors were reported to have fired their weapons but were unable to stop the strikers who, for a short period of time, "took control of the ship." Several strikers entered the hold of the ship, where they were alleged to have destroyed property and attempted to set the ship on fire.[91]

Across the Hudson, the strike was solid though less violent than in New York. But, on June 4, hundreds of strikers, mostly from Hoboken, overran a Jersey City pier and fought with strikebreakers, mostly African Americans, and the police who sought to protect them.[92] Other incidents, smaller in scale, also indicate the intensity of the conflict. On May 17,

Benjamin Vincent, a private detective employed by the Holland-America Steamship Company, said to be associated with the strikebreaker Michael Farley, shot and killed Harry Marshall, a twenty-year-old peddler, in the Columbia Cafe on the Hoboken waterfront. Vincent came into the bar for a drink, but was recognized by strikers. A conflict ensued, and Vincent drew his revolver and shot and killed Marshall. "Scores of longshoremen" chased Vincent from the bar. Someone in the crowd shot him in the leg, but "in the wildest kind of excitement" he escaped. The following Friday, two thousand striking longshoremen joined in the dead man's funeral procession in a "bitter" demonstration, which the *Hoboken Observer* reporter said would "leave a lasting impression on the minds" of all who witnessed it.[93]

Children, "street urchins," were regular participants in the crowds, as were neighbors and the wives of the strikers. Children attacked strikebreakers on Hicks and Union Streets, a predominantly Italian neighborhood in Red Hook. A young boy, John Janeway, eight years old, was shot and killed when Antonio Raffaelle, a strikebreaker, fired at the strike supporters. Police had great difficulty in rescuing Raffaelle from the angry crowd.[94] On May 13, the *New York Times* reported an attack on strikebreakers on West Street: "Scores of strikers . . . and hundreds of street urchins suddenly appeared from where no one seemed to know. The men shouted at the strikebreakers and then the boys began to throw stones."[95] On May 8, in Williamsburg, "400 Italian strikebreakers in a body . . . were assaulted with sticks and stones thrown by sympathizers of the strikers who live in the neighborhood and were standing on the sidewalk as they passed by."[96] Wives and other women joined in the fighting, often from tenement windows, throwing pots and rubbish at strikebreakers in the streets below. On May 14, strikebreakers were attacked by a crowd on Christopher Street in the Village. As one frightened man fled, "from every window peered an angry woman who hurled all kinds of missiles along with their imprecations" at him. Mostly, this involved Irish women, but Italian women may have participated as well.[97] The wives of strikers also marched in support of the strike. On May 8, hundreds of women marched, backing the strikers' claim "that the increased cost of living is the only reason they are asking for more wages." In this they were supported by their "wives, mothers and women relatives and friends."[98] The women also "brought lunches to the hundreds of strikers who are on picket duty along West Street. The women planned to visit the various shipping offices and tell the managers that they cannot keep their families decently upon the wages that their husbands are now getting."[99]

These confrontations also exposed bitter disputes within the ethnic communities and quite possibly offered opportunities to settle scores.[100] In Brooklyn, Sanci Leli, a striker, was killed in a cellar on Columbia Street, "hacked to death," according to the press, by strikebreakers. Leli was reported to have "wanted to continue the strike. He said it was time for all workmen to recognize unionism and American methods." But Markel Basilio, according to police, said he was against the strike; "he was a strikebreaker . . . he was going to make a great deal of money . . . he would become a great padrone." Basilio was charged with the murder.[101] A shooting took place on East 109th Street in Manhattan, when Vito Franolo, a union longshoreman, attempted to kill Phillip Coggiano but hit a bystander, another young boy, instead. Franolo accused Coggiano, identified as a padrone in reports, of supplying strikebreakers for the steamship companies and sought revenge in the fight that followed.[102]

*　*　*

Connors emerged as the strike leader only once it was clear that the strike was solid, including on his own West Side docks. On the fourth day, he called a press conference. He denied the strike was spontaneous and announced that he and LUPA were its leaders. "It is not true that we struck without making any demands. Before we struck a circular with the demands was in the possession of every pier superintendent and we struck because the demands were refused. At the wages we are receiving the longshoremen, who have often to wait days for work, did not average more than $11 a week."[103]

This was not exactly true, of course, but the union gave the strike a center and a voice, and brought formal organization to it. Claiming "The union has a big strike fund on hand and we are bound to win," the union flourished.[104] By mid-May, there was system of "beach walkers" or picket captains, including increasing numbers of Italians, who patrolled the piers. "There are more than 500 of these men doing special duty for the union," wrote Buchanan. "These men met regularly at Greenwich Hall on Christopher Street." On May 15, Buchanan reported that the land pickets had been reinforced by men under the supervision of John Calona, "the importance of this addition . . . will be understood when it is realized that a majority of the strikebreakers . . . are Italians. With a large force of Italian 'beach walkers' the union will now be in a position to deal with this problem." There were also floating picket lines; Buchanan described a trip across the Hudson on a picket boat. The union attempted to monitor traffic in the harbor, especially the movement of strikebreakers.[105]

There were regular mass meetings, including a "monster mass meeting" on May 9, on Hudson Street in Manhattan, addressed by Connors and other union leaders.[106] But the largest meeting was in Brooklyn. The same day, the police estimated seven thousand Italian longshoremen gathered in Prospect Hall, overflowing into the streets. "For three hours" reported the *Brooklyn Eagle*, "they were harangued by Italian orators. . . . Not a word of English was spoken." The strike leaders' speeches were greeted with "the wildest kind of cheering and howling, waving of banners and tossing of hats in the air."[107]

Connors announced at one meeting that he had received requests for 650 additional union badges for Hoboken, and an order for 10,300 from Brooklyn.[108] Certainly this was significant, and an indication of enthusiasm for the union, whatever it may have indicated about the actual level of commitment to the organization on the part of the new members.[109]

One prospect for winning the strike lay in spreading it. In the first days of the strike the union worked to get the backing of the Teamsters and Harbor Boatmen, two groups which could have had a significant impact on the strike. On May 8, Connors issued a statement that the Teamsters and Boatmen's unions would in fact join the strike.[110] But Cornelius Shea of Chicago, the national president of the Teamsters, came immediately to New York to see that such solidarity did not happen. Speaking for the union, John Jennings, the general organizer of the Teamsters, refuted Connors: "We have nothing to strike for. . . . We know nothing of the merits of the [longshoremen's] strike. . . . It is a principle with the union to take no part in a strike in which we have no interests at stake. We are affiliated with the American Federation of Labor, while the Longshoremen's Protective Union is an independent body."[111] The officers of the Boatmen's union admitted "having great difficulty keeping the men from striking. They [the men] object to working on tugs and lighters which carry the strikebreakers to the piers. Last night the crews of several tugs deserted for that reason."[112] Nevertheless, the officers had their way, and there was no sympathy strike. The union also sought solidarity in other ports and sent a delegation of strikers to Philadelphia when there were reports of ships being diverted there and to Baltimore. But in the end, the longshoremen fought alone.[113]

Stopping strikebreakers from working involved both organized picketing and the spontaneous efforts of rank-and-file longshoremen and their supporters on the piers and in the adjacent neighborhoods. While they often succeeded, at least temporarily, the strikers paid a high price— injuries, arrests, and animosities that would long endure. But, there were interesting victories. The union attempted physically to stop the strikebreakers. It also tried to recruit them, sometimes successfully. On May 28, six hundred strikebreakers left the Munson Line on the East River and met with Connors and a delegation of strikers. According to reports, 592 of them signed up and formed Branch No. 15 of the union. In a similar incident, on May 18 "an exodus of strikebreakers took place on the White Star Line when 300 strikebreakers quit in a body and marched to Greenwich Hall, the union's headquarters." Jeremiah Condon, a LUPA delegate, met with them and "it was decided that they should parade to the headquarters of the White Star Line on Broadway. . . . All the strikebreakers being Italian, an Italian flag was obtained and the march began."[114]

In the end, however, the strikers utterly failed to deter the shippers, who were committed to the policy of replacing the strikers. The shippers apparently believed in the effectiveness of the strikebreakers and were willing to employ any number, even though most accounts indicated that they were very poor substitutes for the longshoremen. They were inexperienced, rarely in suitable physical condition, and worked in exceedingly difficult circumstances. The strikebreakers were often housed on the ships themselves or on the piers in crude dormitories; some were kept as virtual prisoners until the job was finished. Most reports indicated that there was very little movement of cargo, at least in the first three weeks of the strike. Nevertheless, the existence of an apparently limitless supply of strikebreakers must have demoralized the strikers, as the violence of the conflict must have exhausted them. Also, this calculated policy of fueling race hatred certainly must have severely strained the strikers' unity.

The longshoremen's strike rapidly propelled LUPA in the direction of industrial unionism quite in keeping with the "One Big Union" sentiment which was developing in the country in decade before the war.[115] The strikers' single demand, one wage increase for all longshoremen, amalgamated the crafts and specializations, including the checkers, in the industry into a single movement. The union's multiracial organizing as well as the strike's immigrant leadership was also characteristic of the times, as was the direct action and the involvement of large numbers of sympathizers. This was not necessarily entirely spontaneous. There is reason to believe that there were significant numbers of longshoremen who believed in multiracial, industrial unionism. According to Connolly, discussing the twelve thousand members of the "independent" union which survived the strike, "Many of the present members were once in the Knights of Labor and they are conversant with the fact partly gained by actual experience in their fights against the employers that the American Federation of Labor is a scab-herding capitalist institution."[116] This may also help explain the failure of the IWW to intervene effectively in the strike, which should have offered it an especially important opportunity to test its new policy of emphasizing economic issues and winning real concessions from employers. But there was nothing comparable to the IWW's interventions in Portland, Oregon, Paterson, and Schenectady that same year. Elizabeth Gurley Flynn created a sensation when she spoke to a big crowd at Dreisbach's Hall in Hoboken, but the leading organizers—Joseph Ettor, from Brooklyn, Fred Heslewood, J. P. Thompson, and Ben Williams—played no role in the New York strike.[117] The fact was, as David Montgomery has suggested, that the Wobblies were not the only players in the field. Even long-standing craft unionists could be swept into the strikes of the period; LUPA filled the vacuum left on the New York waterfront by the skilled workers of the Central Federated Union and provided leadership for a militant, industry-wide, rank-and-file strike which had the support of all of the major ethnic groups. The IWW supported the strike, and the *Daily People,* which at that point supported the IWW, was uncritical of the union leadership during the course of the strike. It reported IWW meetings, paper sales, and recruitment, but offered little tactical advice to the strikers and nothing on alternative forms of trade union organization.[118] In February 1908, nearly a year after the strike, Connolly described LUPA and its twelve thousand members as "industrial and progressive . . . free from the ordinary grafting and corruption elements."[119]

Nevertheless, then, while the majority of the strikers were inexperienced, divided by race and ethnicity, and impoverished, these problems might have been overcome. The shippers, however, were not interested in a settlement. They were united and well organized, and they brought into the contest fantastic wealth and power. The estimates of the cost of the strike to the shippers were staggering, as were estimates of the costs to economy, yet the shippers were able to absorb them.

By 1907, the major shippers had become powerful international trusts, often in partnership with competing nation states, as was the case with the Cunard Line and the British government, and the Hamburg-America Line and the German government. The North Atlantic trade was a great prize, but like the railroads in an earlier period, there were too many ships, and there were destructive rate wars. Cunard's dividends, for example, averaged less than 3 percent between 1883 and 1911.[120] The International Merchant Marine Company (IMM) was the largest of these trusts. Organized by J. P. Morgan in 1902, incorporated in New Jersey, it entered the competition to assert American interests and openly sought to monopo-

lize the industry. George Perkins, Morgan's partner, boasted that the shipping trust would "practically result in stretching our railroad terminals
across the Atlantic."[121] Its ships sailed chiefly under the British flag, including those of the White Star Line, the jewel of the fleet, whose chairman, J. Bruce Ismay, became the IMM's top executive. The trust was never
a success, however, and failed to defeat its German and British rivals. At
the same time, it was accused of having "watered stock" and most of its
investors seem to have lost money, chiefly due to the poor economy of
the North Atlantic shipping business.[122] More importantly, this situation,
frantic competition for diminishing profits, led to great pressure on the
workers. This meant first the sailors but also the workers on the docks,
where the industry was expanding but technically stagnant.[123] In addition,
the races across the Atlantic on tight schedules frequently meant that ships
were forced to leave port with unfilled holds. This was undoubtedly an
important problem for the shippers; and it was another justification for
driving the longshoremen to their limit.[124]

These shippers united and opposed the wage demands from the very
beginning; their "solid front" never cracked. The strikers at one point
naively hoped that Ismay might appear to settle the strike. He did appear,
dramatically, on the elegant new luxury liner, the *Adriatic*. But he did not
try to settle the strike. "I think we have the situation well in hand and no
advances will be made to the striking longshoremen," Ismay announced.
"We can get all the men we want and we do not need more. I did not come
here to settle the strike. I only wanted to make the first trip on the
Adriatic."[125]

In early June, the strike began to disintegrate. The *New York Times* reported Irish women making desperate appeals to the charity societies and
settlement houses.[126] The *Daily People* called it the "old, old story, empty
stomachs . . . against concentrated capital."[127] Connors offered a compromise: thirty-five cents an hour for day work, fifty cents an hour for nights,
and sixty cents on Sundays and holidays. The press reported that the Italians opposed it. It also announced, correctly it turned out, that this was "the
death knell of the strike."[128] The shippers refused to consider the offer.

The strikers went back to work on June 14, when the union leaders
accepted defeat, but they were bitter. The death agony of the strike occurred in the West Side longshoremen's riverfront neighborhoods. On
that date, hundreds of strikebreakers, nearly all blacks and Italians, were
discharged from the White Star Line piers at the foot of Bank Street at
11:00 A.M. They attempted to get to the elevated railway station at Christopher Street, but before they arrived they were intercepted by crowds of

strikers and their supporters. Strikebreakers were attacked with cotton hooks, clubs, and stones. They were dragged into saloons and alleyways. The police found five men lying unconscious in an alley behind Greenwich Street. Crowds of women and children participated in the fighting, and when mounted police arrived to rescue the strikebreakers, they were attacked. Women pelted the police with pots and bottles from their tenement windows. When the police pursued them, they escaped across rooftops and down fire escapes. One woman, Kate Coffey, the wife of a striker, was arrested on riot charges after attacking a policeman with an iron pot. The police reserves were called in, but they succeeded only in shifting the location of the fighting from one street to the next. After a day of "rioting," calm was restored, but only after scores of injured were removed to emergency rooms in St. Vincent's and other nearby hospitals.[129]

* * *

The sudden explosion of the New York longshoremen was an act of great significance. Certainly it deserves a more prominent place in the history of labor struggles in the United States. Still, the strikers were defeated in 1907, as were longshoremen in the harbor before them.

They were not strong enough to overcome the great combination of power and wealth cast against them. They would be defeated again in 1919. This is part of a larger tragedy.[130] Ultimately, sectionalism and highly local trade unionism persisted on the New York waterfront, and industrial unionism failed, however irresistible it sometimes seemed. In the end, unity on the waterfront was imposed from above by the craft unionists of the International Longshoremen's Association (ILA), often by force, and Jim Crow unionism was institutionalized. These defeats, however, were by no means "inevitable," and there is evidence to suggest that the longshoremen could have won in 1907; indeed, they nearly did. Perhaps their greatest weakness was the absence of significant support from labor outside their own ranks. But this conclusion involves speculation and is of limited relevance now. What is not speculation is that the longshoremen proved themselves a powerful group of workers, capable of waging an impressive strike against great odds.

The strike was led by immigrants and rank-and-file workers, who were far from conservative, tractable, and immature. The Italian longshoremen were the dynamic group in the strike. They had the courage, ability, and audacity to transform the local agitations of March and April into a harborwide strike of longshoremen. They were capable, in the course of the strike, of identifying with the other groups of longshoremen and, despite the barriers to common action, they succeeded in drawing them into the general strike. The Italians brought, with their May Day red flags, imagination, commitment, and rebelliousness to the labor movement in the harbor.[131]

African American longshoremen also found a voice in the strike. And despite the violent and unrelenting racism of the times, they tenaciously fought to improve their wages and conditions of work, to increase their numbers, and to be part of waterfront trade unionism, whatever form it would take. The Irish longshoremen joined blacks, Italians, and other immigrants on the basis of occupational and class solidarity. This calls into question recent interpretations of Irish advancement and conservatism in the United States. More realistically, the majority of Irish longshoremen can be understood as belonging to that vast part of the American working class for whom technological innovation and industrial expansion brought only harsh toil and unremitting poverty. This created a growing gap between them and the more skilled workers whose leaders, many of whom were Irish, dominated the AFL's Central Federated Union in New York. It also placed these longshoremen alongside many other workers who comprised an impatient and increasingly class-conscious part of the American working class in the first decades of the twentieth century.

In the wider framework of American working-class history, the 1907 strike can best be understood as one of the first direct action, mass challenges to the employers and their authority, challenges which would continue in progression up to and through World War I. These challenges— labor wars, immigrant strikes, and rank-and-file rebellions—were, even when defeated, links forged in a chain of historical battles which inspired great hope in working people everywhere. The New York longshoremen belong in this setting; their strike was one such link, something Ernest Poole suggested when he called them "lumberjacks come to town."[132] The longshoremen responded to cruel working conditions, chronic unemployment, and low wages in an intensely competitive labor market by joining together to fight for industrial unionism in a very radical strike.

Notes

I would like to thank David Howell, Laurie Flynn, Gil Fagiani, Donna Rae Gabaccia, Dana Frank, Stan Weir, Peter Cole, Eric Arnesen, and Bruce Nelson.

1. Ernest Poole, "The Ship Must Sail on Time," *Everybody's Magazine,* 19 (Aug. 1908), 176–86. Poole goes on: "No shorter hours, no measures to lessen the terrific waste of life" (p. 186).

2. The only account of the 1907 strike is found in the classic investigation of Charles Barnes, *The Longshoremen* (New York: Survey Associates, 1915), pp. 115–21. This is an invaluable source, based on "personal interviews . . . strikers' circulars . . . and various publications," but its interpretation is flawed by the author's antipathy to strikes and his misunderstandings of race and ethnic relations. Edwin Fenton examines the strike and focuses on Italians, but nearly all his evidence comes from Barnes, as do his conclusions. The strike was defeated as a result of "excessive demands" and "poor negotiators." In addition, he calls attention to "the ethnic rivalries which divided the workers and the mores of the Italians [as] all partly responsible for the defeat" (*Immigrants and Unions, a Case Study: Italians and American Labor, 1870–1920* [New York: Arno, 1975], pp. 254–55). David Montgomery calls attention this strike but underestimates its scale and significance. See *The Fall of the House of Labor* (New York: Cambridge University Press, 1987), pp. 106–7.

3. E. J. Hobsbawm, "National Unions on the Waterside," in *Labouring Men* (New York: Anchor Books, 1967), p. 242.

4. For an account of the 1887 strike, see New York State, *Fifth Annual Report of the Bureau of the Statistics of Labor* (Albany, 1887). For the 1919 strike, see Calvin Winslow, "On the Waterfront: Black, Italian and Irish Longshoremen in the New York Harbor Strike of 1919," in *Protest and Survival: Essays for E. P. Thompson,* ed. John Rule and Robert Malcolmson (New York: New Press, 1993), pp. 355–93.

5. See Eric Taplin, *The Dockers' Union: A Study of the National Union of Dock Labourers, 1889–1922* (Leicester, Eng.: Leicester University Press, 1985); and Ken Coates and Tony Topham, *The History of the Transport and General Workers Union,* vol. 1 (London: Basil Blackwell, 1991); and J. Lovell, *Stevedores and Dockers: A Study of Trade Unionism in the Port of London, 1870–1914* (London: Macmillan, 1969), for interesting British comparisons. See David Montgomery, "The 'New Unionism' and the Transformation of Workers' Consciousness in America, 1909–1922" (in *Workers' Control in America* [New York: Cambridge University Press, 1979], pp. 91–112), for patterns of trade unionism in the United States.

6. The best general description of the harbor in this period is in Barnes, *Longshoremen.* Useful contemporary descriptions are found in Poole, "Ship Must Sail on Time," as well as in his novel *The Harbor* (New York: Macmillan, 1915). There is also useful material in the testimony of the longshoremen at the hearings of the Industrial Relations Commission, reprinted in *Commission on Industrial Relations,* vol. 3 (Washington, 1916), hereafter *CIR,* 3; in the Wainwright Commission's report on unemployment, "Report to the Legislature of the State of New York" (New York, 1909); and in the Mayor's Committee on Unemployment, "Report on Dock Employment in New York City" (New York, Oct. 1916).

7. Ron Chernow, *The House of Morgan* (New York: Atlantic Monthly Press, 1990), p. 145. The White Star Line petitioned the city to extend piers to accommodate the *Titanic.*

8. Barnes, *Longshoremen,* p. 3.

9. Barnes, *Longshoremen,* p. 72.

10. "Job control unionism" was a term used by critics of the American Federation of Labor to describe the restrictive polices of the craft unions.

11. Barnes, *Longshoremen,* p. 127.

12. Barnes, *Longshoremen,* p. 57.

13. Barnes, *Longshoremen,* p. 75.

14. Ernest Poole, "The Men on the Docks," *Outlook,* 86 (May 25, 1907), 142–44. Poole wrote, "On the docks of New York are some thirty thousand Irish and Germans, Italians and Negroes, Norwegians and Swedes and Poles. In the six weeks spent among them, I heard many angry demands for more wages, but never for shorter hours or safeguards to lesson the risk" (p. 143).

15. Hobsbawm, "National Unions on the Waterside," p. 274.

16. *Brooklyn Eagle,* May 4, 1907.

17. *New York World,* May 1, 1907.

18. *New York Times,* May 3, 1907.

19. *Brooklyn Eagle,* May 1, 1907. Fenton, *Immigrants and Unions,* p. 253.

20. *Brooklyn Eagle,* May 1, 1907. The unemployment rate in 1907 was about 3 percent and wages on the waterfront had changed little in decades. Barnes estimated the average yearly incomes of longshoremen at from $520 to $624 and noted that investigations had proved that a family of normal size required $800 to $900 annually (*Longshoremen,* p. 92). See also Montgomery on the willingness of workers in these years "to act in defiance of warnings from experienced union leaders" ("'New Unionism' and the Transformation of Workers' Consciousness in America, p. 94).

21. *Brooklyn Eagle,* May 1, 1907.

22. *Brooklyn Eagle,* May 1, 1907.

23. *Brooklyn Eagle,* May 2, 1907.

24. *Brooklyn Eagle,* May 2, 1907.

25. *Brooklyn Eagle,* May 2, 1907.

26. *Brooklyn Eagle,* May 4, 1907.

27. *Brooklyn Eagle,* May 4, 1907.

28. *New York Evening Journal,* May 6, 1907.

29. *Hoboken Observer,* May 6, 1907.

30. The strikebreakers were "cosmopolitan" as well. On the first day of the strike, Italian strikebreakers were being used on the Ward Line piers in Brooklyn to replace black strikers; on the Barber Lines, blacks were replacing Italians. On May 8, the *Eagle* reported Russian Jews, led by a rabbi, replacing Italians on the Atlantic docks in Brooklyn. On May 9, the *Eagle* reported that "scores of scrub women gathered up in the city were performing the work usually done by [striking] stewards." Some Belgian ships carried their own longshoremen (*New York Evening Journal,* May 13, 1907). French sailors were reported doing longshoremen's work (*New York Times,* May 28, 1907). On the notorious Michael Farley, see Edward Levinson, *I Break Strikes* (New York: Arno, 1969), pp. 28–33.

31. *New York Times,* May 5, 1907.

32. *Brooklyn Eagle,* May 4, 1907. On May 8, the *Times* reported that the shippers believed that as soon as "beer money" ran out "the longshoremen will return to work." The same day the *Eagle* commented: "The longshoremen along the waterfront of Greater New York are a shiftless lot as a rule and spend most of their time in the saloons nearest their piers. They live from hand to mouth although making from $3

a day up when there is plenty of shipping which has been the case for the past year. They look on the strike as a diversion."

33. *New York Evening Journal,* May 8, 1907. *New York Times,* May 9, 1907. Barnes, *Longshoremen,* p. 119.

34. *New York Evening Journal,* May 9, 1907.

35. *New York World,* May 11, 1907.

36. *Brooklyn Eagle,* May 29, 1907.

37. *Daily People,* June 4, 1907.

38. Barnes, *Longshoremen,* p. 29.

39. *CIR,* 3, p. 2067.

40. Poole, "Ship Must Sail on Time," p. 183.

41. Barnes, *Longshoremen,* p. 33.

42. Poole, "Ship Must Sail on Time," p. 178.

43. Barnes, *Longshoremen,* p. 16. The Cunard Line was reported to employ some freight handlers in Chelsea the year round on a weekly wage (*Brooklyn Eagle,* May 7, 1907). Not everyone agreed that the Chelsea work was the best. Charles Kiern, a socialist Hoboken longshoremen, told the Committee on Industrial Relations, "I have heard today about the best docks in the city being the White Star dock. The men generally don't consider the best dock where the work is so Taylored that they work a man's life out of him in ten years" (*CIR,* 3, p. 2117).

44. Franklin Frazier, "The Negro Longshoremen" (1921), unpublished manuscript, p. 4, Russell Sage Foundation, New York.

45. See Daniel Bell, *The End of Ideology,* rev. ed. (New York: Free Press, 1962), p. 192.

46. Barnes, *Longshoremen,* pp. 10 and 27.

47. Barnes, *Longshoremen,* p. 3.

48. *New York Times,* May 3, 1907.

49. *Brooklyn Eagle,* May 2, 1907 (emphasis added).

50. *Brooklyn Eagle,* May 2, 1907.

51. George E. Haynes, *The Negro at Work in New York City* (New York: Longman's Green, 1912), p. 75. Haynes counted only seventy-five on the Manhattan waterfront in 1905, though other evidence suggests this was an underestimate, and Haynes says nothing of Brooklyn. See Mary White Ovington on strikebreaking black longshoremen in Brooklyn in "The Negro in the Trades Unions in New York," *Annals of the American Academy of Political and Social Science,* 27 (Jan.–June 1906), 551–58.

52. Sterling Spero and Abram Harris, *The Black Worker: The Negro and the Labor Movement* (New York: Atheneum, 1931), p. 105. Frazier, "Negro Longshoremen," p. 3.

53. Frazier, "Negro Longshoremen," p. 4.

54. *Hoboken Observer,* May 28, 1907.

55. Frazier, "Negro Longshoremen," p. 39 .

56. *New York Times,* May 13, 1907. See Eric Arnesen, "Following the Color Line of Labor: Black Workers and the Labor Movement before 1930" (*Radical History,* 55 [Winter 1993], 53–67), for useful observations on race relations and labor in this period.

57. Barnes, *Longshoremen,* p. 5.

58. Barnes, *Longshoremen,* pp. 7–12.

59. *Brooklyn Eagle,* May 2, 1907. The *Eagle,* in an early report, referred to "three gangs of 'white men,' as others than Italians and negroes are called."

60. The *New York Times,* for example, reported a conflict on the East River where black longshoremen repulsed Italian strikebreakers. "The strikebreakers are Italians," commented the *Times,* repeating popular stereotypes, "and are not nearly so strong as the strikers who are Blacks" (May 8, 1907).

61. Barnes, *Longshoremen,* p. 10.

62. Antonio Mangano, *Sons of Italy* (New York: Missionary Education Movement, 1917), p. 24. See the still-useful study by Isaac A. Hourwich, *Immigration and Labor* (New York: G. P. Putnam's Sons, 1912), for wages and living conditions in New York City.

63. U.S. Census, 1910, NARA, Microfilm Publications, T624, reel 956.

64. Barnes, *Longshoremen,* p. 7.

65. The press frequently referred to Nino Sabbatino as the leader of the Brooklyn Italians. Sabbatino was a Union Street liquor dealer. *Uppingtons General Directory of Brooklyn,* 1908, reel 25, p. 859. On Italian unions, see also *Brooklyn Eagle,* May 14, 1907.

66. *Il Proletario,* May 26, 1907. *Il Proletario,* the Italian American socialist paper, praised the strikers and believed that the strike "dispelled prejudices against Italians." It argued that though the shippers believed that the "Italians would capitulate," instead they conducted "a righteous fight" and delivered "saintly blows" in the cause of "human redemption."

67. *New York World,* May 4, 1907.

68. *Il Proletario,* May 26, 1907.

69. *Brooklyn Eagle,* May 9, 1907. A Dr. Attilo Caccini gave an interesting description of the padrone in a letter to the mayor: "As soon as the Italian arrives in New York, he is met by a fellow-countryman, a padrone, by whom he is directed in every step of his life. This padrone provides the immigrant with work, and abuses him in every possible manner. When he is sick the padrone suggests a doctor. . . . If he has some money he is advised to deposit it in certain bank" (n.d. [1907]), Municipal Archives, MGB—1904–1909, General Correspondence received, #69, Surrogate Court, New York.

70. *Daily People,* May 16, 1907; see Maud Russell, *Men along the Shore* (New York: Brussel and Brussel, 1966), pp. 31–41. Also New York State, *Fifth Annual Report,* for an account of the 1887 strike.

71. See John R. McKivigan and Thomas J. Robertson, "The Irish American Worker in Transition, 1877–1914: New York City as a Test Case," in *The New York Irish,* ed. Ronald H. Bayor and Timothy J. Meagher (Baltimore: Johns Hopkins University Press), pp. 301–20; and Kerby A. Miller, *Emigrants and Exiles: Ireland and the Irish Exodus to North America* (New York: Oxford University Press, 1985). David Brundage emphasizes the numbers and importance of "new" Irish immigrants in a very interesting paper, "The 1920 New York Dockers' Boycott: Class, Gender, Race and Irish-American Nationalism," which examines a boycott by Chelsea dockers which involved not only support from black longshoremen but also the leadership of Irish women in a nationalist boycott of British ships (unpublished manuscript, in author's possession).

72. See, for example, the testimony of social worker Mary Oakly Bay, who worked in the district from Chambers Street to Fourteenth Street, an area "almost exclusively made up of the families of longshoremen." She called it "one of the City's most hopeless" (*CIR*, 3, pp. 2138–39).

73. *Industrial Union Bulletin,* hereafter *IUB,* Feb. 1, 1908, Connolly told the IWW's leaders that "the Germans are considered to be revolutionary socialists; the branches composed of Italians are developing reliable elements for constructive work and the branches composed of Irishmen have among the officers many members and supporters of the I.W.W." Connolly was also soon to launch the *Harp,* aimed at Irish American workers, despite opposition from comrades in the SLP and IWW. See his letters to John Carstairs Matheson, MS. 13906, National Museum of Ireland, Dublin, in particular the letter of Dec. 10, 1907.

74. Barnes, *Longshoremen,* p. 11.

75. See E. P. Thompson on class and consciousness in the preface to *The Making of the English Working Class* (New York: Vintage: 1963), pp. 9–15.

76. *Il Proletario,* for example, railed against Italian bankers and businessmen for their role in defeating the strike (May 26, 1907).

77. New York State, *Fifth Annual Report.*

78. See Russell, *Men along the Shore,* pp. 48–52. McHugh was a follower of Henry George, the single taxer; he was an advocate of racial equality. The American Longshoremen's Union rules stated "all men are brothers." According the Barnes, "There was to be no distinction of race, creed, color, or nativity." Membership was open to "every man employed about the piers or docks in any capacity in connection with the shipping or carrying industries" (*Longshoremen,* p. 111).

79. Barnes, *Longshoremen,* p. 127.

80. Barnes, *Longshoremen.* p. 127. Barnes continued on reasons for the defeat: "Add to these a lack of permanent solidarity among the men, jealousy and bickering between the unions and among men individually, different rates of wages in different parts of the port and at different piers, and you have a picture of conditions which inevitably lead to failure."

81. *New York Evening Journal,* June 4, 1907.

82. *Nation,* May 16, 1907.

83. *Il Proletario,* June 2, 1907.

84. *New York World,* May 15, 1907.

85. *New York World,* May 12, 1907.

86. *New York World,* May 12, 1907.

87. E. J. Hobsbawm, "The New Unionism in Perspective," in *Workers: Worlds of Labor* (New York: Pantheon, 1984), p. 158.

88. *New York World,* May 8, 1907.

89. *New York World,* May 8, 1907 (emphasis added).

90. *New York World,* May 8, 1907.

91. *New York Times,* May 11, 1907.

92. *Hoboken Observer,* June 4, 1907.

93. *Hoboken Observer,* May 17, 1907.

94. *New York Evening Journal,* May 24, 1907.

95. *New York Times,* May 13, 1907 (emphasis added).

96. *Brooklyn Eagle,* May 9, 1907.

97. *New York Evening Journal,* May 9, 1907. *Brooklyn Eagle,* May 14, 1907. *Il Proletario* carried an account of Italian wives attacking strikebreakers in June 1907 (July 5, 1907).

98. *New York Evening Journal,* May 9, 1907.

99. *New York Evening Journal,* May 9, 1907.

100. *New York Evening Journal,* May 13, 1907.

101. *New York Evening Journal,* May 13, 1907.

102. *New York World,* May 9, 1907.

103. *New York World,* May 9, 1907. But this was not true. According to Buchanan, "It cannot be said that the strike is due to the influence of walking delegates or labor agitators . . . about 90 percent [of the strikers] were not connected with any union." Buchanan also believed the Brooklyn Italians led the strikes. Nevertheless, Connors told reporters he "wished to correct the idea that the strikers are an unorganized body. They belong to the Longshoremen's Protective Union," he said, "which has existed for ten years as an independent body and has fourteen branches in New York and New Jersey" (*New York Evening Journal,* May 12, 1907).

104. *New York Evening Journal,* May 12, 1907. As late as June 2, 1907, the *Brooklyn Eagle* reported "the union is steadily gaining ground," giving as an example the Australasia Line where longshoremen were paid higher, forty cents and sixty cents an hour but still went out.

105. *New York Evening Journal,* May 15, 1907.

106. *New York Times,* May 10, 1907.

107. *Brooklyn Eagle,* May 9, 1907.

108. *New York Evening Journal,* May 16, 1907. The fact that a year later LUPA still had 12,000 members seems to offer evidence that the recruitment figures were reasonably accurate.

109. *Brooklyn Eagle,* May 9, 1907.

110. *New York Times,* May 12, 1907.

111. *New York Times,* May 8, 1907.

112. The International Longshoremen's Association, centered in the Great Lakes, seems to have taken no interest in the strike, except insofar as it became difficult for its small New York affiliate, Local 658, Lumber Handlers, only accidentally connected to the strike, to settle a dispute with the lumber dealers (ILA, *Proceedings of the Fifteenth Convention of the Longshoremen's Association,* July 1907, Detroit, Mich.).

113. *New York World,* May 28, 1907.

114. *New York Times,* May 14, 1907.

115. The fact that the checkers and tally men of White Star and Cunard Lines struck, demanding the same scale as longshoremen, was seen as a sign of strength for the union, according to union leader Dennis Delaney. It is more evidence of an industry-wide movement (*New York Evening Journal,* May 9, 1907). On workers' movements in this period, see Montgomery, "'New Unionism' and the Transformation of Workers' Consciousness in America," pp. 91–112.

116. *IUB,* Feb. 1, 1907. The Knights of Labor were defeated in the waterfront strike

of 1887, but the men who struck were still represented among the longshoremen in 1907. They may have carried the tradition of multiracial unionism, industrial unionism, into the twentieth century, as did the McHugh organization. This is evidence, it seems to me, that there were workers, though a minority of course, on the New York Harbor waterfront who opposed the dominant tendencies in the labor movement of the time. Workers, in Herbert Gutman's words, who "were stifled by the defensive strategy of organized labor . . . as well as the rising tide of racism within the labor movement and throughout the country" ("The Negro in the United Mine Workers of America," in *Work, Culture, and Society in Industrializing America* [New York: Vintage, 1977], p. 208). In 1907, and again in 1919, class conflict erupted on an enormous scale on the New York waterfront, and in both cases there was considerable support among longshoremen for multiracial, democratic trade unionism.

117. On the IWW, see Melvyn Dubofsky, *We Shall Be All* (New York: Quadrangle, 1969).

118. After the strike the IWW blamed the defeat on lack of support from other marine and harbor workers, as well as "the treachery of the A.F.L." (*IUB*, Oct. 24, 1907).

119. *IUB*, Feb. 1, 1908.

120. Taplin, *Dockers' Union*, p. 11.

121. Chernow, *House of Morgan*, pp. 100–102. According to John Hutchins, the shipping companies were "huge." In 1914, for example, six German firms owned 220 steel liners; in Holland, eleven companies owned 210 ships; the British Peninsular and Oriental Steam Navigation Company alone owned 306 (*The American Maritime Industries and Public Policy: 1789–1914* [Cambridge: Harvard University Press, 1941], p. 487).

122. Vincent P. Carosso, *The Morgans: Private International Bankers* (Cambridge: Harvard University Press, 1987), pp. 481–86.

123. Hobsbawm, "National Unions on the Waterside," p. 172.

124. Carosso, *Morgans*, p. 492; Hobsbawm, "National Unions on the Waterside," p. 172.

125. *New York World* May 17, 1907. Chernow writes that Ismay was an "abrupt and ill-mannered man," according to colleagues. He survived the sinking of the *Titanic*, "the crowning disaster for the shipping trust," but was forced to resign as a result of the "public drubbing" he took in New York (*House of Morgan*, p. 146).

126. *New York Times*, June 2, 1907.

127. *Daily People*, June 18, 1907. Connolly blamed defeat on the lack of solidarity, the result of "the treachery and deceit advocated and practiced by the American Federation of Labor," as well as European workers who worked the ships including some who were members of "progressive unions" (*IUB*, Feb. 1, 1907). *Il Proletario* attributed defeat to the power of the shippers, "the colossus of the shipping trust" (June 30, 1907).

128. *New York Times*, May 29, 1907.

129. *New York Evening Journal*, June 14, 1907, *New York Times*, June 15, 1907. There were similar scenes in other parts of the port, according to Barnes, *Longshoremen*, p. 120.

130. See Winslow, "On the Waterfront."

131. While we still know too little about these workers, the evidence suggests that their behavior should not surprise us. Other groups of Italians in America, about whom we know more, acted much the same, in part because they carried with them the radical traditions of late nineteenth-century southern Italy and Sicily. See Donna Rae Gabaccia, *Militants and Migrants: Rural Sicilians Become American Workers* (New Brunswick: Rutgers University Press, 1988). Also Rudolph J. Vecoli, "Italian American Workers, 1880–1920: Padrone Slaves or Primitive Rebels?" in *Perspectives in Italian Immigration and Ethnicity,* ed. S. M. Tomasi (New York: Center for Immigration Studies, 1977), pp. 25–49.

132. Poole, "Ship Must Sail on Time," p. 176.

3 Radical Possibilities? The Rise and Fall of Wobbly Unionism on the Philadelphia Docks

Howard Kimeldorf

In the spring of 1913, when some two thousand longshoremen in Philadelphia joined the Industrial Workers of the World (IWW), hardly anyone outside the Quaker city even noticed. Understandably, the nation's attention was focused on another labor struggle taking place a few miles to the east, in Paterson, New Jersey, where the Wobblies were leading a "general strike" of twenty-five thousand silk workers. The Paterson conflict had all the elements of good drama that the public had recently come to expect from the IWW: stark portrayals of defenseless immigrant laborers and rapacious capitalists, impassioned pleas for justice heavily laced with "subversive" rhetoric, and a sparkling cast of radical celebrities, all culminating in a final, desperate showdown between the forces of good and evil.[1] If the story line varied somewhat from strike to strike, the underlying plot was by now a familiar one. Only a few months before, the IWW had made national headlines in Akron, Ohio, after leading a similarly dramatic walkout of nearly twenty thousand rubber workers. But the incident that really put the IWW on the map was the 1912 textile strike in Lawrence, Massachusetts. Accomplishing what the craft unions deemed impossible, the Wobblies welded the city's "unorganizable" polyglot labor force—consisting of no fewer than fifteen distinct nationalities speak-

ing in forty-five different dialects—into a solid mass of twenty-three thousand strikers. With considerable fanfare, and much publicity, the IWW
scored its first major victory that winter, when Lawrence's textile manu-
facturers, traditionally some of New England's most intransigent employers, granted significant concessions in wages, job security, and conditions.[2]

But the promise of Lawrence, Akron, and Paterson was never realized.
By the end of 1913, local IWW chapters in each city were in total disarray.
In Lawrence, membership in the National Industrial Union of Textile
Workers plummeted from sixteen thousand dues-paying members shortly
after the strike to around seven hundred less than a year later.[3] Akron experienced an equally precipitous drop, from close to twelve thousand
members at the height of the walkout to fewer than fifty active supporters in the space of six months. Such organizational volatility seemed to be
the fate of the IWW, as local after local, particularly in the industrialized
East, rose and fell in meteoric fashion.[4]

In Philadelphia, meanwhile, the longshoremen continued their union-
building efforts on the docks. While events in Lawrence, Akron, and Paterson were capturing the headlines, the city's dock workers, organized into
Local 8 of the Wobblies' Marine Transport Workers (MTW), were qui-
etly capturing the waterfront. By the fall of 1913, with the big eastern locals on the verge of collapse, Local 8 appeared stronger than ever. The
secretary of the MTW pointed with pride to Philadelphia as "the only
local in good standing" with the national organization. And, with almost
three thousand dues-paying members, Local 8 was larger than all of the
other Wobbly marine locals combined. As a delegate to the 1913 IWW
convention admitted, "the Philadelphia local practically makes up" the
entire national membership of the MTW.[5]

Local 8 pressed ahead. Honoring the IWW's policy against signing
agreements with employers, the longshoremen relied not on the sanctity
of the contract but rather on their own solidarity to gradually extend the
union's control over the waterfront, advancing from pier to pier by forcing stevedores to hire only those men wearing the MTW work button.
After three years of such direct-action tactics, Local 8 controlled virtually all of the city's sixty-five or so piers engaged in intercoastal and foreign shipping. The task of organizing the port was finally completed in
1920, when Local 8 mopped up the remaining coastwise longshoremen,
bringing its membership to around seven thousand. The Wobbly local was
now in the driver's seat. With formal recognition from the United States
Shipping Board, a large and stable treasury, an extensive network of job
delegates operating throughout the port, and an unusually capable staff

of union officers, Local 8 seemed set for life. Less than three years later, however, in April 1923, the longshoremen abandoned the IWW and, after briefly functioning as an independent union, moved en masse into the AFL-affiliated International Longshoremen's Association (ILA), their longtime and bitter rival.

Local 8's association with the IWW from 1913 to 1923 made it the single most durable example of Wobbly unionism at the time. During that same span of years, literally hundreds of IWW locals passed into and out of existence: hardly any lasted beyond a particular strike or job action; those that did typically survived as paper organizations, with wildly fluctuating memberships and few regular dues-payers.[6] In contrast, Local 8 remained viable throughout its ten-year existence, maintaining a stable and growing membership along with its commitment to a variant of "revolutionary industrial unionism."

The history of Local 8 thus provides a rare opportunity to observe Wobbly unionism in practice over a period of several years. Whether the "Philadelphia model" deserved to be emulated for its envious record of accomplishments and exceptional durability or instead repudiated—as some national IWW leaders urged—for its alleged economism, Local 8 was, in the words of Walter Nef, one of its early leaders, "an outstanding example of what the I.W.W. could do if permanent organization were more pushed."[7]

The issue of organizational stability raised by Nef remains one of the great "what if" questions dogging IWW historiography. While there are many versions of this question, they all boil down to the proposition that the Wobblies' failure was primarily organizational. In this view, what sank the IWW was not that its syndicalism was too radical or its confrontational methods too extreme, but rather that, as labor historian David Saposs long ago observed, "its innate urge to propagandize at the expense of stability" undermined any efforts aimed at organizational consolidation. If only the Wobblies had taken the task of union-building more seriously, the argument goes, they might have survived in places like Lawrence, Paterson, and Akron to spearhead the organization of basic industry, perhaps paving the way for an earlier, more aggressive industrial union movement in the United States.[8]

As with all such counterfactual claims, questions about what might have been can only be answered, if at all, by investigating what was in fact historically possible. Local 8's rise and consolidation, resting on an unusual combination of left-wing leadership, organizational stability, and popular support, sheds considerable light on the possibilities of working-class insurgency during the first quarter of the twentieth century, just as its eventual demise illuminates the limitations. Contrary to received theorizing on the failure of American labor radicalism, the history of Local 8 suggests that leftist union leadership, sound "business" methods, and rank-and-file support were not necessarily incompatible; indeed, they may even presuppose one another, as they did years ago on the Philadelphia docks where the longshoremen embraced a Wobbly leadership that was as militant about its revolutionary vision as it was pragmatic about building a mass-based organization.

Baptism of Fire: The Emergence of Local 8

When the Wobblies began agitating on the Philadelphia docks in the spring of 1913, there was little cause for optimism. The port's longshoremen did not seem to have much of an attachment to unions, as borne out by the repeated failures to organize the waterfront. The Knights of Labor were the first to taste defeat when their local assembly of dock workers, organized in 1895 with under two hundred members, folded after only a few months.[9] The following year, Edward McHugh, an international organizer with the British Dockers' Union, launched his American Longshoremen's Union (ALU) in several East Coast cities. In Philadelphia, excitement generated by the ALU's presence spilled over into a spontaneous walkout in the summer of 1898. McHugh, viewing the longshoremen's struggle as key to organizing the North Atlantic ports, placed his entire treasury at the disposal of the strikers. But upon applying to the union's general treasurer for funds, McHugh learned that all monies had been secretly diverted to the secretary, who had recently left town. Lacking external funding, the walkout collapsed, and along with it the scandalized ALU. Except for a brief flurry of activity initiated by the AFL in 1909, the Philadelphia waterfront remained unorganized and impenetrable to unions.[10]

Without union protection, conditions on the docks went from bad to worse. Although the ten-hour day was the rule, stretches as long as fifty hours or more were not uncommon. Jack Walsh, who helped organize Local 8, told a federal judge in 1918 of one gang that was forced to work 110 consecutive hours without rest. Two of the men, Walsh reported, were "carried up dead in the tugs and a few more of them, they ain't able to walk yet."[11] The long hours of work, coupled with the extraordinary physical demands of the job itself, placed longshoremen at considerable risk to life and limb. Yet, however dangerous it was, most men eagerly took what little work they could find. At quitting time, Walsh recalled, "The boss would order the men back again, and he would tell you if you would not come back, 'You don't need to look for work there any more.'"[12] Nor was this an idle threat, for the casual nature of longshore employment—marked by its irregularity and resulting dependence on employer favoritism—made the blacklist an unusually effective weapon of labor discipline. In the absence of union protection, chronic economic insecurity was enough to keep most men on the job for as long as needed, subject to miserable conditions, rarely earning more than twenty-five cents an hour.[13]

After suffering in silence for so many years, the longshoremen finally found their voice. On May 10, 1913, Wobbly leaders in Philadelphia received word that the port's dock workers were interested in organizing, possibly under their banner. Although admittedly "at a loss" to explain the sudden interest in their organization, the Wobblies immediately dispatched an organizer, Edward Lewis, down to the docks to sign up new recruits. But after canvassing the waterfront, Lewis came back empty-handed, unable to find even a single supporter. That might have been the end of the story had not a small group of longshoremen happened upon a meeting of striking sugar workers who were being addressed by George Speed, national IWW organizer. After Speed concluded his formal remarks to the strikers, the longshoremen in attendance approached the stage to ask for his assistance in organizing the waterfront. In agreeing to help, Speed laid the foundations for what would become one of the most durable associations in IWW history.[14]

Speed met with the longshoremen the following morning at IWW headquarters where they hammered out three demands. At the top of the list was money, with the longshoremen seeking to increase the hourly wage from the current "sliding scale" of twenty to twenty-five cents to a uniform rate of thirty-five cents for all categories of day work. A second wage demand, calling for the establishment of overtime rates of pay, was actually a thinly disguised attempt to limit the length of the working day to ten hours. For safety reasons alone, the longshoremen probably would have preferred to ban all work beyond ten hours. But such restrictions were not likely to be accepted by time-conscious stevedores whose job it was to get ships in and out of port as fast as possible. So instead of trying to legislate the length of the working day outright, they sought to make "overtime" less attractive to their employers by demanding time and a half after 6 P.M. and double time for Sundays and holidays. And finally, the longshoremen demanded union recognition, not of the IWW but of a "standing committee" of dock workers.[15]

The demands spread rapidly along the waterfront. On May 13, apparently without waiting for a response from the stevedores, the men began leaving their jobs. After three days, more than two thousand longshoremen were out, stranding twenty vessels along a ten-mile stretch of the Delaware River from Port Richmond to Girard Point. Other ships, particularly those on tight schedules, were forced to sail without their full complement of passengers or cargo. As activity ground to a halt, several large shipping lines rerouted their vessels to nearby ports, discharging cargo in Baltimore and New York for eventual shipment by rail to Philadelphia. In response, the strikers fired off telegrams to longshoremen in other cities asking them not to service any vessel that had been diverted from Philadelphia. Both sides then dug in for what one local newspaper described as "a fight to the finish."[16]

At this point the leadership of the walkout was still unresolved. Although the Wobblies claimed to be in charge, only a handful of strikers actually belonged to the IWW. The vast majority were unorganized. With the rank and file up for grabs, the ILA sent organizers down to the docks in an effort to wrest control of the walkout away from the IWW. But beyond their ritualistic denunciation of the IWW as an "anarchistic . . . insidious organization," ILA organizers had nothing to offer the strikers except the promise of "frank discussion with the shipowners." In contrast, the Wobblies called on the rank and file to act now and talk later. "We will continue your fight until you get what is your right share," Lewis vowed. "We are strong enough to do anything, and we will surely do this. . . . Our great power lies in being able to sit with our hands folded and do nothing." The choice was clear: open mouths or folded arms. After weighing both strategies, the longshoremen declared for the IWW. Over the next few days, more than fifteen hundred strikers poured into the recently chartered Local 8 of the MTW. To handle the flood of new recruits, the Wobblies suspended the usual $2.00 initiation fee.[17]

The Wobblies' emergence elicited a predictable response from local stevedores, who vowed to fight as long and as hard as necessary to keep the IWW off the docks. Shipowner Frederick Taylor, representing one of the port's largest lines, dismissed the IWW as merely "a business proposition" and confidently predicted a short strike. But as the walkout entered its second week, Taylor's optimism waned. Although still confident of ultimate victory, he realized that the stevedores had a real fight on their hands. To combat the growing strength of the union, Taylor convinced the port's employers to create "an independent nucleus of power" on the docks by establishing nonunion beachheads on several piers. From these staging areas, skeletal crews were put to work under constant police protection.[18]

Introducing strikebreakers destabilized what had been up to that point an orderly and peaceful walkout. The calm was broken late in the afternoon on May 21, when about fifty strikebreakers, heading home after work, were confronted by a larger group of pickets. The men began arguing, then fighting, freely exchanging blows with fists, clubs, and lead pipes. Close to one thousand residents of the neighborhood flowed into the streets, turning an otherwise limited altercation into a full-scale riot. The police arrived but, according to press accounts, "were powerless. The crowd filled the street and the pavements and many of them took sides with the strikers. Bricks and bottles were hurled from windows and alleys." Five men, all of them strikers, were taken into custody and many more were injured. A few hours later, in apparently unrelated incidents, two men suspected of strikebreaking were beaten by roving bands of pickets.[19]

The rioting polarized the city along class lines. While Philadelphia's leading daily newspaper called upon its middle-class readers to aggressively "root out" the Wobblies, others, notably workers, came to their defense. Union carpenters, who had been building eating facilities for the strikebreakers, walked off the job. Members of the various marine trades stopped reporting for work. As cargo handling slowed to a crawl, even Taylor had to admit that strikebreaking efforts had become largely symbolic, amounting to little more than "putting up a bold front." The following day Taylor called three former employees into his office to discuss the impasse. He argued that a wage increase was not really in the men's best interest since it would only serve to divert shipping from Philadelphia to low-wage ports such as Baltimore and Montreal. The men apparently found this argument convincing, and agreed to take Taylor's offer of thirty cents per hour, plus time and a half for overtime with double time for Sundays and holidays, back to the membership for consideration. That evening the longshoremen voted to accept Taylor's proposal. When word of a possible agreement reached the strikebreakers, they responded by immediately calling a strike of their own. The employers wasted no time in firing the ringleaders while allowing the others to stay on until the original strikers returned to reclaim their former jobs.[20]

The walkout produced no clear winner. Although the shipowners succeeded in shaving a nickel off of the original wage demand, the men won a uniform rate of thirty cents an hour, thus doing away with the highly unpopular "sliding scale." Of the two remaining demands, the longshoremen secured the ten-hour day but failed to win union recognition.[21] Both sides claimed victory but neither the Wobblies nor the stevedores were satisfied with the outcome.

Dissension arose first among the employers. Shortly after the men returned to work, the port's leading shipping interests sat down together for the first time since the walkout to discuss the terms of the recent settlement. Taylor, being its principal architect, was assailed from all sides for conceding the ten-hour day. Leading the charge was a representative from the International Mercantile Marine Company, who urged those present to set their own independent wage rates for evenings, Sundays, and holidays. Taylor vigorously dissented, warning that such action would "have the effect of maintaining the I.W.W. in the field." But no one else in the room seemed to take the IWW threat seriously. No doubt cognizant of past failures to unionize the port, the shipowners dismissed the Wobblies as "a huge joke."[22]

The longshoremen, however, were not laughing. With about half of the port's thirty-five hundred dock workers enrolled in Local 8, the Wobblies wasted no time putting their syndicalist beliefs into practice when all 250 men employed by the International Mercantile Marine Company quit work rather than remove their union buttons as ordered by the head stevedore. At stake here was not only the men's freedom of expression but also, more importantly, their recently acquired control over the job. In the absence of a written contract—which neither the shipowners nor the Wobblies were willing to sign—Local 8's survival following the May walkout depended on cornering the local labor market. This was accomplished by pressuring the port's stevedores, under threat of a renewed strike, to hire only those men displaying a union work button. Where this practice was adopted, as it was on most piers, membership in the MTW became a condition of employment, thereby securing the union's presence on the docks. Local 8's success in establishing job control without the usual encumbrances of craft exclusiveness, high dues, or restrictive contracts made it—for a time, at least—the darling of national IWW leaders, who pointed to the "Philadelphia model" as a solution to the perennial problem of building a union movement that was capable of protecting its members without succumbing to the sins of the AFL.[23]

Local 8 also departed from the typical business union in vigorously promoting economic equality across its diverse membership. Such equity considerations clearly informed the strikers' original demand for a single, uniform rate of pay. When the stevedores finally agreed to a universal wage of thirty cents per hour, it applied not only to the deep-sea longshore-men but to everyone else on the dock, from the lowliest water boy to the most skilled winch driver. In later years, other ports around the country would introduce plans for equalizing earnings within particular maritime occupations, but nothing so inclusive as the universal wage was ever adopted outside of Philadelphia.[24]

Local 8's commitment to equality was further demonstrated in its han-dling of ethnic and race relations. Prior to the Wobblies, attempts to or-ganize the docks had been routinely frustrated by the shipowners' skill in playing one nationality off against another. Americanized Irish were regularly pitted against foreign-speaking Poles and Lithuanians, while at other times all three ethnic groups banded together in opposition to Af-rican Americans, who accounted for around 40 percent of the port's long-shoremen. By promising first one group and then another the easiest jobs, steady work, or special treatment of some kind, the stevedores fueled distrust and dissension among the men. The Wobblies met this challenge head-on. In the course of the May walkout, MTW leaders made it a point to include representatives of each nationality on all of the important strike committees. This simple act was enough to hold the men together dur-ing the two-week walkout.[25] Afterwards, in an effort to solidify their ranks, Local 8 inaugurated a policy of rotating the union's top elected positions between black and white officers: one month, an African American served as president, assisted by a white vice president; the next month this pat-tern was reversed. In addition, Local 8's bylaws stipulated that at least one of its two secretaries, who directed the union's daily activities, was to be a black member in good standing.[26]

In an industry otherwise known for its segregationist practices,[27] Lo-cal 8's commitment to racial equality was a most remarkable achievement. Much of the credit goes to the union's indigenous black leadership, par-ticularly Benjamin Fletcher. Born and raised in Philadelphia, Fletcher first came in contact with the IWW in 1911 on the city's docks, where he was working as a longshoreman.[28] The following year, while the Lawrence textile strike dragged on, a steady stream of IWW partisans—most no-tably Elizabeth Gurley Flynn, whose fiery oratory earned her the nick-name "Rebel Girl," and Patrick Quinlan, a hotheaded Irishman who later turned up on the payroll of the ILA—passed through Philadelphia, oc-casionally stopping long enough to address the longshoremen.[29] Although these periodic agitational efforts failed to produce permanent organiza-tion on the docks, the Wobblies' gospel of militant interracial unionism converted men like Fletcher. Shortly thereafter, he joined the IWW, becoming the corresponding secretary for Local 57, a "mixed" local made up of workers employed in various industries throughout the city.[30]

Local 8's commitment to interracial leadership together with its policy of rotation in office generated a large cadre of experienced black activists—men like Charles Carter, Alonzo Richards, Dan Jones, and Glenn Perrymore, who along with Fletcher were often at the center of the union's ongoing factional struggles. The quality of white leadership was more suspect, at least initially. National IWW organizer George Speed's revolutionary fervor alienated many longshoremen, while Ed Lewis, the main spokesman during the recent strike, had a fondness for alcohol that made him less than reliable. When both men were eventually forced to leave Philadelphia late in 1913, however, Local 8 found extremely capable replacements in Jack Walsh and Walter Nef.[31]

That both Walsh and Nef, as IWW stalwarts, were deeply wedded to the cause of interracial unionism helped considerably in forging an unusually close and, by all accounts, trusting relationship between them and their black counterparts in Local 8. Philadelphia's integrated Wobbly leadership was thus able to lead by force of example, effectively countering ILA demands for separate white and black locals by demonstrating the viability of collective action. Repudiating the ILA's racial separatism and occupational exclusiveness, Local 8 was unwilling to rest until it controlled not just the docks but, as Walsh explained, every "transport worker aboard ship, truck, railroad, or street car." The first in line were the harbor boatmen, who affiliated with Local 8 as Branch #4 following a successful strike for higher wages. Next came the seamen. Led by Spaniard Genaro Pazos, a marine fireman and fervent syndicalist, the port's two hundred or so Spanish-speaking sailors gravitated to Local 8 as a temporary base of operations before eventually striking out on their own as Local 100 of the MTW. By the middle of 1914, with the city's streetcar workers reportedly "on track for the I.W.W. special," the Wobblies' goal of "One Big Union for Philadelphia's transport workers" seemed within reach.[32]

The rising tide of labor solidarity swept across the city's grain docks where, early in 1915, several hundred men began agitating for a wage increase. Taking their cue from the mostly African American grain handlers, over three thousand longshoremen walked off the job on the morning of January 25, demanding an increase in the hourly rate from thirty to forty cents for day work and corresponding adjustments in overtime pay.[33] By nightfall, most of the port's stevedores had come around, with the notable exception of Frederick Taylor. Still smarting from charges that he had caved in to union pressure during the last strike, Taylor refused to even meet with Local 8 officers. When the men began reporting for work the following morning under the new wage scale, Taylor notified his employees that their services were no longer required.[34] Undeterred by picket lines, Taylor launched his own nonunion operation, which he maintained through mid-February, when Local 8—considerably weakened by a recent drop-off in shipping activity—finally threw in the towel and ordered the remaining strikers back to work under the old wage scale. This was no ordinary defeat, however, for the union's control over hiring had been broken, first on Taylor's piers and then throughout the entire port. Once Local 8 was unable to provide any semblance of job security, its membership almost vanished, plummeting from around twenty-five hundred men to a hard core of twenty-seven IWW loyalists who continued paying dues throughout the lean months of 1915.[35]

Renewal and Consolidation: Building Revolutionary Unionism on the Docks

The economic recovery of East Coast shipping, spurred by the growing allied demand for war materials overseas, breathed new life into the skeletal remains of Local 8. Early in 1916 the Wobblies led a walkout against the anti-union Southern Steamship Company, returning to work a short time later as "union men, proudly wearing the I.W.W. work button." Their success triggered similar actions on other piers until Local 8 had been restored to its former self, complete with job control.[36] In April, after ignoring the Philadelphia waterfront for over a year, *Industrial Solidarity* reported that Local 8 was back in business with "over 3,000 members . . . in good standing."[37]

The longshoremen then went after the stevedores with the same wage demand that had cost them their union the year before. Again, the struggle broke out on the Southern line after a company spokesman refused to consider any increase in the hourly rate. In disgust, the entire work force of three hundred men immediately walked off. For the second time in recent months, a picket line went up around the Southern line piers.[38] But this time the employers were ready. With the appearance of the first picket, they converted one of the struck piers into "an emergency camp" capable of accommodating upwards of two hundred strikebreakers, who were lured "with food of excellent quality, soft, springy cots to sleep on and clean sheets three times a week."[39]

The strike remained orderly and peaceful for the first few weeks. But beneath the surface calm, pressure was slowly building. The lid finally blew off in early July, when Thomas Kenney, a Wobbly and ardent strike supporter, was shot through the heart by Warner Madox, one of several African Americans who had been hired to cook for the strikebreakers.[40] The next day, according to eyewitness John Walsh, "The police organized a frame-up. A colored detective was disguised as a scab. . . . A picket, Klen [Glenn] Perrymore, asked him what he was doing on the dock. Instead of showing his shield, he answered it was none of Perrymore's business, and pulled his gun. Perrymore grappled with him. He emptied his gun of five shots; while the rest of the police and detectives started in, Perrymore was hit on the head with a blackjack five times."[41]

The courage displayed by Perrymore, a prominent African American leader of Local 8, in confronting the "colored detective" underscored the class dimensions of the conflict, thereby preventing an even bloodier confrontation from erupting along racial lines. As it was, a "short but spirited" fight ensued between police and pickets. Several shots were fired. One picket was hit in the leg, while another miraculously escaped with only a minor flesh wound when a bullet fired at close range glanced off of a metal spectacles case that he carried in his breast pocket. Casualties from two days of fighting included five union men seriously injured and "one killed outright." Partly out of respect for the dead and injured, Local 8 continued the strike against the Southern line for several months before admitting defeat. When it was over, the longshoremen returned to work at the former wage scale and without job control.[42]

Local 8's humiliating defeats at the hands of the anti-union Southern line might have proved fatal had it not been for World War I. By the spring of 1917, following President Wilson's formal declaration of war against Germany, shipping activity along Philadelphia's Delaware River had reached a frenetic pace. As production of military hardware swung into high gear, the docks became congested with cargo destined for allied forces overseas. Working around the clock, the labor force was stretched to the breaking point. Experienced cargo handlers were in such demand that the navy, whose port surveillance team characterized Local 8 as "extremely dangerous potentially," was forced to go through the union hall in requesting civilian longshoremen to load munitions and other military supplies.[43] When the first members of Local 8 reported for work at the navy yard, they were ordered, at the point of drawn bayonets, to relinquish their "subversive" IWW work buttons. As in the past, the longshoremen refused and, after a brief standoff, they were put to work under the watchful eye of naval intelligence officers.[44]

With the existing dockside labor force depleted by military conscription on the one hand, and the lure of high-paying defense jobs on the other, a widening gap appeared between the declining number of longshoremen and the growing demand for their services.[45] Into the breach stepped several hundred African Americans. Swept up by the massive wartime exodus from the South, many black migrants arrived on the docks fresh from similar employment in New Orleans, Mobile, and other eastern Gulf ports, while others followed a more circuitous route by way of southeastern Pennsylvania's booming steel and construction industries.[46] Fed by this stream of new arrivals, Local 8 grew dramatically, initiating sixty to seventy new members every week. By summer the membership, now approaching five thousand, was around 60 percent black.[47]

Local 8's rebounding success did not escape the watchful eye of government officials. On September 5, 1917, agents with the Department of Justice staged simultaneous raids on forty-eight IWW locals across the country, including the MTW hall in Philadelphia, seizing several truckloads of "evidence" purporting to demonstrate IWW subversion of the war effort, mostly in the form of letters, newspapers, pamphlets, and other documents. Included in the nearly five tons of confiscated material were all of Local 8's membership records, account books, correspondence, and literature, as well as most office supplies, including the union's only working typewriter. Federal indictments were issued later that month against 166 leaders of the national IWW who were charged with violating the Selective Service Act, the Espionage Act, and the constitutional rights of employers, among other offenses. Government repression took a heavy toll in Philadelphia, where Fletcher, Walsh, Doree, and Nef were arrested and incarcerated while awaiting trial.[48]

Leadership of Local 8 passed into the hands of William "Dan" Jones, a black longshoreman, and Joseph Green. Reviewing Jones's performance in office, an informant for the War Department characterized him, quite accurately, as "more conservative" than his predecessor, Ben Fletcher, who, along with his codefendants, was facing a lengthy sentence in Leavenworth federal prison following their convictions. Jones and Green proved to be competent but uninspiring caretakers, lacking both the vision and intellectual depth of the men they had replaced. After completing his first year in office, Green stepped down amidst allegations of financial improprieties. His successor, Paul "Polly" Baker, seized the reins of local leadership and never let go.[49]

Baker's uncompromising militancy reinvigorated Local 8. Embracing the syndicalist traditions of the union's founders, Baker's presence at the helm lifted the men's spirits and turned things around. But success was not without its costs. With Local 8's renewed growth came a host of ideological and organizational dilemmas which, framed in the polarizing language of "reform" versus "revolution," created a deepening rift between the port's longshoremen and their national organization.

The first run-in with national MTW leaders occurred in February 1918 when the United States Shipping Board—the wartime agency charged with regulating industrial relations in the maritime industry—offered to recognize Local 8 as the port's exclusive bargaining agent. The ball was now in the Wobblies' court. Although Local 8 was anxious to secure union recognition, some of the government's terms, particularly the stipulation that the union select one representative with full authority to negotiate wages and conditions, flew in the face of IWW organizational guidelines governing democratic participation. Turning to the national IWW in Chicago for advice, Local 8 appealed to the General Executive Board, which, after condemning the proposal as "autocracy and a violation of IWW principles," reluctantly gave its consent—provided that Local 8's representative was elected by the entire membership, remained at all times "under their instruction and supervision," and was subject to recall. In agreeing to these terms, the Philadelphia MTW cleared the way for formal recognition from the Shipping Board.[50]

The fact that another branch of the federal government was at that very moment committed to putting the national IWW leadership—including four prominent members of Local 8—behind bars did not prevent the longshoremen from milking their relationship with the Shipping Board for all it was worth. In October, they received a substantial increase in the hourly wage from forty to sixty-five cents for day work.[51] One month later, the armistice was signed, ending World War I, and the cozy relationship between Local 8 and the government came to an end. With the return to "normalcy," the Shipping Board assigned a full-time undercover operative to Philadelphia with specific instructions to monitor the activities of the port's longshoremen. As reflected in the intelligence reports of special agent J.K., the new year brought a growing realization that with peace overseas, it was back to business as usual along the waterfront.

By the spring of 1919, the deepening postwar slump in shipping activity was generating fierce competition for work, pitting established union members with access to steady work against "floaters," many of whom had recently arrived in Philadelphia from more severely depressed ports on the Pacific Coast, including a large contingent from Seattle where local shipowners had begun screening Wobbly activists off the docks. Working as little as two days a week, the floaters began pressuring Local 8 to adopt something like Seattle's system of "rotary hiring," in which men were dispatched to jobs on a rotating basis from a central hiring hall. Secretary Jones promptly dismissed rotational hiring as impractical in a large port like Philadelphia. Rejecting such arguments as a product of the conservative "job trust mentality" now guiding Local 8, the floaters continued agitating for a more equitable distribution of work. In response, MTW leaders, viewing the demand for work equalization as part of a widening attack on their coveted job control, did what any self-respecting trade unionist would do: they raised the initiation fee from $2.00 to $25.00 as a means of restricting entry into the already saturated waterfront labor market.[52]

Raising the initiation fee failed to silence the floaters since many of them entered Local 8 not as raw recruits but as transferees from other MTW locals. Over the summer, agent J.K. observed, the floaters joined with the port's Wobbly seamen in agitating for a general maritime strike in October when their agreement with the Shipping Board was due to expire.[53] As the deadline for renewal approached, union leaders—under pressure from the floaters and their allies—called for almost doubling the hourly rate from sixty-five cents to $1.25, recognition from the port's civilian operators, a closed shop under MTW jurisdiction, and prohibitions against foremen shouting at the men. The stevedores countered by offering seventy cents an hour and nothing more. After several stormy union meetings, in which the membership was bitterly divided over the wisdom of striking, a last-minute compromise was effected, giving the longshoremen eighty cents an hour along with the promise to be treated in a respectful manner on the job.[54]

Local 8's modest gains, coming at a time when virtually all other marine unions were in full-scale retreat, served as a powerful recruiting magnet, attracting longshoremen from around the country. From the West they transferred in as members of sister MTW locals in Seattle, Portland, and San Pedro, thus dodging the high initiation fee. African Americans from the South worked a similar angle by joining local Gulf Coast branches of the MTW for a mere $2.50 before immediately transferring into Local 8. By 1920 there were more than seven thousand men roaming the docks in search of work. With no corresponding increase in demand, the waterfront labor market was decidedly skewed in favor of local stevedores.[55]

It was hardly the best time to launch a major strike. But with the neighboring ports of New York and Boston hit by wildcat strikes, Local 8 was pressed into action. On May 26, with coastwise traffic tied up along the Atlantic seaboard, four thousand deep-sea longshoremen in Philadelphia—virtually the entire membership of Local 8—walked out, demanding an increase in wages from eighty cents to $1.00 an hour. Bolstered by the refusal of marine firemen to supply steam for running "scab winches," more than one thousand coastwise longshoremen streamed into Local 8 by nightfall. The next day the strike was tight as a drum, as nothing moved across the docks. Taking advantage of a specially reduced $1.25 initiation fee, unorganized cargo handlers kept pouring into Local 8 until its membership reached almost eight thousand. Represented by the Wobblies, the coastwise strikers demanded an equivalent twenty-five percent wage increase from sixty-five cents to eighty cents an hour.[56]

If the work stoppage came at a bad time for the union, it was even worse timing for the city's commercial interests. With over 150 vessels already in port waiting to be serviced and another 117 freighters on their way to Philadelphia after being rerouted from strike-ridden New York, the walkout was "indeed an unfortunate occurrence," observed the municipal director of wharves, docks, and ferries. "Never before in the history of Philadelphia," he added, "has the port enjoyed such prosperity as it had up until the strike was called."[57] Local shipowners, operating from a position of greater strength, took immediate steps to end the walkout, beginning with a free citywide taxi service for transporting strikebreakers to the docks. After the "scab cabs" failed to bring in enough replacement workers, individual stevedores approached the union for help. But their pleas fell on deaf ears. When a request to load flour for "the starving people in Belgium" was brought up on the floor of a union meeting, Walsh—who along with Fletcher, Neff, and Doree had recently been released on bail from Leavenworth pending an appeal—urged the men to "let it perish," according to FBI agent J. McDevitt, who was in attendance that evening. "It don't belong to us," McDevitt recorded in his notes. "It belongs to the bosses. If the bosses want it unloaded, let them pay $1.00 per hour. Men, I ask you to stick. Stick, if it takes every man in this organization to sacrifice his blood. Stick, for if the stevedores ever land this victory over you, you are going right back to slavery days."[58]

And "stick" they did, time and time again. When the longshoremen were asked to unload four thousand crates of lemons at the desired rate of $1.00 an hour, they voted unanimously not to break ranks. When the Poles were promised free liquor and preferential employment if they returned to work, they refused—as did the Italians, who were at one point offered $1.20 an hour, or twenty cents more than what the union was demanding.[59] The only soft spot in the strikers' ranks was among some African Americans who reportedly lacked sufficient savings to endure a protracted walkout. Yet, despite their economic hardships, the port's black longshoremen initially backed the strike.[60]

Such solidarity was possible as long as the union was winning. Then, on June 4, the Shipping Board finally broke its silence, issuing a public statement condemning the union's demands as "unjustified and arbitrary." Throwing the full moral and material weight of the federal government behind the stevedores, the board instructed its local shipping agents to support the port's commercial operators in resisting any wage increase. With momentum slipping away from the union, the men's resolve weakened, as small contingents of strikers began drifting back to work.[61]

Violence was not far behind. On the evening of June 10, Louis Townsend, a black strikebreaker, and two companions were on their way home when they ran into a group of pickets. Townsend, armed with a loaded revolver, had apparently been drinking. After forcing his way past the pickets, he "went mad," as one eyewitness described it, pulling his gun, wheeling around, and firing indiscriminately into the crowd. With enraged union men in hot pursuit, Townsend ran down the main waterfront artery, "shooting at everyone in sight," injuring two small children and an elderly bystander before fatally wounding Stanley Darylak, a striking longshoreman.[62] Townsend was charged with murder, which, while applauded in the pages of *Solidarity*, further undermined the morale of the more race-conscious African American longshoremen. "I talked with several negroes," special agent J.K. reported a few days later, and "individually they are ready to go back to work."[63]

The strike, punctuated by sporadic violence, gradually petered out. When the men finally returned to work on July 7, they did so under the former wage scale. The Wobblies, however, refused to admit defeat, pointing with great pride to the addition of some five thousand new members of Local 8. "That is POWER," they told the longshoremen. "LET US KEEP IT."[64] But the new recruits, most of whom were employed in the coastwise trade, showed little interest in being power brokers—or even good unionists. Returning to work in many cases without their Local 8 buttons, "they are," as two veteran longshoremen observed at the time, "breaking down every principle and rule established by the union."[65]

These newer members contributed to Local 8's growing isolation by plunging the union into a serious clash with the national organization. In early August, an unnamed AFL source from Philadelphia cabled the head of the Soviet embassy that Local 8 was loading the *Westmount,* an American steamer, with a shipment of shrapnel bound for General Wrangel's anti-Bolshevik forces operating in Poland. The Soviet ambassador immediately contacted James Scott, national secretary-treasurer of the MTW, and, according to Scott, threatened to expose the "traitorous" actions of the Wobbly longshoremen. Scott then rounded up his supporters on the General Executive Board (GEB) and headed for Philadelphia. At a hastily called "rump meeting" of Local 8, he lashed out at the port's dock workers, calling them, as one participant recalled, "scabs and traitors and every conceivable form of mean and dirty things." Scott was followed to the platform by two GEB members, who summarily ordered the longshoremen to stop all work on the *Westmount.* The sixty men in attendance agreed to take the matter up at their next regularly scheduled union meeting in four days.[66]

Local 8's Wobbly leaders, although critical of Scott's abrasive style, generally supported his position. Fletcher, accompanied by business agent Baker, had already visited the *Westmount,* trying to persuade their members not to handle munitions. But being "mostly new men recruited during the recent strike," few were listening.[67] As loading continued, Doree, who had just been released on bail from Leavenworth, threatened to bring his home local up on charges before the GEB. At the next regular union meeting set aside to discuss the *Westmount* controversy, Scott took the floor and gave a repeat performance, hurling one accusation after another at the longshoremen, and vowing to "expel you all tomorrow" if munitions are still being loaded. But the men were not about to be stampeded. With many newer members dragging their feet, the union voted to defer any action until hearing from the GEB. The longshoremen did not have long to wait. The next day, just as Scott had promised, they were expelled.[68]

The longshoremen made amends at their next weekly union meeting, voting unanimously "not to load any munitions in the Port of Philadelphia" and to immediately expel any member found doing so. Still, Local 8's fall from grace continued. With the munitions incident resolved, national IWW leaders lifted the suspension order in October, just in time to shift their attack to constitutional grounds, citing the longshoremen for numerous violations of IWW bylaws and giving them until December 1 to comply or face expulsion for a second time.[69] Many of the specific complaints concerning financial transactions with the central office arose from simple misunderstandings and were easily cleared up. But not so with the union's $25 initiation charge, which openly violated the IWW's universal $2.00 entrance fee.[70] The ensuing debate over Local 8's initiation policy struck at the heart of IWW philosophy, consuming the national organization in a heated, often bitter, controversy over the meaning of Wobbly unionism.

What had begun a few years earlier as the much celebrated "Philadelphia model" had now become the infamous "Philadelphia controversy." As in the recent *Westmount* incident, the GEB took a hard line, with newly installed board chairman Roy Brown excoriating the longshoremen for practicing what he termed "the A.F. of L. kind of job control," which relies on "high initiation fees" to pay business agents who then police the contract. "If the right sort of education had been given the membership," he argued, "by now they would have understood that real job control, as the I.W.W. understands it, is not accomplished by the dictation of salaried business agents. . . . I.W.W. control is the kind that is maintained by the *members on the job*" who rely on direct action to win conditions.[71]

Local 8 replied through a four-page leaflet, authored by Doree, that was reprinted in *Solidarity* and distributed to the leaders of the major industrial unions. Unless the GEB yields, Doree began, "a month from now, the Philadelphia M.T.W. will have passed out of existence, either as part of the I.W.W. or else as a 'shop control' organization." While freely admitting that the $25 fee violated the IWW constitution, Doree argued for greater flexibility so as to avoid any "straight-jacketing of experiments." Then, turning to the substance of the GEB's criticism, Doree responded to Brown's AFL-baiting head-on. "The A.F. of L. has high dues, we hear. The I.W.W. low fees. Who," he asked, "has the members? The I.W.W. whose fees are 'not prohibitive' or the A.F. of L. whose fees are 'prohibitive?'" Part of the difference in membership, he noted, was due to the fact that "the A.F. of L. is conservative and the bosses don't fight it as they do the I.W.W." But, he added, "the bosses are at this moment giving the A.F. of L. a real battle—and the A.F. of L. hangs on—on to no great ideal, no great philosophy—hangs on to shop control." For Doree, it all boiled down to a simple aphorism: "Because the A.F. of L. tries to protect the job, members stick to it; because the I.W.W. does not, members do not stick."[72]

On the Philadelphia waterfront, Doree continued, "we now have seven members to every job." Such a huge surplus, as the AFL has shown, is inimical to effective job control. But the federation's solution of "closing the books" is not the only answer. Instead, Doree argued, we can erect "reasonable safeguards around our already existing unions" by charging a high enough entrance fee to discourage "every Tom, Dick and Harry" from simply paying the union $2.00 for the privilege of working. During the last strike, Doree observed, it was "this job-hungry, non-principled bunch of low-fee artists who gave us hell. We are just now beginning to get back some of the many things these new members rob us of."[73]

The parallels with Gomperism—in logic as well as language—proved too much for the majority of Wobbly loyalists whose ideological purity came before all else. At the next IWW convention in the spring of 1921, following two full days of discussion devoted to the "Philadelphia controversy," the delegates voted 774 to 96 against reinstating the longshoremen.[74] Local 8 would now have to survive, or perish, on its own.

Brotherhood Is Not Enough: The Demise of Local 8

Seizing on Local 8's latest setback, the long-dormant AFL sprung into action. ILA Local 1116, which had been chartered only a few months before as the port's first "colored" local, began hammering away at the MTW, harping on the failed 1920 strike, the continuing controversy over initiation fees, and the longshoremen's resulting organizational isolation. At the same time, several African American leaders spoke out publicly for the first time, directing unspecified criticisms at Local 8's confrontational "tactics" and urging their followers to affiliate with the all-black ILA. The longshoremen were finally listening. By summer, Local 1116 reportedly had over one thousand members. Noting the growing "number of colored longshoremen . . . leaving the IWW" for the ILA, an FBI informant wrote in July of Local 8's imminent demise.[75]

But the Wobblies fought back. In August, they expelled twenty-five to thirty African Americans—including such prominent figures as Glenn Perrymore, one of the heroes of the 1916 strike—for fraternizing with the ILA.[76] Local 8 then began weekly educational forums aimed initially at shoring up its black membership. After attending one of the forums, a reporter for the *Messenger* wrote approvingly that "the Southern bugaboo" of interracial contact "has been routed by the plain, unvarnished workers" of Local 8. "Here," added another correspondent, "was a living example of the ability of white and black people to work, live and conduct their common affairs side by side. There were black and white men and black and white women in this meeting. No rapes, no lynchings, no race riots occurred! Isn't it wonderful!" With between six and seven hundred members usually in attendance, invited guests spoke on a variety of topics, in each case condemning "the doctrine of race firstism," whether in the guise of union autonomy or nationalism.

Support for "race firstism" among African American longshoremen appeared to be a reaction largely to rising racial tensions within the wider society.[77] The conditions giving rise to biracial unionism in other ports—most notably racial discrimination in hiring and competition for work—were not much in evidence on the Philadelphia waterfront. On the contrary, contemporary accounts from IWW supporters and oral histories conducted many years later describe a racially integrated setting in which "mixed" gangs were quite common, and where both employment opportunities and job assignments were typically distributed without regard to race.[78] Confirmation for this view also comes from a most unlikely source: the more than one hundred field reports filed by otherwise critical government informants and ILA organizers alike, none of which contains even the slightest suggestion of racial discrimination at the hands of Local 8 officials. Of course, it is possible, perhaps likely, that many covert forms of racism and discrimination escaped the eyes of these predominantly white informants. Nonetheless, it seems clear that Local 8's Wobbly leaders made a sincere effort to practice what they preached when it came to race relations. Determined to root out all manner of "separatist tendencies," the port's longshoremen have "entered the vanguard of American labor," as the *Messenger* put it. "No finer spirit of brotherhood can be found anywhere."[79]

Brotherhood alone was not enough, however. In the face of stepped-up ILA agitation and a deepening slump in commercial shipping, Local 8 decided it was time to rejoin the IWW. Reducing their initiation fee to $2.00, the port's longshoremen, after a year's hiatus, became Wobblies once again.[80] Under pressure from the national organization, Local 8 implemented an expanded educational program. Meeting several times a week during the slack winter months of 1922 to discuss IWW philosophy and methods, the longshoremen seemed at long last on the road to becoming Wobblies in thought, not just deed. "The ice has been broken here along educational lines," a Local 8 activist announced in February. "In the near future no one in the Wobbly movement will say that the longshoremen of Philadelphia don't understand their organization."[81]

The longshoremen had an opportunity to apply what they had learned a few months later. In early October, with the expiration of the current "agreement," Local 8 demanded a reduction in the length of the working day from nine to eight hours, seeking to limit straight time to the hours from 8 A.M. to 4 P.M. When the stevedores balked, the men took matters into their own hands. Reporting for work as usual at 7 A.M., they stood by idly for the first hour, refusing to begin until being assured of receiving the overtime rate of $1.00 an hour. One or two of the smaller stevedoring firms immediately caved in and began paying overtime from

7 A.M. The larger operators, however, remained intransigent, repudiating not only the men's demand but their union as well. After formally breaking off all contact with Local 8, the port's steamship interests announced their intention to "treat with the men as individuals."[82]

The longshoremen, recalling the debacle of 1920, responded cautiously. When a motion was made to authorize a portwide strike on October 14, only twenty-four votes out of several hundred cast were in favor. "We are not looking for a fight," union spokesman Baker announced to the press that evening. "But," he added, "we won't quit."[83] Alongside Baker, Alonzo Richards emerged as a forceful leader of Local 8's black majority. Sensing the mood of the rank and file, Richards—himself a former ILA backer—scrupulously avoided any hint of radical rhetoric, attempting instead to reach the men through the language of fairness. "We have never had a square deal from the bosses," he told the membership. "We work hard and our work is dangerous as every one knows. We should have fought for an eight hour day and had it long before this. Nearly every other class of men have it and why shouldn't we."[84]

While many veteran dock workers found Richards's arguments persuasive, others, particularly newer African Americans, were content simply to have a job. Seeking to exploit such sentiments, ILA organizers continued scouring the waterfront for new recruits. When the longshoremen failed to respond, the ILA turned to its many friends in high places. The former international president of the ILA, T. V. O'Connor, having recently been appointed by President Harding to head the Shipping Board, offered to provide the port's employers with a government vessel to house strikebreakers in the event of a work stoppage.[85] O'Connor's like-minded successor, Anthony Chlopeck, then conferred with local stevedores, reportedly offering to supply as many "replacement" workers as needed from neighboring ports. The following day the shipowners issued an ultimatum that work would begin at 7 A.M.. the next morning or not at all. When the longshoremen reported one hour after the deadline, they were locked out, immediately stranding thirty vessels and idling five thousand men.[86]

While ILA president Chlopeck was making good on his earlier promise by delivering five hundred strikebreakers from New York, Local 8 members began drifting back to work. With cargo moving once again, Baker returned to the membership seeking authorization to put up picket lines around the offending piers. Voting largely along racial lines, the black majority turned down Baker's latest proposal.[87] Local 8, observed "operative #2," another Shipping Board informant, was now "like a house divided," with many men no longer paying dues, tempers flaring, and fist fights breaking out on the floor of the union hall. As Richards began speaking out against any escalation of the conflict, Baker became increasingly isolated. "Many of the negro longshoremen are anxious to depose him," operative #2 reported a few days later.[88]

While Local 8's leaders were regrouping, considering what to do next, the waterfront exploded in rioting that left one man dead and two more seriously wounded. Accusing outside radicals of deliberately fomenting violence, Richards confided to operative #10 that he and other elected union officers had lost control of the walkout. The longshoremen evidently sensed as much and began returning to work. Although the Wobblies maintained a brave front, issuing regular "strike news bulletins" in the days that followed, most longshoremen had abandoned the walkout long before it was officially called off on November 18.[89]

Local 8 was in ruins. Philadelphia, the country's third busiest port behind New York and New Orleans, had become an open shop, as the formerly ubiquitous union button was nowhere to be seen. In its place the men were now required to carry a work permit issued by the stevedore's recently established Employment Bureau. Modeled after the infamous "Seattle Plan," the bureau's principal function was to "stabilize" the labor force by weeding out "undesirables"—a term usually reserved for union activists, many of whom were blacklisted and eventually driven from the docks, forced to find employment aboard ship or elsewhere along the waterfront in one of the large sugar refineries or in the shipyards.[90]

Local 8, which had been held together by the thinnest of threads, began unraveling after the first of the year. At a regular business meeting on January 9, Earl Yeager, a Wobbly veteran, rose to speak. Flashing credentials from the main office of the MTW, he accused Local 8 of withholding dues from the national organization and demanded their charter, seal, and all stationery. The longshoremen refused. The next day a leaflet appeared, signed by the IWW, warning the port's dock workers about "fakirs" masquerading as Wobblies, and announcing the opening of a new MTW hall, located several blocks away from Local 8's headquarters. For the next few months, the longshoremen had not one but two IWW locals claiming to represent them.[91]

The stalemate was finally broken in April, when Ben Fletcher—for many years one of the Wobblies' most ardent supporters as well as a founding member of Local 8—led his remaining followers out of the IWW. Looking back over the past ten years of affiliation with the IWW, Fletcher acknowledged the "more than 500" members who were "arrested upholding the principles of the organization," along with those who paid even more dearly, with life and limb.[92] "The history of the Philadelphia Longshoremen's connection with the I.W.W. is one of unswerving loyalty to its fundamental principles," he insisted. But the national organization's continuing "interference in local affairs," its lack of material support during the last two major strikes, and its preoccupation with collecting dues at the expense of organizing other ports, left them "no other course of action." With that, the independent Philadelphia Longshoremen's Union was born.[93]

Parting ways with Fletcher, Walsh threw his support behind the recently chartered MTW union, which showed definite signs of life in early 1923. Unable to restore Local 8's former job control, however, members soon drifted away and stopped paying dues. By the end of the year the situation had become desperate.[94] At the 1923 IWW convention in November, the Philadelphia Wobblies, led by Walsh, submitted a resolution urging the national organization to lend immediate assistance in the form of advice and financial support. "It is our action or inaction here," it read, "that will decide whether we have completely lost the longshoremen of this port . . . or whether we have just lost them temporarily." Insisting that the IWW is "deep rooted" among the men, the resolution concluded "that we have lost the longshoremen more through our fault than theirs"—a statement remarkable not only for its candor but also for its veiled criticism of IWW orthodoxy.[95]

Walsh was prepared to go it alone if necessary, and that is just what he did when the national IWW turned down his request for support. In early 1924 the MTW launched a portwide organizing drive. Following a particularly successful open air meeting in February, many longshoremen promised "to join the IWW as soon as they can raise the money." But promises do not pay rent. Without a steady dues-paying membership, the longshore branch of the Philadelphia MTW was forced to close its doors a few months later. Moving their operation into the local seamen's hall, Walsh and a handful of followers were all that remained of the once powerful Wobbly longshoremen.[96]

ILA leaders then launched an organizing campaign of their own. Targeting Fletcher's independent union, they appealed specifically to his African American followers, holding out vague promises of preferential treatment in Local 1116's segregated atmosphere. But, in the absence of meaningful job control, the ILA's racial separatism was no more attractive than the IWW's industrial radicalism. "The I.L.A. has nothing to offer," observed the *Marine Worker,* national organ of the MTW. "Philadelphia with an open shop and no organization has the same wages and better working conditions than New York, Baltimore or Boston with I.L.A. control."[97]

All three unions—the independent, MTW, and ILA—were now on a collision course. Early in 1925, with the ILA campaign in high gear, Fletcher brought his remaining followers back into the MTW, thus redrawing the original battle lines between the Wobblies and the AFL. Joining Fletcher were several familiar faces, including George Speed and former Local 8 officer Paul Baker. The MTW was back on its feet, holding its first regular business meeting a few weeks later in April. Following a rousing speech by Fletcher, more than one hundred men signed up, "mostly old members who are coming back to the I.W.W." Almost one thousand IWW work buttons were then distributed all along the waterfront to dues-paying members and supporters alike. "To date," the *Industrial Worker* reported on April 5, "very little opposition has been reported by the boss stevedores."[98] The next day, however, the powerful Jarka Stevedoring Company—apparently acting on orders from O'Connor of the Shipping Board—dismissed several gangs for refusing to remove their IWW work buttons. At an emergency union meeting with five hundred members present, the men voted to set up picket lines around all Jarka piers. Later that same evening, the company's white gang bosses walked out in sympathy with nearly three hundred strikers, leaving behind only three African American bosses to supervise the remaining operation.[99]

The ILA countered this latest MTW offensive by recruiting strikebreakers, who were promptly escorted by a heavily armed police convoy from their union hall down to the waterfront, past Wobbly pickets, and onto the piers. A week later, MTW leaders, charging the ILA with "deliberate and open scabbing," called off the strike. But the battle was far from over.[100] Now it was the ILA's turn to prove itself. Joseph Ryan, international vice president in charge of the North Atlantic district, was brought into town. At the ILA's next meeting, Ryan presented his plan for organizing the port of Philadelphia. Appropriating the IWW's two key demands from 1922, Ryan called for a reduction in the work day from nine to eight hours and a uniform starting time of 8 A.M. Striking an uncharacteristically militant pose, the ILA chieftain then promised a strike if their demands were not met by May 1.[101]

The ILA's strike deadline conveniently coincided with a previously announced work stoppage that had been called by the MTW in honor of May Day. But in late April, Wobbly leaders abruptly canceled their plans, fearing that a walkout on May 1 would only strengthen the ILA's bargaining position with the port's stevedores.[102] The arrival of May Day—a time normally reserved for celebrating working-class solidarity—found Philadelphia's dock workers more divided than ever, with "radical" Wobblies busily at work as hundreds of "conservative" ILA men stood by in disbelief. Playing up the possibility of trouble, Ryan appealed to the local representative of the Shipping Board, who promised to take up the eight-hour day demand in the fall while in the meantime guaranteeing ILA members preference in hiring.[103] When Ryan presented his prize to the membership, Alonzo Richards, aligned once again with the ILA, grudgingly lent his support.

Richards's defection turned the tide decisively in favor of the ILA. In time, even Wobbly stalwarts like Baker were forced to admit defeat. Accepting an offer from Ryan in the summer of 1926 to become head ILA organizer for Philadelphia, Baker "went right to it," stopping first at local ILA headquarters. What he found was not really a union "but a social club," recalled veteran longshoremen James Moocke in a 1980 interview. "They had no contracts or nothin' at the time." The mythically powerful ILA turned out to be a small, almost exclusively black organization. Making contact with former Wobblies Glenn Perrymore, Alonzo Richards, Dan Jones, and other ILA leaders, Baker began reaching out to the port's white longshoremen, encouraging many of them to join by implementing Local 8's policy of maintaining a racially balanced leadership. With growing numbers of whites flocking to the ILA, the struggling MTW local was driven out of business by the end of the summer.[104]

Although the Wobblies were gone, their methods of organizing remained for some time. In October, after the stevedores refused to recognize the rejuvenated ILA, Baker instinctively responded with direct action, distributing some two thousand union work buttons throughout the port as a way of forcing recognition. When that failed, he called a general strike. As in past walkouts, O'Connor from the Shipping Board intervened, but this time, significantly, he sided with the longshoremen. Joining Ryan, O'Connor prevailed upon the shipowners to not only recognize the ILA but to concede the eight-hour day as well. Once "the 8 hour day went into effect," Ryan later recalled, "the rest of the job was easy." By the end of the year, almost all of the port's longshoremen had joined the ILA, thus bringing to a close the Wobblies' decade-long supremacy on the Philadelphia waterfront.[105]

* * *

A unique species of Wobbly unionism ruled the Philadelphia docks for more than a decade around World War I. Local 8's unwavering commitment to racial equality, membership inclusiveness, and democratic participation stood in marked contrast to the segregationist, restrictionist, and bureaucratic policies that characterized the mainstream of American labor earlier in this century. At the same time, Local 8 demonstrated that militant mass-based unionism, led by self-professed revolutionaries, held a strong appeal to at least some segment of workers in the United States. That the Wobblies' efforts in Philadelphia (as elsewhere) ultimately met with defeat will come as no surprise to those students of American labor who have routinely attributed the left's failure to the bedrock "conservatism" of American workers. In this formulation, more conservative unions like the AFL won because, in Selig Perlman's celebrated phrase, its limited economism "fitted" the narrow "job consciousness" of the rank and file.[106]

The history of Local 8, however, offers at most qualified support for the conventional view of the left's failure. Although few longshoremen of either race "possessed the idealism of the IWW," as Fletcher conceded years later,[107] most men firmly embraced the Wobblies' practical expression of syndicalism—as evidenced in Local 8's solidaristic mobilization that transcended occupational and racial barriers, its militant direct action confined to the point of production, and its principled rejection of contracts and all manner of "industrial legalism" in favor of worker self-activity. However lacking in "idealism," the port's longshoremen pursued their workplace aspirations in ways unknown to most craft unionists.

Local 8, then, did not falter because of its idealism, much less because of its militant syndicalism. It failed only after the relations of force on the docks became decidedly unfavorable. In marked contrast to the ILA, Local 8 faced a powerful and unrelenting opposition: federal prosecutors, whose wartime roundup of Wobblies deprived Local 8 of its most talented leaders; the port's stevedores, whose intransigence kept Local 8 always on the defensive; the Shipping Board, whose every move under O'Connor's administration was calculated to benefit the ILA; and even national leaders of the IWW, whose sectarianism led to Local 8's expulsion, its growing isolation, and its resulting inability to resist the ILA's postwar offensive. Local 8 failed, in short, not because the longshoremen resisted its syndicalist orientation but because hostile political forces operating outside the union successfully mobilized to put it out of business. On the Philadelphia docks, the Wobblies' "failure"—if it can be called that—was clearly one of power rather than organizational practices.

Notes

This essay is part of a larger project on the role of syndicalism in the American labor movement. I am most grateful to my fellow contributors Colin Davis, Bruce Nelson, and Cal Winslow for their helpful and constructive comments.

1. Philip S. Foner, *History of the Labor Movement in the United States,* vol. 4: *The Industrial Workers of the World, 1905–1917* (New York: International Publishers, 1965), pp. 351–72; Robert Zieger, "Robin Hood in the Silk City: The IWW and the Paterson Silk Strike of 1913," *Proceedings of the New Jersey Historical Society* 84 (July 1966), 182–95; Robert Biagi, "Rip in the Silk: The 1912 and 1913 Paterson Textile Strikes" (Ph.D. dissertation, Wayne State University, 1971); Anne Tripp, *The I.W.W. and the Paterson Silk Strike of 1913* (Urbana: University of Illinois Press, 1987); Melvyn Dubofsky, *We Shall Be All: A History of the Industrial Workers of the World,* 2d ed. (Urbana: University of Illinois Press, 1988), pp. 263–85; and Steve Golin, *The Fragile Bridge: Paterson Silk Strike* (Philadelphia: Temple University Press, 1988).

2. On the Akron strike see Foner, *Industrial Workers of the World,* pp. 373–83; Dubofsky, *We Shall Be All,* pp. 286–87; Roy T. Wortman, "The I.W.W. and the Akron Rubber Strike of 1913," in *At the Point of Production: The Local History of the I.W.W.,* ed. Joseph R. Conlin (Westport, Conn.: Greenwood Press, 1981), pp. 49–60; and Daniel Nelson, *American Rubber Workers and Organized Labor, 1900–1941* (Princeton: Princeton University Press, 1988), pp. 23–43.

The Lawrence strike, being one of the few IWW success stories, has attracted considerable attention from labor historians; see, for example, Foner, *Industrial Workers of the World,* pp. 306–50; Dubofsky, *We Shall Be All,* pp. 227–62; Paul Brissenden, *The IWW: A Study of American Syndicalism,* Columbia University Studies in History, Economics, and Public Law, no. 193 (New York: Columbia University Press, 1919), pp. 281–96; and Patrick Renshaw, *The Wobblies: The Story of Syndicalism in the United States* (Garden City, N.Y.: Doubleday and Co., 1967), pp. 133–49.

3. Foner, *Industrial Workers of the World,* p. 349; Dubofsky, *We Shall Be All,* p. 255.

4. Wortman, "I.W.W.," p. 53. For a discussion of the IWW's failed eastern campaign, see John S. Gambs, *The Decline of the I.W.W.* (New York: Columbia University Press, 1932).

5. "Stenographic Report—8th Annual Convention, Industrial Workers of the World, 1913," box 2, folder 2-1, p. 6, Industrial Workers of the World Papers, Archives of Labor and Urban Affairs, Wayne State University, Detroit, Mich. (hereafter cited as IWW Papers).

6. The high rate of turnover of IWW locals was openly discussed in the Wobbly press at the time; for a summary of such discussions, see Foner, *Industrial Workers of the World,* pp. 462–70.

7. Correspondence from W. T. Nef to Agnes Inglis, dated July 3, 1936, Agnes Inglis Papers, Joseph Labadie Collection, Harlan Hatcher Graduate Library, University of Michigan, Ann Arbor, Mich.

8. David Saposs, *Left Wing Unionism: A Study of Radical Policies and Tactics* (New York: International Publishers, 1926), p. 174. The issue of organizational stability is also emphasized in accounts by Sidney Lens, *Left, Right, and Center: Conflicting Forces*

in American Labor (Hinsdale, Ill.: Henry Regnery, 1949), p. 153; William Preston, "Shall This Be All? U.S. Historians versus William D. Haywood et al.," *Labor History* 12 (Summer 1971), 445; and David Montgomery, "The 'New Unionism' and the Transformation of Workers' Consciousness in America, 1909–1922," *Journal of Social History* 7 (Summer 1974), 522.

9. Jonathan Garlock, *Guide to the Local Assemblies of the Knights of Labor* (Westport, Conn.: Greenwood Press, 1982), p. 454.

10. The ALU's role in Philadelphia is briefly discussed in Maud Russell, *Men along the Shore* (New York: Brussel and Brussel, 1966), pp. 50, 248. On McHugh's arrival in this country, see *New York Times*, Sept. 28, 1896, p. 8.

11. Testimony of John J. Walsh, box 114, folder 5, p. 9331, "U.S. vs. William D. Haywood et al.," Trial Transcript, IWW Papers (hereafter cited as Trial Transcript).

12. Walsh testimony, box 114, folder 5, p. 9333, Trial Transcript, IWW Papers.

13. For a general discussion of the casual nature of longshore work, see Charles P. Larrowe, *Shape-Up and Hiring Hall: A Comparison of Hiring Methods and Labor Relations on the New York and Seattle Waterfronts* (Berkeley: University of California Press, 1955); and Vernon H. Jensen, *Hiring of Dock Workers and Employment Practices in the Ports of New York, Liverpool, London, Rotterdam, and Marseilles* (Cambridge: Harvard University Press, 1969). For a more richly textured account of hiring practices on the West Coast, both before and after regularization of hiring, see Bruce Nelson, *Workers on the Waterfront: Seamen, Longshoremen, and Unionism in the 1930s* (Urbana: University of Illinois Press, 1988); Herb Mills and David Wellman, "Contractually Sanctioned Job Action and Workers' Control: The Case of San Francisco Longshoremen," *Labor History* 28 (Spring 1987), 167–95.

14. *Solidarity,* Oct. 4, 1913, p. 1.

15. *Solidarity,* May 24, 1913, p. 2.

16. *Philadelphia Public Ledger* (hereafter cited as *PPL*), May 18, 1913, n.p., found in Newspaper Clipping file, Urban Archives, Temple University, Philadelphia, Penn. (hereafter cited as Clipping File).

17. *Philadelphia Evening Bulletin* (hereafter cited as *PEB*), May 20, 1913, n.p., Clipping File.

18. Correspondence from F. W. Taylor to Mr. Eugene O'Neill, dated May 24, 1913, Fred Walter Taylor Papers, "River Front Strike 1913" folder, Historical Society of Pennsylvania, Philadelphia, Penn. (hereafter cited as Taylor Papers). Correspondence from F. W. Taylor to Messrs. Furness, Withy, and Co., Ltd., June 3, 1913, Taylor Papers.

19. *PPL,* May 24, 1913, n. p., Taylor Papers. *PEB,* May 22, 1913, n.p., Clipping File.

20. Correspondence from F. W. Taylor to Messrs. Furness, Withy, and Co., Ltd., June 3, 1913, Taylor Papers.

21. *Solidarity,* Oct. 4, 1913, p. 1.

22. Correspondence from F. W. Taylor to Messrs. Furness, Withy, and Co., Ltd., June 11, 1913, Taylor Papers.

23. Prior to 1920, and occasionally thereafter, the pages of *Solidarity* are filled with nothing but praise for Local 8.

24. The "universal wage" did not apply to cargo handlers employed in the coastwise trade, who remained outside of Local 8 until 1920, and then joined only briefly.

For a survey of income equalization efforts in other ports, see Lester Rubin, *The Negro in the Longshore Industry* (Philadelphia: Industrial Research Unit, The Wharton School, University of Pennsylvania, 1974).

25. Foner, *Industrial Workers of the World,* p. 126. On the ethnic representativeness of the 1913 strike committee, see *Solidarity,* May 24, 1913, p. 2.

26. Philip S. Foner, "The IWW and the Black Worker," *Journal of Negro History* 55 (Jan. 1970), 51.

27. Rubin, *Negro;* Daniel Rosenberg, *New Orleans Dockworkers: Race, Labor, and Unionism 1892–1923* (Albany: State University of New York Press, 1988); Eric Arnesen, *Waterfront Workers of New Orleans: Race, Class, and Politics, 1863–1923* (1991; rpt. Urbana: University of Illinois Press, 1994); and Arnesen's insightful contribution elsewhere in this volume.

28. For more on Fletcher's personal life, see William Seraile, "Ben Fletcher, I.W.W. Organizer," *Pennsylvania History* 46 (July 1979), 214; and Irwin Marcus, "Benjamin Fletcher: Black Labor Leader," *Negro History Bulletin* 35 (Oct. 1972), 138–40.

29. In addition to Flynn and Quinlan, Fletcher's early years in Philadelphia may have put him in contact with many leading radicals of his day, among them John Reed and Joe Hill; see unsigned correspondence (from Fred Thompson?) to Sam and Esther, Jan. 6, 1967, box 12, folder 26, Fred Thompson Collection, IWW Papers.

30. On Fletcher's early contact with the IWW, see correspondence from John B. Campbell to the Director of Military Intelligence, cover letter dated Oct. 27, 1919, Records of the War Department General Staff, Military Intelligence Division, Correspondence, 1917–41, Record Group 165, box 2776, file no. 10110-1460-2, National Archives, Washington, D.C. (hereafter cited as Military Intelligence Papers); Fletcher's position as corresponding secretary is from *Solidarity,* Aug. 10, 1912, p. 3.

31. "Stenographic Report—8th Annual Convention, Industrial Workers of the World, 1913," box 2, folder 1, p. 28, IWW Papers.

32. *Solidarity,* Aug. 1, 1914, p. 1; Aug. 23, 1914, pp. 1,4; and Nov. 28, 1914, p. 1. On the harbor boatmen, see *Voice of the People* (New Orleans), Oct. 16, 1913, p. 1.

33. *PPL,* Jan. 28, 1915, p. 8.

34. *Solidarity,* Feb. 13, 1915, p. 1.

35. "The Philadelphia Controversy," box 79, folder 20, p. 1, IWW Papers (hereafter cited as Philadelphia Controversy).

36. Philadelphia Controversy, p. 1.

37. *Solidarity,* Apr. 15, 1916, p. 1

38. *Solidarity,* July 15, 1916, p. 1.

39. *PPL,* July 7, 1916, p. 1.

40. *PPL,* July 6, 1916, p. 1.

41. Walsh is quoted in *Solidarity,* July 15, 1916, p. 1.

42. Philadelphia Controversy, p. 1.

43. "Investigation of the Marine Transport Workers and the Alleged Threatened Combination between Them and the Bolsheviki and Sinn Feiners," Confidential Report from the Office of Naval Intelligence, Dec. 23, 1918, pp. 32, 33, microfilm reel 8, *U.S. Military Intelligence Reports: Surveillance of Radicals in the United States, 1917–1941* (Fredrick, Md.: University Publications of America, 1984).

44. Philadelphia Controversy, cover page.

45. An estimated six to seven hundred members of Local 8 served in the military during World War I; see John D. Dunn testimony, box 117, folder 7, p. 11986, Trial Transcript, IWW Papers.

46. On the wartime migration of black labor from the south to Pennsylvania, see U.S. Department of Labor, Office of the Secretary, Division of Negro Economics, George E. Haynes, Ph.D., Director, *Negro Migration in 1916–17* (Washington: USGPO, 1919; rpt. New York: Negro Universities Press, 1969), pp. 123–25.

47. The number of weekly initiates is from Records of the Federal Bureau of Investigation, Record Group 65, microfilm reel 555, case file no. 160053, dated July 14, 1917, National Archives, Washington, D.C. (hereafter cited as FBI Papers). Estimates on the proportion of black members are from Seraile, "Ben Fletcher," p. 217, and John J. Walsh Testimony, box 114, folder 5, p. 9356, "U.S. vs. William D. Haywood et al.," Trial Transcript, IWW Papers.

48. Renshaw, *Wobblies,* pp. 215–42; on the raid's effect in Philadelphia, see untitled report, box 99, folder 12, IWW Papers.

49. Report on "Radicalism and Race Riots," by Castle M. Brown, Oct. 28, 1919, Military Intelligence Papers.

50. Correspondence between Local 8 and the GEB is found in "Philadelphia—memo from old notes taken years before," n.d., pp. 3, 4, typed manuscript, box 10, folder 9, Thompson Papers.

51. United States Shipping Board, *Marine and Dock Labor: Work, Wages, and Industrial Relations during the Period of the War,* Report of the Director of the Marine and Dock Industrial Relations Division, United States Shipping Board (Washington, D.C.: USGPO, 1919), p. 137.

52. The activities of the "floaters" are from an intelligence report filed by special agent J.K., May 7, 1919, Records of the United States Shipping Board, Record Group 32, Investigated Cases Files of the Home Office, case file no. 1494 (hereafter cited as Shipping Board Papers). Secretary Jones is quoted in a report by agent J.K., May 14, 1919, case file no. 1494, Shipping Board Papers.

53. Report of agent J.K., Aug. 2, 1919, case file no. 1494, Shipping Board Papers.

54. *PPL,* Oct. 15, 1919, pp. 1, 8.

55. Report from agent J. F. McDevitt, Mar. 18, 1920, case file no. 366145, microfilm reel 806, FBI Papers.

56. *One Big Union Monthly* 2 (July 1920), 1. On the economic situation facing coastwise shipping, see *New York Times,* June 6, 1920, sec. 7, p. 14.

57. *PPL,* May 28, 1920, p. 6.

58. Report of agent J. F. McDevitt, June 17, 1920, p. 4, case file no. 366145, microfilm reel 806, FBI Papers.

59. *Solidarity,* June 19, 1920, p. 6.

60. Report from agent J.K., June 17, 1920, case file no. 1484, Shipping Board Papers.

61. *Philadelphia Inquirer,* June 5, 1920, p. 4; *PPL,* June 10, 1920, p. 12.

62. *Solidarity,* June 19, 1920, p. 1.

63. Report from agent J. F. McDevitt, June 17, 1920, case file no. 366145, microfilm reel 806, FBI Papers.

64. *Solidarity*, July 17, 1920, p. 3.

65. Philadelphia Controversy, p. 7.

66. Philadelphia Controversy, p. 4.

67. On efforts by Fletcher and Baker to persuade the men not to load weapons, see Philadelphia Controversy, p. 19. The quote on "new men" is from *Solidarity*, Aug. 21, 1920, p. 4.

68. Doree's threat is reported in Philadelphia Controversy, p. 5. Details of the union meeting are from Philadelphia Controversy, pp. 5, 6.

69. The expulsion campaign waged by the national IWW against Local 8 was motivated by more than philosophical differences. It was also driven by the naked political self-interest of Scott, who saw Fletcher and his seven thousand voting members of Local 8 as a potential threat to his leadership of the national MTW, and a minority of pro-Communist GEB members whose blind allegiance to the Soviet Union explains their vendetta against Local 8. This interpretation is drawn from a report from agent J. F. McDevitt, Sept. 20, 1920, case file no. 366145, microfilm reel 806, FBI Papers; correspondence from Fred Thompson to Susan Dawson, dated July 30, 1982, p. 2, box 10, folder 6, Thompson Papers.

70. Philadelphia Controversy, pp. 21, 22. *Solidarity*, Dec. 4, 1920, p. 3.

71. *Solidarity*, Dec. 18, 1920, p. 3.

72. *Solidarity*, Dec. 4, 1920, p. 3.

73. *Solidarity*.

74. *Minutes of the 13th Convention of the Industrial Workers of the World*, May 9–27, 1921, Chicago, p. 9, IWW Papers.

75. On the ILA's escalating attack on Local 8, see report of agent H. S. White, Aug. 22, 1921, case file no. 202600-1084, microfilm reel 936, FBI Papers. The quote on "colored longshoremen" is from a report by agent S. Busha, July 15, 1921, case file no. 202600-1084, microfilm reel 936, FBI Papers.

76. Report of agent H. S. White, dated Aug. 22, 1921, case file no. 202600-1084, microfilm reel 936, FBI Papers.

77. For a more extensive discussion of race relations on the Philadelphia waterfront, see Howard Kimeldorf and Robert Penney, "'Excluded' by Choice: Dynamics of Interracial Unionism on the Philadelphia Waterfront 1910–1930," *International Labor and Working-Class History* 51 (Spring 1997), 50–71.

78. Electronically recorded interview with Joe Kane conducted by Howard Kimeldorf, May 2, 1989, Philadelphia; electronically recorded interview via telephone with Edward Kelly conducted by Howard Kimeldorf, Mar. 10, 1990, Ann Arbor, Mich.

79. *Messenger*, July 1921, pp. 214, 215; Aug. 1921, p. 234; and Oct. 1921, pp. 262, 263. The only article-length study of the Philadelphia longshoremen concludes that "the IWW's non-discrimination policies enabled black workers to obtain a voice unheard of in industrial affairs of the day." See Lisa McGirr, "Black and White Longshoremen in the I.W.W.: A History of the Philadelphia Marine Transport Workers Industrial Union Local 8," *Labor History* 37 (Summer 1995), 377–402.

80. *Solidarity*, Nov. 5, 1921, p. 1.

81. *Solidarity,* Feb. 4, 1922, p. 6.

82. *PPL,* Oct. 14, 1922, n.p., clipping found in Department of Justice Records, Record Group 60, case file no. 61-2353, National Archives, Washington, D.C. (hereafter cited as Department of Justice Papers).

83. The vote totals are from the report of agent #10, Oct. 29, 1922, case file no. 1494-4, Shipping Board Papers. Baker is quoted in *PPL,* Oct. 15, 1922, p. 16.

84. Richards is quoted in a report from agent #2, Oct. 16, 1922, p. 1, case file no. 1494-4, Shipping Board Papers.

85. ILA activities are detailed in an unsigned report (agent #2?), Oct. 17, 1922, case file no. 1949-4, Shipping Board Papers. O'Connor's offer is reported in *Solidarity,* Nov. 18, 1922, p. 1.

86. On Chlopeck's role in providing strikebreakers, see *Solidarity,* Oct. 28, 1922, p. 1; *PPL,* Oct. 17, 1922, p. 2.

87. The use of New York strikebreakers, presumably members of the ILA, is from a report by agent J. F. McDevitt, dated Oct. 16, 1922, p. 2, case file no. 61-2353, Department of Justice Papers. A similar account of "non-union men" being sent from New York to Philadelphia appears in *Industrial Worker,* Nov. 4, 1922, p. 1. The vote against Baker is from an unsigned report (agent J. A. Sullivan?), Oct. 24, 1922, p. 2, case file no. 1494-4, Shipping Board Papers.

88. On growing tensions within Local 8, see reports from agent #2, Oct. 19 and 20, 1922, p. 1, case file no. 1494-4, Shipping Board Papers; and report from agent #10, Oct. 19, 1922, case file no. 1494-4, Shipping Board Papers. Opposition to Baker is from a report by agent #10, Oct. 23, 1922, p. 2, case file no. 1494-4, Shipping Board Papers.

89. On the waterfront riot, see *PPL,* Oct. 30, 1922, p. 2. Richards is quoted in a report by agent #10, Oct. 30, 1922, p. 1, case file no. 1949-4, Shipping Board Papers.

90. *PPL,* Nov. 21, 1922, p. 24. Abraham Moses interview with Greg Williams and Ed Kirlin, May 12, 1980, Philadelphia, Penn., electronic tape #00011, Philadelphia Maritime Museum, Philadelphia, Penn.

91. Fletcher, "The Facts," box 79, folder 23, p. 3, IWW Papers. During the 1922 strike, Yeager was described as "the biggest agitator the whites have and a vicious fighter," in an unsigned report (agent J. A. Sullivan?), Oct. 30, 1922, case file no. 1494-4, Shipping Board Papers.

92. Fletcher, "The Facts," box 79, folder 23, p. 2, IWW Papers.

93. The quote about unswerving loyalty is from the *Messenger* 5 (June 1923), 741. On the IWW's "interference" see Fletcher, "The Facts," pp. 2, 3.

94. The decline of the MTW is followed in the pages of *Solidarity,* Apr. 7, 1923, p. 6; May 12, 1923, p. 6; and May 19, 1923, p. 8.

95. *Minutes of the 15th General Convention of the Industrial Workers of the World,* Nov. 12–Dec. 3, 1923, no location indicated (Chicago?), p. 50.

96. The quote on promising to join is from *Solidarity,* Feb. 16, 1924, p. 1. In May 1924, the Philadelphia MTW submitted dues receipts from the port's seamen but not for the longshoremen, indicating that the longshore branch was no longer functioning; see "General Office Bulletin," May 1924, p. 24, box 31, folder 24, IWW Papers.

97. On the ILA's promise of preferential treatment, see *Marine Worker,* July 31,

1924, p. 1; *Marine Worker,* Aug. 28, 1924, p. 1; both available on microfilm, New York Public Library, New York City, N.Y.

98. Both the reaction to Fletcher's speech and the report dated Apr. 5 are in *Industrial Worker,* Apr. 18, 1925, p. 2.

99. Developments in the Jarka strike are reported in *Industrial Worker,* Apr. 18, 1925, p. 1; Apr. 22, 1925, p. 1; and Apr. 25, 1925, p. 1.

100. The police convoy is reported in *Industrial Worker,* Apr. 22, 1925, p. 4. The quote on "scabbing" is from *Industrial Worker,* Apr. 29, 1925, p. 1.

101. Correspondence from J. F. Dewey to Mr. H. L. Kerwin, Apr. 16, 1925, p. 2, Records of the Federal Mediation and Conciliation Service, Record Group 280, dispute case file no. 170-2936, Washington National Records Center, Suitland, Md.

102. *Solidarity,* May 13, 1925, p. 4.

103. Report from J. F. Dewey, "Summary of Final Report of Commissioner of Conciliation," May 21, 1925, microfilm reel 1, *Black Workers in the Era of the Great Migration, 1916–1925,* Harlan Hatcher Graduate Library, University of Michigan.

104. This account is based on James Moocke interview, n.d. (1980?), name of interviewer not indicated, electronic tape #00123, Philadelphia Maritime Museum, Philadelphia, Penn.; *Proceedings of the Twenty-ninth Convention of the International Longshoremen's Association,* July 11–16, 1927, New York, N.Y., p. 135 (hereafter cited as *Proceedings of the Twenty-ninth Convention*).

105. *Proceedings of the Twenty-Ninth Convention,* pp. 15, 135, 136.

106. Selig Perlman, *A Theory of the Labor Movement* (New York: Macmillan, 1928).

107. Correspondence from "BHF" (Benjamin Fletcher) to Mr. Abram Harris, July 29, 1929, pp. 3, 4, handwritten letter in Abram Harris Collection, Moorland-Spingarn Research Center, Howard University, Washington, D.C.

4   "All I Got's a Hook": New York Longshoremen and the 1948 Dock Strike

Colin J. Davis

During the late 1940s and early 1950s, New York City longshoremen engaged in a series of explosive wildcat strikes that challenged both their employers and union leaders. Prompting such action were poor wages and working conditions, and an unresponsive and often oppressive trade union whose officers seemed more interested in lining their pockets than in defending the membership. In turn, the longshoremen developed a series of strategies to sidestep and challenge these union leaders. Tactics adopted included the creation of rank-and-file organizations, judicial offensives, and wildcat strikes. Outside organizations also played a key role in spurring on or framing the longshoremen's militancy. Labor priests and Communists battled hard to improve the working conditions of New York's longshoremen. In the process federal agencies became entwined in the lives of the longshoremen. Labor legislation became a crucial factor in this federal involvement, as did decisions by the U.S. Supreme Court and the actions of President Harry S Truman. Thus, the longshoremen's battles to improve their lot moved beyond the immediacy of a local workforce to incorporate an array of intersecting forces.

The New York longshoremen fit the mold of an industrial workforce that was mostly casual, lacked formal power in its representative trade union, and lived and worked under the dual threats of unemployment and gangster violence. This study examines the hostile work environment the longshoremen faced and the militant oppositional identity they forged in response, as well as the reaction of trade union leaders, framed by increasing federal involvement. Above all, this study will analyze how the longshoremen captured the attention not just of their employers and trade union but also of the federal government and the general public. Such attention culminated in a series of investigations of the New York waterfront and federal and state attempts to clean up the union. The post–World War II New York waterfront was therefore a cauldron of competing power blocs.

The New York longshoremen labored in a port that extended for seven hundred miles, encompassing the coastlines of Manhattan, Brooklyn, Staten Island, Jersey City, and Hoboken. The port consisted of seven bays and the mouths of four rivers and four estuaries. *Fortune Magazine* calculated that the "entire port of Antwerp could be stuffed into Jersey City." From the early twentieth century on, New York longshoremen had experienced little fundamental change in their working conditions. Much of the work still required a strong back and the skillful use of the hook to move cargo in and out of the ship's hold. Basic machinery such as winches still transferred cargo by sling from dock to hold or vice versa. What had changed since World War II, however, was the sling load. Heavier bearing winches ensured increased sling loads. As one longshoreman complained: "Before the war we worked with a one-ton draft—2,240 pounds. Today the sky is the limit." The problem for the longshoremen was the increased threat of injury because of the collapse of such slings. As the same longshoreman commented, "[There are] lots of accidents because there are no safety provisions and often the gear is rotten, the ropes frayed." Other on-the-job dangers included hernias, falls, and cuts from unwieldy cargoes; all this made the longshoremen's work environment extremely hazardous. Indeed, other than the lumbering and mining industries, dock work had the highest accident rate. When the severity of injuries is factored in, longshoring held the dubious distinction of being the most dangerous occupation in the nation.[1]

Beyond the constant danger of accidents, the most prominent fear of the men was the exploitative and inequitable method of obtaining work. Unlike their brothers on the West Coast, the New York longshoremen continued to shape-up for work. Through strike action in 1945 the men had at least obtained the partial victory of two instead of three shapes per day, one at 6:55 A.M. and the other at 12:55 P.M.[2] The continuation of the practice can be laid at the door of the International Longshoremen's Association (ILA), the union that represented dock workers on the Atlantic and Gulf coasts. Under the leadership of Joe Ryan, the ILA accepted the system because it ensured power over the membership. The ILA controlled the system by choosing the hiring boss or having a union official present at the shape-up. The advantages for the union officials were two-fold: it gave the corrupt union control of who got work and constituted a lucrative kickback scheme. Because they had to appear for work twice a day, the workmen fully realized the necessity for compliance with union demands. Anyone who questioned the union's actions could easily be overlooked for employment. An attorney representing rank-and-file longshoremen testified in 1948 to the Senate Committee on Labor and Public Welfare that a union leader successfully maintained his power "because he is able to discipline any man who dares to raise his voice in a union meeting. . . . That man does not work anymore." The power of hiring ensured that so-called troublemakers were kept "off the waterfront simply by not picking them in the shape-up."[3] The shape-up system and its corresponding surplus of labor guaranteed subservience and ensured employment insecurity. Even the chief counsel for the ILA, Louis Waldman, was forced to conclude that "this is one of the rare exceptions in modern industrial relations to have men come to the employer's establishment [each day] and make themselves ready and willing to work with no obligation on the part of the employer whatever to take them."[4]

The shape-up also encouraged rampant discrimination against African American workers. Blacks for the most part were located in Brooklyn and segregated in the Jim Crow Local 968. Daily competition with white longshoremen at the shape-up exposed black longshoremen to the racism of the hiring boss and attendant union official. One black longshoreman described the humiliating experience: "Sometimes standing on the pier with my union button and my union book, the hiring boss acts like he hates me. . . . It happens all the time."[5] The "hate," of course, culminated in the man's not obtaining a job for the shift. Cleophas Jacobs, president of Local 968, charged that the "shipping companies . . . in collaboration with various local union officials and the hiring bosses, have an agreement whereby the available work is given to the other nine [white] locals in Brooklyn, to the exclusion of our men." Accentuating the problem was the lack of representation in the ILA, where not one African American had been appointed organizer even though Local 968 had a membership of one thousand men. Jacobs complained bitterly to Ryan but was rewarded with a chilling silence. Protection of jobs, then, was combined with racist sentiment. President Morgan of Philadelphia Local 1291 highlighted the racist attitude by stating that blacks could not be trusted as regular workers: "Negroes accept most of the dirty work on the riverfront because of economic necessity due to their own lack of frugality. Many of them work for one or two days, draw their pay, go on a spree and do not return to work until their funds are exhausted." Such a perspective could not help but reinforce the stereotype of the lazy black longshoreman who should not be given steady work.[6]

Although the ILA did not officially bar blacks from the union, their complaints of discrimination were ignored. Having their own local helped some but other blacks throughout the port were forced to accept shorter and dirtier work. To some extent the ILA's relative acceptance of blacks was tactical, to protect against strikebreakers. As one black union official testified, "We are in the union today because the white man had to take us in for his own protection. Outside the organization the Negro could scab on the white man. Inside he can't."[7] What existed in New York was a combination of biracial unionism and free-floating black members. Mirroring the ethnic locals of Italians and Irish, blacks were either forced to create their own or accept what was available. What separated black locals, however, was embedded racism and their inability to control a pier to ensure regular employment.[8]

Officials used discrimination and insecurity to line their pockets with kickbacks. It was standard practice to pay a bribe to either the foreman or a union official to get picked from the shape-up. The form the bribe took depended upon the system established on each pier. In some cases it was an individual activity, a straight money payment, buying of drinks before or after the shape, or purposely losing card games. One longshoreman known only as "John Doe" testified to the 1952 New York State Crime Commission (NYSCC) that he paid the hiring foreman two dollars per week and "once in a while on Fridays—buy him a pint of whiskey." The kickback and the buying of whiskey was expensive. "[It was] more than I could afford," John Doe explained, "but in order to keep the job and support my family you got to do those things."[9] Kickback clubs were also used. Situated in apartments, saloons, barbershops, or storefronts, the clubs would gather cash from prospective workers before adding their names to the call-up list. Pat Wilson explained to the NYSCC how for years following World War II men would shape-up in his basement. In an astonishing admission Wilson explained that his wife would pick up the identification checks or discs, and collect the wages from the payroll office. Although he denied that he or his wife received kickbacks, it was obvious that some form of payment was made.[10]

Thus the shape-up was for the most part a sham. As one observer testified, "You will find that 99 out of a hundred times . . . names were submitted to that hiring boss before the men go to the shape-up." One longshoreman pointed out, "you pretend to shape-up . . . and the other fellows waiting there think they have a chance. But they don't." In some cases the "toothpick gimmick" was used; the hiring boss could recognize those to be chosen from the position of the toothpick in the mouth or behind the ear.[11] Union officials also lined their pockets by inventing workers known as "phantoms" or "carried." Fictitious names were given the hiring boss and each week the wages were collected. Thomas Maher, a stevedoring superintendent for the Huron Stevedoring Corporation, testified that Timmy O'Mara, a boss loader, regularly collected the wages of a Mr. Ross, which totaled $25,000 for the period of 1943–51. Payments to O'Mara guaranteed "labor peace" because he "settled strikes."[12]

Little wonder that gangsters were attracted to the New York waterfront. Thugs and members of organized crime fought each other for the distinction of becoming hiring bosses. Since the beginning of the twentieth century a series of crime figures had attempted to strong-arm their way onto the docks. By the 1920s and 1930s Irish gangs in Manhattan and Italian gangs in Brooklyn and Jersey City had gained control on the waterfront. But such control did not guarantee peace, as challengers shot and murdered their way into the loading and kickback rackets.[13] Not only kickbacks were at stake but also loan-sharking, bookmaking, payroll padding, and contributions to "charitable" causes or testimonial dinners.

Such criminal schemes ensured that for the most part the membership went along with the wishes of their leaders. Loan-sharking was a good example of this phenomenon. It was a common practice, forcing the men to borrow heavily in order to obtain a job. One longshoreman explained that if a loan shark approached him and asked if he needed money, "if I refused, I didn't get the job." Even those workers fortunate enough to pay off the loan discovered once again that they could not obtain work "unless they borrow some more and get into debt again." The system was a lucrative one for the loan shark; even after he paid off the hiring boss for the privilege of working a particular dock, the 10 percent weekly interest charge made for a profitable enterprise.

Local union leaders used a more direct method for obtaining cash; they demanded cash contributions for testimonial dinners or to aid a sick worker. Longshoremen felt obliged to buy the $5 dollar tickets or kick in the odd dollar or two. In some cases up to fifteen thousand tickets would be "sold" even though the hall hired for the event would only hold one hundred people. Obviously, the longshoremen were not expected to attend the "dance" or dinner. When propositioned for a cash contribution, the man who refused "might find he couldn't get work, or he might get kicked around. A man soon gets the idea; he doesn't refuse more than once."[14]

The criminal exploitation of the longshoremen could not have occurred without a critical alliance between the ILA and gangsters. In many cases the line between the two was blurred. Malcolm Johnson, a crusading journalist for the *New York Sun,* described the Port of New York as "an outlaw frontier." Even the structure of the industry played a role in encouraging criminal activity. Any delay in loading or unloading a ship cost the stevedore money. The stevedore was therefore more than likely to pay cash to offset any threat of a work stoppage.

To a large extent the assimilation of gangsters corresponded with Joe Ryan's presidency of the ILA.[15] Working as a longshoreman for a few years until injury forced him to stop, Ryan maneuvered his way through the ILA hierarchy, becoming president in 1927. He cemented his control in 1943 by getting elected international president for life.[16] Just like his gangster allies throughout the New York City port, Ryan also gained financially from his union position. Through a complex web of semiofficial organizations, testimonial dinners, and outright plundering of ILA funds, Ryan accumulated expensive suits, golf club memberships, automobiles, and paid vacations around the world. The most explicit gain came from direct payoffs from the employers, the stevedoring companies. John William McGrath, president of McGrath Stevedoring Corporation, and Frank Nolan, president of Jarka Stevedoring Corporation, both testified that they paid Ryan cash every year. After intense questioning by the NYSCC, James C. Kennedy, president of Daniels & Kennedy Corporation, admitted that he too paid Ryan $1,500 annually to ensure labor peace. Once a year, Kennedy explained, he visited Ryan's office and handed over the cash in an envelope. Incredibly, Kennedy stated the only word exchanged between them was "Hello."[17]

Ryan also welcomed convicted felons into the union and appointed them as organizers and, in some cases, as presidents and secretaries of locals throughout the port. His initial justification was that he was giving the men a second chance, but after being pressed during a Senate inquiry, he admitted hiring convicts to fight Communist influence and maintain his power. As Ryan exclaimed, "Some of those fellows with the bad criminal records were very handy out there when we had to do it the tough way." One ex-convict, Dominick Genova, later testified to the NYSCC that he had made his first contact with the ILA while serving a prison sentence in Sing Sing. After his release he appeared at the docks, introduced himself, and was given a union book, though he paid no dues. He was not alone: "Oh, after working there I found many men in the same circumstances as myself, who were ex-prisoners, ex-convicts."[18] Arthur Tischon, who had also served time in Sing Sing, suggested to the NYSCC, "Well, I guess the worst record you have, I guess the easier [it was] to get the job." Tischon testified that he never shaped-up but just walked in after the morning shape and "played cards, and looked to steal something." Contrary to Ryan's insistence that employing ex-convicts gave them a chance to reform, Tischon argued it achieved the opposite effect: "I don't believe in sending a man to work where his friends are the same friends he had in prison. . . . You're looking for a fast buck [as are] people you are hanging around with . . . the temptation is so much greater than if you worked with a legitimate concern."[19]

Organized theft was rampant, threatening both cargo and passenger valuables. In one daring episode ten tons of steel were stolen. Jones F. Devlin, general manager for the U.S. Shipping Lines testified to the NYSCC, "That was the most remarkable case of pilferage (Laughter) . . . Yes sir, ten tons disappeared off the pier. It is remarkable how one can get away with it." Individuals also took their share. Longshoreman Charles Strang explained how one man attempted to steal silk: "the fellow coming out one night got quite a bit of silk wrapped right around his body and he had so much, and he looked so fat that when the customs stopped him and asked him to bend, he couldn't bend at all (Laughter)." Watchmen were present throughout the port but threats of violence encouraged them not to enforce the rules. In one case where a watchman prevented the theft of some cases of meat, the hiring foreman approached him with a dollar bill in his hand. The watchman explained that the foreman told him, "he was making a collection for flowers for me and that I was going to be throwed overboard."[20]

A collection of Irish and Italian gangs carved up the waterfront into a series of fiefdoms. In Brooklyn, particularly the Red Hook area, the ILA locals were under the control of the Anastasia brothers. Following a 1939 investigation by the Brooklyn district attorney, William O'Dwyer (later to become mayor of New York), Ryan promised to clean up the Red Hook locals; it became apparent a few years later, however, that the same group still held power. On the New Jersey waterfront, Charlie Yanowsky had controlled the locals and thereby the various criminal activities until assassinated in 1948. Edward Florio took his place as the kingpin along the Jersey shore. Florio's ascendancy coincided with the election of Fred M. DeSapio as mayor of Hoboken. To pay off political favors for his electoral victory, DeSapio with Florio's blessing obtained jobs for supporters on the Jersey shore.[21] On the West Side of Manhattan, the Bowers gang had gained tenuous control by the 1940s. Their inability to dominate the area led to widespread bloodshed as the respective gangs fought for control, causing one West Side local to gain the infamous nickname the "Pistol Local." Testifying to the widespread criminal activity on the waterfront, John Corridan, the "waterfront priest," noted that the standard joke on the docks was that when longshoremen read of murderers in the local newspapers they remarked: "If he can beat that rap he has a good job down here."[22]

The presence of tough guys throughout the port deeply affected the longshoremen's work existence. Beyond the numerous criminal schemes, gangsters were also on the docks to maintain order. The criminals and ex-cons were hired by the shipping companies not just to guarantee peace but to ensure the maximum amount of work from the intimidated longshoremen. The employment of gangsters as hiring bosses was explicitly affirmed by one company official who revealed that "if I had the choice of hiring a tough ex-convict or a man without a criminal record I am more inclined to take the ex-con. Know why? Because if he is in a boss job he'll keep the men in line and get the maximum work out of them. They'll be afraid of him." After Frank Nolan, president of the Jarka Stevedoring Corporation, was pressed for an explanation why the notorious Anthony Anastasia was hired by his company, Nolan replied, "He is resourceful and tireless on the job. He preserves discipline and good order on the part of the men."[23] Clearly, longshoremen both obtained employment and performed their work in an atmosphere of fear and intimidation. Their daily lives were marked by the twin anxieties of job insecurity and unsafe working conditions.

The lack of any democratic institutional structures within the union hampered efforts to challenge the corruption. Union meetings and elections were rarely held and barely advertised. Mitch Berenson, a longtime Brooklyn rank-and-file reformer, testified in 1949 to the House Committee on Education and Labor, "You know, there are elections and [there are] elections." It was common that the corrupt "guys will put a little notice on a store window and they will say, 'Elections tonight.' And they get 15 or 20 guys together in the local, all in favor of Joe Blow, to be delegate. And that is the end of it." To attend such meetings was to place your life in peril: "They will get 15 or 20 gorillas together in a local, and it is your death to get into that local." Furthermore, ILA officials kept no records of the meetings. An illuminating interchange between the 1952 New York State Crime Commission and John J. Gannon, secretary-treasurer of Manhattan Locals 824-1 and 901-1 and president of the New York District Council, highlighted the lack of democracy:

Commr. Proskauer: Have you got any minutes of your meetings prior to 1951?

The Witness: I can't locate them.

Q. They have gone too?

A. Yes sir.

Commr. Proskauer: Gone with the wind. . . .

Q. Didn't you testify that the last election in that local [901-1] was maybe ten, twelve, or more years ago?

A. I would say that.

Q. How about 824-1?

A. We had one there in around 1944, '45; I'm not too sure which. . . .

Q. Since then you have never had a meeting?

A. We had a few meetings, but I don't recall the dates.[24]

The system did not, however, go unchallenged. Some brave longshore-men confronted these conditions but were quickly silenced—their pun-ishments examples of what awaited those who dared challenge the ILA's and the gangsters' grip on the waterfront. Prior to World War II, Pete Panto, a Brooklyn longshoreman, organized a vibrant rank-and-file movement. As a result of his activism he was murdered by Albert Anastasia, the re-puted head of Murder, Inc., and dumped in a lime pit in New Jersey.[25] By 1945, however, the rank and file rebelled against ILA rule and embarked on an unofficial strike. Following the strike, two of the leaders, William E. Warren and Sal Barone, were viciously beaten, thrown out of the ILA, and warned to steer clear of the docks thereafter.[26]

Neither violence nor the absence of democracy within the ILA prevented a core of longshoremen from challenging the union's leadership and their criminal allies. But following Pete Panto's murder, such opposition had to be organized secretly, with the aid of outside supporters. The potential "outside" organizations were the Communist Party of America and the Xavier Institute of Industrial Relations, run by labor priests from Fordham University. Although bitterly opposed to one another, the two organizations provided the only outlet for a frustrated rank and file. As Father John Corridan, the principal priest working the docks (who was portrayed by Karl Malden in the film *On the Waterfront*), explained: "The only constant information dispensed on the waterfront comes from either the Commu-nist Party or from this school." Like other labor priests, Corridan vigorously fought the Communist Party. In a Labor Day speech in 1948 he described "Communist control" as a "stench" rising out of the waterfront.[27]

The establishment of the Xavier Institute was symptomatic of the Catholic church's "social action" crusade of the 1930s. The catalyst for the movement was the Great Depression and the rising strength of the Communist Party. A series of papal encyclicals formed the basis of the Catholic attack. In 1931, Pope Pius XI issued his encyclical *Quadragesimo anno,* calling for "social justice" so that "riches . . . ought to be distributed among individual persons and classes that the common advantage of all . . . will be safeguarded."[28] The American priesthood was quick to take advantage of such a call. Although there were significant differences between many of the groups, ranging from the rabid anti-Semite Father Joseph Coughlin to the Christian Socialists led by Dorothy Day, between 1932 and 1940 the Jesuits established labor schools such as the Xavier Institute to educate Catholics about the twin evils of capitalist exploitation and Communist infiltration of the labor movement in the United States.[29]

The Xavier Institute attempted to attract longshoremen to its evening classes but the organizing was dangerous and for most part had to be achieved in a surreptitious manner. In many cases leaflets had to be left alongside the dock or in toilets. Labor priest Father Philip Carey described the method and effect of placing such literature in the men's toilet: "[we] pasted up the paper on the inside door of all the conveniences—Which served a double purpose, it gave a man freedom from fear while he was reading it and number two, it gave him sufficient time to reflect on its contents."[30] For the most part, though, up until late 1948 the Xavier Institute played an observer's role and it was the Communist Party that took the initial lead in organizing an institutional opposition to the ILA.

The Communist Party focused on the longshoremen as potential recruits because of their bad working conditions and inattentive union. Harry Bridges's International Longshoremen and Warehousemen's Union (ILWU) viewed the situation also as an opportunity to expand their influence on the East Coast. Consequently Sam Madell, a Communist Party member and organizer with the ILWU, began working with the New York longshoremen. He picked the issue of pay to galvanize them, starting with a movement to obtain back pay owed the longshoremen under the 1938 Fair Labor Standards Act.[31] Working with lawyers, Madell first "started a petition" among the men and by 1947 the tenuous alliance was cemented when attorneys helped longshoremen file suits for back pay. Madell explained that the men "were very much interested in this thing because it meant millions and millions of dollars in back pay would be due longshoremen."[32] Back-pay committees were formed in Brooklyn and Hoboken, New Jersey, and also in Baltimore. According to William Glazier, Washington, D.C., representative of the ILWU, the Brooklyn back-pay committee was the "strongest," with meetings drawing over eighteen hundred attendees. Brooklyn

blacks formed their own committee, closely associated with all-black Local 968. The "back pay movement," according to Glazier, had become the
"first mass anti-Ryan development" since the 1945 strike.[33] This amalgam
of rank-and-file action and legal collaboration made for a potentially strong
bond that would culminate in the 1948 strike.

Fueling the movements were increasing unemployment during 1947 and
1948, increasing sling loads and the corresponding speed-up, and favoritism at the shape-up. More pertinent was the interpretation of the Fair Labor Standards Act by longshoremen and their allied attorneys. The issue
revolved around overtime payments. Throughout 1947 rank-and-file longshoremen and their attorney allies inaugurated a series of suits demanding back pay owed under the auspices of the Fair Labor Standards Act. Since
1916, contracts negotiated between the ILA and shippers had established the
regular workday as from 8:00 A.M. to 12 noon, and 1:00 P.M. to 5:00 P.M. All
work outside those hours was to be remunerated as overtime at time and a
half. Longshoremen commonly worked outside of the regular hours, in
some cases working twelve to fourteen hours at a stretch. The back-pay
attorneys produced considerable evidence that men who had worked
through the night into the daytime hours were denied overtime pay. For
example, if a longshoreman worked through to 8:00 A.M. he was paid time
and a half, but if he continued working after 8:00 A.M. he would be paid
the regular rate for hours worked thereafter. The longshoremen's attorneys
therefore argued, using the provisions of the Fair Labor Standards Act, that
work during the evenings was shift work, and the longshoremen should be
paid overtime on top of the time and a half payment.[34]

The suits of the back-pay committees were contested by the ILA and
the shippers all the way to the Supreme Court. The shippers' opposition
was simply predicated on reluctance to pay overtime wages. As for the ILA,
Ryan argued that the courts should not rule on contract provisions negotiated by the union. He and the ILA leadership clearly feared direct
judicial challenge to their decision-making powers. The Supreme Court,
in October 1947, agreed with the back-pay committees that night work
was indeed shift work and any longshoremen working in excess of eight
hours should be paid time and a half. The ILA and shippers responded
by attempting to persuade the relevant congressional committees to
amend the Fair Labor Standards Act.[35]

As the issue wound its way through the Senate Committee on Labor
and Public Welfare, negotiations for a new contract between the ILA and
New York Shipping Association (NYSA) began in early June 1948. Many
of the rank and file, emboldened by the back-pay suits and the Supreme

Court decision, watched the process closely. Experience had shown that Ryan and other ILA leaders had generally taken what was offered by the shippers, usually settling for just enough to quiet rank-and-file opposition. One stevedoring operator described the bargaining routine as follows: "We call Ryan in once a year or so and say, 'Joe, how much of a raise do you need to keep the boys in line?'"[36] Although Ryan's perfidy was common knowledge during bargaining talks, what gave the 1948 negotiations such potency was the overtime issue. The rank and file believed, with justification, that the issue was to be negotiated away. Indeed, the overtime question was a major stumbling block in the negotiation process. Although both sides agreed on a small wage increase, Ryan threatened that a strike might follow if an overall agreement was not reached. For the most part, his threat was merely a gesture to the members that he was hanging tough. At this point of impasse, the federal government took the dramatic step of involving itself in the controversy.

The government's involvement was motivated by worry about the disruptive effect on the economy that a New York City dock strike would have. With its three hundred deep-sea piers, the port of New York handled nearly as much cargo as all the other Atlantic and Gulf Coast ports combined. As many as two hundred thousand New York City area workers were directly employed in the longshore industry, not counting insurance and financial companies.[37]

The enormous size of the port and the immense amount of tonnage that flowed through it guaranteed that the federal government would take seriously any threat to its operation. Using the recently passed Taft-Hartley Act, President Harry Truman created a board of inquiry to investigate the dispute and recommend action to avoid overt labor conflict. Formed on August 17, four days before the expiration of the contract, the board found that the issue of overtime on overtime was the major stumbling block and feared that without an agreement a strike would take place on August 21. Again, using provisions of the Taft-Hartley Act, Truman obtained a federal injunction barring the ILA from engaging in strike action for a period of eighty days (the order would expire on November 9) and ordering the contending parties to resolve the dispute through collective bargaining. Truman also reconvened the board of inquiry to hold hearings and attempt to get the two parties to settle. Conciliators from the Federal Mediation and Conciliation Service (FMCS) were also ordered in to support the board members.[38]

Throughout September and October a series of separate meetings were held, with FMCS conciliators shuttling back and forth between the two sides. The sticking point continued to be the overtime on overtime question. The employers also rejected the idea of a welfare fund for injured longshoremen. With the injunction due to expire on November 9, by late October the parties appeared ready to sign an agreement. The NYSA held fast and put forth its final offer on October 26, agreeing to a 10-cents-per-hour increase and a vacation plan (with eligibility reduced from 1,350 hours per year to 1,250). The critical segment of the agreement concerned the overtime issue. The employers demanded that the agreement be placed under terms of Section 7 (B) (1) of the Fair Labor Standards Act, which would exempt the employers from the act's overtime provisions.[39] The ILA, although unhappy that a welfare fund had been rejected by the NYSA, nonetheless appeared ready to accept the offer.

Complicating approval, however, was the fact that the National Labor Relations Board (NLRB), as directed by the Taft-Hartley Act, supervised the ballot of the membership. Scheduled for November 6–7, the ballot contributed to rank-and-file resistance to the agreement. The NLRB had based eligiblity to vote on a vacation list that ended on June 30, 1948. Only 12,664 New York and 2,500 Philadelphia and Boston longshoremen were on the list, excluding approximately 30,000 East Coast longshoremen, most of whom were unable to obtain steady work, in some cases because they opposed the ILA leadership, and thus could not qualify for the vacation list. The ILA had provided the list and had used the opportunity to exclude those they regarded as a threat to their power. The ILA also used tried and true tactics of distilling the potential vote by advertising the vote late and holding a series of "quickie meetings" to forestall any opposition. To further counter opposition to the contract, Ryan insisted that it was "a very fine agreement" and only "disruptive elements" opposed it.[40] The rank and file, unhappy with the agreement and incensed that the vote had been fixed, embarked on strike action on November 10, leaving in their wake an embarrassed leadership that had supported the agreement.

To some extent the wildcat strike was but a reflection of the longshoremen's lack of power and corresponding frustration. Sam Madell pointed out that the men "would go along with all of these terrible things for a period of time, and then there would be an explosion, and the docks would be tied up." Father Carey echoed Madell's observation by stating the "waterfront was very much like Mount Etna . . . [the longshoremen] had no real way to get their grievances answered." As frustration increased, "building up a head of steam," it would eventually "blow up all over."[41]

ILA leaders had seriously misjudged the temper of their members and their own power to control an angry rank and file. A dramatic shift in power had occurred, and the members no longer fatalistically accepted their lot. Years of oppressive hiring practices and the concomitant corruption, increasing sling loads, and unemployment had taken their toll. Empowerment through the back-pay committees also made the members less likely to blindly accept their leaders' promises and threats. Just as vital were the inequities of federal power. Longshoremen had been hampered from taking strike action through injunctive law under the Taft-Hartley Act, while their ILA leaders and the NYSA ignored the Supreme Court decision on overtime payments. As Alfred Corbett, a member of the New Jersey back-pay committee, later testified: "It is hard for us to understand why an injunction against labor . . . can be immediately enforced, whereas a United States Supreme Court ruling can be openly flaunted by the shipping interests."[42] As the strike progressed, however, the rank and file quickly learned the precariousness of their position. Having little institutional power within the union and no recognizable leaders, the men quickly fell victim to a union leadership intent upon reestablishing its hegemony.

Within days of the wildcat strike the ILA leadership scrambled to regain control of the situation. Hampering their efforts was a local leader within their own ranks—Eugene Sampson, the powerful leader of Local 791 in Manhattan who had long coveted Ryan's presidency. Sampson was a traditional labor boss in the mold of Ryan, a leader who could more accurately be said to hold court than office. Just like other locals, Local 791 had no record books of expenses or of the membership. When questioned on the issue Sampson had replied that the membership figures were "under his hat." Unlike the 1945 strike, in which Sampson had supported the rank-and-file revolt only to be outmaneuvered by Ryan and other ILA leaders, this time he had a real opportunity to openly challenge Ryan's iron rule. Shippers attributed the 1948 strike "to the long-standing feud between Mr. Ryan and the so-called pretender to the Ryan 'throne,' John J. (Eugene) Sampson." The conflict between the two leaders reached a fever pitch on the first day of the strike, when Sampson and Ryan clashed publicly. After engaging in a shouting match, and aware that such public acrimony would undermine his leadership position, Ryan ordered the reporters present to "Get out . . . we are going into executive session."[43] The public tirade would be the last open conflict between the two throughout the remainder of the strike, as Ryan scrambled to regain control.

Ryan, given a black eye from the unofficial walkout and the public tongue-lashing from Sampson, embarked on a path to master the explosive situation. In an effort to overpower opposition from the strikers, Ryan did a complete about-face and declared the strike legal for all East Coast ports, making it the first official longshore strike since 1919. His strategy then was to channel rank-and-file anger and thereby neutralize it. By quieting opposition from the rank and file, Ryan could simultaneously counter the challenge by Sampson. The success of such a policy highlighted the skills of a master manipulator.

To avoid further embarrassing public outbursts and to nullify internal criticism, Ryan clamped down on press releases. He ordered that the ILA press committee could only make statements in the presence of six members of the eleven-man committee.[44] Thus he hoped to stifle institutional opposition and keep the members in the dark concerning negotiations. One other, and perhaps more important, method for repressing dissent was to curtail strike activity. No picket lines were set up, nor were informational meetings held. On its surface the tactic appeared logical because the NYSA had not planned to recruit strikebreakers. In any event, with a reputation for toughness and ruthlessness, the ILA correctly believed that any potential strikebreaker would think twice before trying to obtain work on the waterfront. The more substantial reason was that by not providing a fighting strike organization, the union deliberately left its members isolated and uninformed of strike strategy. The men instead were left to meet in bars and street corners throughout the port to discuss strike events. They were thus scattered and unable to formulate their own demands and organization.

All was not lost for the rank and file, however, since interviews with journalists could at least bring their grievances to the public's attention. A longshoreman identified only as "Bill, a giant of a man," highlighted the inequities of the shape-up: "I only got about four hours that week [just before the strike], even though I was up every morning at 6 for the goddam shapeup." Another striker, characterized as a "grey-haired, rugged docker," blamed the conflict on the shape-up: "It's a dog-eat-dog affair without rhyme or reason except that it pads the pockets of the stevedores with profits." One aged "docker with five grandchildren" compared his existence with that of other workers: "we are ordinary average workingmen with one big difference. We average a hell of a lot less than most workers."[45]

Strategically supplementing the individual grievances were oppositional organizations, namely, the back-pay committees. An alliance of the committees was formed under the title of the Rank and File Committee and a meeting was planned for November 16 at Manhattan Center. Ryan, correctly sensing the threat that such a meeting could hold for his tenuous control, declared that no longshoremen would be present, and as for those "communists" attending, "our men will throw them in the river." Ryan, with ILA goons and members of the AFL Seafarers Union, attempted to storm the building. Although they were able to leave leaflets declaring the meeting a Communist plot "to seek control of the ILA and to sabotage the Marshall Plan," Ryan's forces were outnumbered and had to beat a hasty retreat. Those present at the meeting included rank-and-file members, back-pay attorneys, and indeed some Communists. The *New York Times* reported that Ryan's "name was booed lustily." A series of strikers outlined their respective grievances and James Longhi, an attorney representing the Brooklyn back-pay committee, applauded the "rank and file longshoremen in pressing their demands for wages, lighter sling loads and back pay through the years." The meeting also observed a minute of silence in memory of Pete Panto, and then ended with a call to fight to the finish and to send a delegation to Washington, D.C., to press for back pay.[46] Although those in attendance had been able to repel Ryan's physical attack, the meeting nonetheless marked the end of the militant longshoremen's active involvement in the strike. Throughout the remainder of the strike the ILA leaders and the federal government would take center stage in the unfolding drama. The rank and file and their allies, excluded from critical involvement, were forced to stand on the sidelines as frustrated observers.

Government involvement in the strike was predicated above all on the serious effect of the stoppage on the greater economy, and in part on the exportation of Marshall Plan goods. The board of inquiry spelled out this concern in October when it declared the employers and longshoremen had a "responsibility . . . to the people of the United States and the world, whose welfare would be seriously impaired by a cessation of work in this most vital industry."[47] The initial casualties were passengers who arrived in the port on the first day of the strike. Newspapers reported that the actress Helen Hayes and others were forced to carry their own luggage. Railroads serving the port also placed embargoes on freight and in turn laid off an estimated eleven hundred freight handlers by November 16. Fifteen hundred tugboat men were idled by the stoppage, and numbers of freight forwarders and custom brokers joined the ranks of the unemployed.[48] The greatest impact of the strike was the curtailment of mail and cargo. The *New York Times* reported on November 19 that "150,000 bags of outbound mail were piled up awaiting settlement of the strike." General cargo, including $130,000 worth of bananas and $500,000 worth of chestnuts, was languishing in the holds of ships. Particularly annoying to the federal government was the curtailment of Marshall Plan goods. An official of the Economic Cooperation Administration estimated that twenty thousand tons per day were backing up on East Coast docks. The standstill of Marshall Plan cargo forced Paul G. Hoffman, economic cooperation administrator, to appeal to Ryan to release the cargo. Ryan responded that only "army supplies to garrison troops overseas" would be handled. The number of strike-bound ships in the port numbered eighty-four and reached a total of 179 vessels on the Atlantic seaboard. The *New York Times* reported an "unusually small" number of ships trapped in the port of New York, noting that shippers had already loaded ships and "dispatched [them] on the last day before the strike, in anticipation of trouble."[49]

The strike dramatically expanded to other Atlantic ports; spreading by November 13 to Boston, Philadelphia, Baltimore, and Norfolk, Virginia. Mirroring the New York situation, rank-and-file dissension was also present in these ports, fueling the men's determination to strike. Some of these men explained how they formed back-pay committees and voiced their anger toward a union leadership judged to be superfluous. Joseph Kane, a Philadelphia longshoreman, explained how the men in his port formed a back-pay organization after the Supreme Court decision concerning overtime on overtime. As Kane pointed out, "we realized we had been deprived. . . . Thirty-five hundred men in Philadelphia immediately filed for back pay." Fueling Kane's frustration was the distinct lack of democracy in the ILA. The Philadelphia men, Kane contended, "have no constitution books, we have no bylaw books, we have no agreement books." For Kane the situation smacked of conspiracy: "I believe they keep us in a state of ignorance in order to dominate us."[50] Like their New York brothers, however, the Philadelphia men were forced to witness the strike from the sidelines. The ILA leadership continued throughout the strike to hold a tight rein on policy and tactics.

The ILA, for example, ordered its Gulf Coast locals to continue working at Jacksonville, Florida; Mobile, Alabama; Galveston, Texas; and New Orleans. The reasoning behind the decision was to guarantee Marshall Plan shipments, and thereby avoid a more aggressive government response. Shippers, however, tried to use these ports as an opening to sneak their goods into the country. Ryan responded by threatening "ship companies that any more diversions of ships or cargoes will result in tying up the South Atlantic and East coast Gulf ports."[51] Ryan also had problems with the Canadian members of the ILA. Although they were not party to the agreement, sympathy action by Canadian dockers made for an effective strike. In the walkout's early stages, shipping companies had begun disembarking passengers at Halifax, Nova Scotia, and transferring them to trains bound for New York City. Ryan responded by ordering ILA members in the port to boycott any ships that used Canadian ports to bypass East Coast docks. The order resulted in disruption within the Canadian ILA leadership. Under pressure from the Canadian government, J. J. Campbell, the president of the Halifax ILA local, argued that to continue the boycott was contrary to Canadian labor law and ordered his members to work incoming ships.[52]

Although the Canadian situation concerned the ILA leadership, it was not unduly threatening. The Atlantic ports remained sealed shut. With a critical blockade of cargo in place, the federal government took an active role in settling the strike. The Federal Mediation and Conciliation Service had already dispatched its assistant director, William N. Margolis, to New York City. Just like his regional counterparts, Commissioner Thomas Steutel and Regional Director Howard E. Durham, Margolis was unable to break the impasse between the ILA and the NYSA. Neither was Cyrus Ching, the FMCS director, who flew to New York City from Washington to confront the issue. Ching was hampered by lack of power to force an agreement. As he declared to reporters, "We have no authority to make them get together but we want to give them a nudge."[53]

Although lacking tangible power, Ching was the official representative of the Truman administration and intended to use every limited weapon at his disposal, including bluff. By November 26, after a series of hectic back-and-forth meetings with the ILA and the NYSA, an agreement seemed in sight. Yet the ILA and the NYSA refused to settle. Ching then played a new card, threatening Joe Ryan and John V. Lyon, chairman of the NYSA, with government action. When Ryan and Lyon both asked, "What is the Government going to do?" Ching replied, "I'll tell you at four o'clock." Ching was bluffing: as he explained later to Truman, "they didn't know what further weapons the Government had, and they didn't realize that the Government didn't have any."[54] Unsure of the threat posed by Ching, Lyon and Ryan hammered out an agreement giving the longshoremen a 13-cents-per-hour increase, one week of paid vacation after working eight hundred hours per year, two weeks of paid vacation after working 1,350 hours per year, and, crucially, a welfare fund. While a majority of locals accepted the agreement, in Brooklyn rank-and-file resistance remained strong, with four locals voting down the agreement. Public meetings were held to discuss the issue but with the rest of the port's longshoremen, and those in Baltimore, Philadelphia, and Boston voting for acceptance, the men drifted back to work.[55]

The outcome of the strike confirmed the rank and file's latent power to affect change in contract and working conditions. The resulting pay increase, improved vacation time, and welfare fund highlighted the potency of a workforce perceived as crushed and of no consequence. Although government action did much to frame the longshoremen's working world through the Supreme Court decision recognizing their back-pay claims, the presidential ordering of a cooling-off period, and the FMCS settlement of the strike, the rank and file still held the vital power of withdrawing their labor. As the strike progressed, however, it affirmed the rank and file's weakness (and that of their allies) in the face of union and government action that critically divorced them from decision making. The back-pay committees remained in existence and continued to press their claims, although in late 1950 the U.S. Court for the Second District decided against the suits. The Communist Party suffered greatly from the decision. As Sam Madell explained, the issue "was the closest that I ever really came to accomplishing something [on the docks]."[56] Father Corridan and the Xavier Institute carried on its program of evening classes for dockers and pushing the New York state and the federal governments to reform the industry. It would take another wildcat strike in 1951, and a barrage of Crime Commission hearings, for the longshoremen to rid themselves of the humiliating shape-up system. The 1948 strike then, set the scene for a move toward democratic control of the ILA and a more secure and safe work environment. Rank-and-file action was critical in this process of challenge and accommodation, but without clear avenues of control within the ILA such a movement would be on the outside looking in.

Notes

1. "On the Beach," *Fortune Magazine,* Feb. 1937, p. 75; *Daily Worker,* Nov. 19, 1948, p. 4; "Work Injuries in the United States, 1948," *Monthly Labor Review* 69 (Oct. 1949): 385–86, 388. A special study discovered that "70 to 75 percent of all longshore accidents occur aboard ship" (*Longshore Safety Survey: A Survey of Occupational Hazards in the Stevedoring Industry,* Maritime Cargo Transportation Conference Publication 459, National Academy of Sciences-National Research Council [Washington, D.C., 1956], p. 1). The New York Shipping Association, the employer organization, shifted the blame for the high accident rate onto the prior physical condition of the longshoremen: "These longshoremen subject themselves and their fellow workers to definite risks not concomitant with their employment, and in doing so subject the employer to extra occupational risk" (Senate Committee on Labor Public Welfare, *Longshoremen and Harbor Workers Act—Amendments,* 80th Cong., 2d sess., 1948, S.2237, p. 55).

2. Howard Kimeldorf, *Reds or Rackets: The Making of Radical and Conservative Unions on the Waterfront* (Berkeley: University of California Press, 1992), pp. 154–55.

3. "Testimony of Julius E. Bagley," Senate Committee on Labor and Public Welfare, *Fair Labor Standards Act, Amendments, Part 1*, 80th Cong., 2d sess., p. 994. The second quote is from Charles P. Larrowe, *Shape-Up and Hiring Hall: A Comparison of Hiring Methods on the New York and Seattle Waterfronts* (Westport, Conn.: Greenwood Press, 1976), p. 74.

4. "Excerpt from Testimony of Louis Waldman in Arbitration Proceedings before William H. Davis, November 21, 1945," International Longshoremen's Association, box 3, folder Hiring Hall, 1942–54, Tamiment Library, New York University. Hereafter cited as ILA-TAM.

5. Malcolm Johnson, *Crime on the Labor Front* (New York: McGraw-Hill, 1950), p. 116.

6. "Testimony of Cleophas Jacobs," Senate Committee on Labor and Public Welfare, *To Clarify the Overtime Provisions of the Fair Labor Standards Act of 1938, As Amended,* 81st Cong., 1st sess., 1949, pp. 488–91; "Notice—To All Members of Local 1291," James I. (Carfare) Keys, ILA-TAM, box 3.

7. Sterling Spero and Abrahm L. Harris, *The Black Worker: The Negro and the Labor Movement* (Port Washington, N.Y.: Kennikat Press, 1931), 199.

8. For excellent discussion of biracialism among longshoremen see, of course, Eric Arnesen, *Waterfront Workers of New Orleans: Race, Class and Politics, 1863–1923* (1991; rpt. Urbana: University of Illinois Press, 1994). For the mix of ethnic and racial groups see Cal Winslow, "On the Waterfront: Black, Italian and Irish Longshoremen in the New York Harbor Strike of 1919," in *Protest and Survival: Essays for E. P. Thompson,* ed. John Rule and Robert Malcolmson (New York: New Press, 1993).

9. "Testimony of John Doe," *New York State Crime Commission—Public Hearing, No. 5, Port of New York (Waterfront),* vol. 3, pp. 1802–3. Hereafter cited as *NYS Crime Commission.*

10. *NYS Crime Commission,* vol. 3, pp. 1807–12.

11. "Testimony of Ross J. DiLorenzo," Senate Committee on Labor and Public Welfare, *To Clarify the Overtime Compensation Provisions of the Fair Labor Standards Act of 1938,* p. 272; Larrowe, *Shape-Up and Hiring Hall,* p. 55.

12. "Testimony of Thomas Maher," *NYS Crime Commission,* vol. 1, pp. 257–60.

13. Daniel Bell, *The End of Ideology: On the Exhaustion of Political Ideas in the Fifties* (Glencoe, Ill.: Free Press, 1960), 159–90; Bernard B. Turkus and Sid Feder, *Murder, Inc.: The Story of the "Syndicat"* (London: Victor Gollancz, 1952).

14. Johnson, *Crime on the Labor Front,* pp. 113–15; "Testimony of Julius E. Bagley," Senate Committee on Labor and Public Welfare, *Fair Labor Standards Act, Amendments, Part 1,* p. 995; Larrowe, *Shape-Up and Hiring Hall,* pp. 56–57. In some cases the loan shark had direct access to the payroll department and would obtain the money owed direct from the payroll clerk (Citizens Waterfront Committee, *The New York Waterfront: A Report to the Public of New York City by the Citizens Waterfront Committee Setting Forth Our Oldest and Most Urgent Civic Problem—The Condition of the Waterfront* [New York, 1946], p. 28).

15. Johnson, *Crime on the Labor Front,* p. 91.

16. Bruce Nelson, *Workers on the Waterfront: Seamen, Longshoremen, and Unionism in the 1930s* (Urbana: University of Illinois Press, 1988), p. 142; Larrowe, *Shape-Up and Hiring Hall*, p. 26.

17. "Testimony of John McGrath, Frank Nolan, and John Kennedy," *NYS Crime Commission*, vol. 1, pp. 43–44, 568, and 94–102.

18. "Testimony of Joe Ryan," Senate Committee on Interstate and Foreign Commerce, *Waterfront Investigation. Part 1: New York-New Jersey Waterfront*, 83d Cong., 1st sess., p. 447; "Testimony of Dominick Genova," *NYS Crime Commission*, vol. 3, pp. 2144–47.

19. "Testimony of Arthur Tischon," *NYS Crime Commission*, vol. 1, pp. 551–53.

20. "Testimony of Jones F. Devlin, General Manager, U.S. Shipping Lines," *NYS Crime Commission*, vol. 1, p. 162; "Testimony of Charles Strang," *NYS Crime Commission*, vol. 2, p. 1058; "Testimony of Thomas Launders," *NYS Crime Commission*, vol. 5, p. 3249.

21. "Testimony of George Joseph Fitzpatrick, County Commissioner, Hudson County," *NYS Crime Commission*, vol. 2, p. 933.

22. "Testimony of Edward A. Heffernan," *NYS Crime Commission*, vol. 5, pp. 1548–59; Larrowe, *Shape-Up and Hiring Hall*, pp. 22–23; Johnson, *Crime on the Labor Front*, pp. 210–13, 165–82; "Testimony of Father John Corridan," Senate Committee on Interstate and Foreign Commerce, *Waterfront Investigation. Part 1: New York–New Jersey Waterfront*, p. 569.

23. Larrowe, *Shape-Up and Hiring Hall*, pp. 19 and 63.

24. "Testimony of Mitch Berenson," House Committee on Education and Labor, *Amendments to the Fair Labor Standards Act of 1938*, vol. 1, 81st Cong., 1st sess., 1949, pp. 611–12; "Testimony of John J. Gannon," *NYS Crime Commission*, vol. 3, pp. 2000–2001.

25. It was reported later that Panto, after being lured to a house in Staten Island, realized he was in danger and attempted to escape. But as mobster Mendy Weiss explained, "It was a lucky thing I was there, he would have got away. I grabbed him and mugged him, and when I mugged him, he started to fight and he tried to break the mug, and that's when he scratched me, but he didn't get away" ("Testimony of Edward A. Heffernan," *NYS Crime Commission*, vol. 5, p. 1563; *New York Herald Tribune*, Dec. 19, 1952, p. 1; *New York Times*, Dec. 19, 1952, p. 1; Kimeldorf, *Reds or Rackets*, pp. 124–25).

26. The Rank and File Committee, *This Is Our Story*, located in ILA-TAM, box 3. Father Benjamin L. Masse recounted that "The day after the strike ended, Warren reported for work—and fell and hurt himself; i.e., he was beaten up. Nice place, the New York waterfront" (quoted in Johnson, *Crime on the Labor Front*, p. 158).

27. Letter to Hon. Christopher C. McGrath, House of Representatives, from John Corridan, June 6, 1949, Records of the Xavier Institute of Industrial Relations, series 2—Father John M. Corridan, S.J., box 10, folder 15. Hereinafter cited as XIIR. "Labor Day Speech, 1948, Father John Corridan," XIIR, box 11, folder 30. For the anti-communism of labor priests, see Joshua Freeman and Steve Rosswurm, "The Education of An Anti-Communist: Father John F. Cronin and the Baltimore Labor Movement," *Labor History* 33 (Spring 1992): 217–47, and Monsignor Charles Owen Rice, "Confessions of an Anti-Communist," *Labor History* 30 (Summer 1989): 449–62.

28. David J. O'Brien, *American Catholics and Social Reform: The New Deal Years* (New York: Oxford University Press, 1968), 17.

29. Aaron I. Abell estimated that twenty-four labor schools had been formed by Jesuits, while diocesan authorities established thirty-two (*American Catholicism and Social Reform: A Search for Social Justice* [Notre Dame, Ind.: University of Notre Dame Press, 1963], pp. 278–79; Dorothy Day, *The Long Loneliness: The Autobiography of Dorothy Day* [New York: Curtis Books, 1972]). The more radical anti-Communist organization was the Association of Catholic Trade Unionists; see Douglas Seaton, *Catholics and Radicals: The Association of Catholic Trade Unionists and the American Labor Movement, from Depression to Cold War* (Lewisburg, Pa.: Bucknell University Press, 1981); Neil Betten, *Catholic Activism and the Industrial Worker* (Gainesville: University Presses of Florida, 1976).

30. Interview with Father Philip Carey, Oral History—Collection Title: New Yorkers at Work, Wagner Labor Archives. Hereinafter cited as NYAW.

31. The 1938 Fair Labor Standards Act had been passed to regulate minimum wages and overtime payments of time and a half for work done after forty hours (A. Howard Myers, *Labor Law and Legislation* [Cincinnati: South-Western Publishers, 1968], pp. 764–839; John S. Forsythe, "Legislative History of the Fair Labor Standards Act," *Law and Contemporary Problems* 6 (Summer 1939): 464–90). For the relationship between the act and homework, see Eileen Boris, "The Regulation of Homework and the Devolution of the Postwar Labor Standards Regime: Beyond Dichotomy," *Labor Law in America: Historical and Critical Essays,* ed. Christopher L. Tomlins and Andrew J. King (Baltimore: John Hopkins University Press, 1992).

32. Interview with Sam Madell, NYAW.

33. Report to Harry Bridges from William Glazier, Aug. 19, 1948, ILA-TAM, box 1.

34. "Testimony of Julius Bagley," House Committee on Education and Labor, *Amendments to the Fair Labor Standards Act of 1938,* vol. 1, p. 621; Vernon H. Jensen, *Strife on the Waterfront: The Port of New York since 1945* (Ithaca: Cornell University Press, 1974), pp. 54–59.

35. For the shippers' and Ryan's opposition to the overtime on overtime issue see, "Testimony of Frank Nolan, Chairman, Stevedoring Committee, NYC," Senate Committee on Labor and Public Welfare, *Fair Labor Standards Act, Amendments, Part 1,* pp. 381–421; "Statement of Joseph Ryan," ibid., pp. 1063–79. For the original suit and the following decisions through to the Supreme Court, see "Statement of Louis Waldman, General Counsel, ILA," Senate Committee on Labor and Public Welfare, *To Clarify the Overtime Compensation Provisions of the Fair Labor Standards Act of 1938,* pp. 4–35.

36. Quoted in Citizens Waterfront Committee, *New York Waterfront,* p. 13.

37. New York State Crime Commission, *Study of the Port of New York* (New York, 1953), p. 27; Benjamin Chinitz, *Freight and the Metropolis: The Impact of America's Transportation Revolution on the New York Region* (Cambridge, Mass.: Harvard University Press, 1960), p. 2.

38. *Report of Board of Inquiry—Maritime Industry (East Coast Longshoremen)* (Washington, D.C.: GPO, 1948); *Final Report of Board of Inquiry, October 21, 1948* (Washington, D.C.: GPO, 1948), pp. 1–2. Under the terms of the Taft-Hartley Act the

federal government had the power to order a cooling-off period and create a board of inquiry to investigate the dispute (R. Alton Lee, *Truman and Taft-Hartley: A Question of Mandate* [Lexington: University of Kentucky Press, 1966], p. 76).

39. "Status Report of Thomas R. Steutel," Oct. 26, 1948, Federal Conciliation and Mediation Service, Dispute Case Files, 1913–1948, RG 280, box 2357, National Archives, Washington, D.C.; "Last Offer of Settlement by the New York Shipping Association and the International Longshoremen's Association, submitted to the Presidential Board of Inquiry, Thursday, October 21, 1948," Federal Conciliation and Mediation Service, Regional Dispute Files (Nationally Significant), 1948–1950, Category One, RG 280, box 2522; *Final Report of the Board of Inquiry*, pp. 3–6.

40. *Daily Worker*, Nov. 14, 1948, p. 1; *New York Times*, Nov. 10, 1948, p. 59; Larrowe, *Shape-Up and Hiring Hall*, p. 32.

41. Interviews with Sam Madell and Father Philip Carey, NYAW.

42. "Statement of Alfred Corbett, Chairman, New Jersey Back Pay Committee," Senate Committee on Labor and Public Welfare, *To Clarify the Overtime Compensation Provisions of the Fair Labor Standards Act of 1938*, p. 341.

43. Sampson's hold on Local 791 is discussed in Larrowe, *Shape-Up and Hiring Hall*, p. 34. For the public clash between Ryan and Sampson see *New York Times*, Nov. 11, pp. 1 and 31; *New York Telegram*, Nov. 10, 1948, p. 5.

44. *New York Times*, Nov. 13, 1948, p. 1; *New York Sun*, Nov. 12, 1948, pp. 1 and 10; *New York Times*, Nov. 17, 1948, p. 3.

45. "Shapeup, Unemployment Main Issues in Longshore Strike," Fred Zeserson, Federated Press, Eastern Bureau, Nov. 18, 1948, ILA-TAM, folder Agreements, Negotiations & Strikes, box 1.

46. *New York Telegram*, Nov. 10, 1948, p. 1; Larrowe, *Shape-Up and Hiring Hall*, p. 34. I must thank Bruce Nelson for bringing the quote concerning the leaflets to my attention. *New York Times*, Nov. 16, 1948, p. 35; *Daily Worker*, Nov. 16, 1948, p. 6; ibid., Nov. 17, 1948, pp. 2 and 11; *New York Sun*, Nov. 16, 1948, pp. 1–2.

47. *Final Report of Board of Inquiry*, p. 15.

48. *New York Telegram*, Nov. 10, 1948, p. 5; *New York Times*, Nov. 16, 1948, p. 35; ibid., Nov. 17, 1948, pp. 1 and 49.

49. *New York Times*, Nov. 19, 1948, p. 23; ibid., Nov. 18, 1948, p. 19; ibid., Nov. 17, 1948, pp. 1 and 49; ibid., Nov. 16, 1948, p. 1; ibid., Nov. 11, 1948, p. 31.

50. "Testimony of Joseph Kane, Member of the International Longshoremen's Association," Senate Committee on Labor and Public Welfare, *To Clarify the Overtime Compensation Provisions of the Fair Labor Standards Act of 1938*, pp. 255–63.

51. *New York Times*, Nov. 14, 1948, p. 48; *San Francisco Chronicle*, Nov. 18, 1948, p. 1.

52. "Canadian ILA Leader Knuckles Under to Pressure," by Tom Carlson, ILA-TAM, box 1; *New York Times*, Nov. 19, 1948, 1; *New York Sun*, Nov. 17, 1948, pp. 1–2.

53. "Report, William N. Margolis," Dec. 8, 1948, Records of the FMCS, Regional Dispute Files (Nationally Significant), 1948–1950, Category 1, RG 280, box 2522; *New York Times*, Nov. 18, 1948, pp. 1 and 19; *New York Times*, Nov. 25, 1948, p. 1.

54. "Cyrus Stewart Ching," Columbia University Oral History Collection, part 2, no. 35, card 7 of 9, pp. 575 and 577; "Report, William N. Margolis," Dec. 8, 1948,

Records of the FMCS, Regional Dispute Files (Nationally Significant), 1948–1950, Category 1, RG 280, box 2522.

55. *New York Times,* Nov. 28, 1948, pp. 1 and 66. Eugene Sampson's Local 791 voted overwhelmingly for the agreement, 635 to 81.

56. Interview with Sam Madell, NYAW.

5 The "Lords of the Docks" Reconsidered: Race Relations among West Coast Longshoremen, 1933–61

Bruce Nelson

During the years from the mid-1930s through the late 1940s, the unions affiliated with the Congress of Industrial Organizations (CIO) emerged as formidable challengers to the conservative, narrowly job-conscious, and often racist unionism of the American Federation of Labor (AFL). Given the inclusive character of industrial labor markets, CIO leaders were well aware that they had to organize blacks as well as whites if their unions were to survive. Moreover, unlike the AFL, the early CIO included a substantial number of left-wing activists—mainly Communists and Socialists—who had a strong commitment to the goal of racial equality. Thus, at its founding convention in 1938, the CIO declared its "uncompromising opposition to any form of discrimination, whether political or economic, based on race, color, creed, or nationality." In language that reflected a widespread—but finally inadequate—understanding of the roots and role of racism in American society, the new federation denounced racial prejudice as an employer weapon designed to "create false contests between Negro and white workers."[1]

In recent years there has been a lively debate among labor historians about the CIO's record on race. Although no consensus has emerged, the poles of the argument are clear enough. On the one side are those who argue that in spite of its real failings and the daunting obstacles it faced, the CIO's record was essentially a positive one. The industrial union federation "hardly created a racially integrated society," says Lizabeth Cohen in a prize-winning study of workers in Chicago, "but it went further in promoting racial harmony than any other institution in existence at the time." On the other side are those who point to a negative continuity, emphasizing that historically organized labor, including the CIO, has served as a vehicle for defending the relatively privileged position of white workers vis à vis their minority competitors in the labor market. The best known advocate of this perspective is Herbert Hill, a scholar at the University of Wisconsin, who came to know the trade union movement intimately through his many years of service as NAACP labor secretary. Hill maintains that "the great promise of the CIO, the promise of an interracial labor movement, was never realized."[2]

How does the history of the International Longshoremen's and Warehousemen's Union (ILWU) fit within the framework of this argument? Did the leadership of ILWU president Harry Bridges, his undeniable association with the Left, and his union's "Red" reputation mean that the ILWU's record on race was significantly better than that of more conventional CIO unions? Moreover, did the remarkable power achieved by the self-proclaimed "Lords of the Docks" at the "point of production" lead to a new willingness to incorporate African Americans into a labor force that had long been "lily white"? This essay will seek to answer these questions by focusing on the ILWU's history, from its emergence in the labor insurgency of the 1930s to the signing of the Mechanization and Modernization Agreement of 1961 (which would lead to a dramatic decline in the number of dock workers on the West Coast).[3] In particular, it will examine the ILWU international leadership's stance on race and compare it with the record of one of the union's most important affiliates, Local 13 in San Pedro, which represented longshoremen in the port of Los Angeles. In addressing these necessary but narrowly focused questions, I want also to raise a larger one about working-class "agency," about the "making" of white working-class identity in ways that reflected—and reinforced—the racial fault lines of American society.[4]

* * *

The place to begin is with an assessment of the long-term evolution of race relations on the waterfront. Over a period of many years, dock workers developed their own special pattern with regard to race and ethnicity. On the Atlantic and Gulf Coasts, the International Longshoremen's Association (ILA) found it necessary to embrace a mosaic of nationality

groups and above all to find a way of achieving an accommodation between blacks and whites. In some ports, whites predominated; in other
ports, the two races divided the work equally; in still others, African
Americans constituted the overwhelming majority of the labor force. In
these circumstances, said scholars Sterling Spero and Abram Harris in
1931, the black worker "probably plays a more important role [in the ILA]
than he does in any other labor union." But the accommodation that
occurred was only partial, and it sometimes gave way to bitter conflict.
In New York, the nation's largest port, Spero and Harris noted that "the
Negro's presence . . . is now accepted by the white man. He has a right to
be there; he has a right to work; he has a right to belong to the union. Yet
he is by no means regarded as an equal." Thirty years later, black trade
union leader A. Philip Randolph could still charge that "with increasing
severity Negro longshoremen are being denied equal job rights and are
made the victims of race violence and intimidation on the piers of New
York."[5]

On the West Coast, before the renaissance of unionism in 1933 and the
founding of the ILWU in 1937, there had been very little accommodation
between blacks and whites. Here, the black population was much smaller
than in the Atlantic and Gulf ports, and, operating squarely within the
white supremacist craft traditions of the AFL, white dock workers and
their unions had succeeded in excluding African Americans altogether,
or nearly so. Insofar as black workers found a place on the West Coast
waterfront before the famed "Big Strike" of 1934, it was mainly as strikebreakers, and then—for the most part—only temporarily. According to
census data, African Americans constituted 1.4 percent of the dock labor
force in California in 1930, and an even smaller percentage in the Pacific
Northwest. Economist Herbert Northrup reported that on the eve of the
1934 strike, there were only twenty-three black ILA members along the
entire West Coast.[6]

From the standpoint of official union policy, this situation would
change dramatically during and after the Big Strike, the eighty-three-day
walkout that began in May 1934 and ended in a great victory for the union
(at that time, the Pacific Coast District of the ILA). The strike victory led
not only to union recognition but to a coastwide agreement, union control of hiring, the six-hour day, and—overall—a remarkable turnaround
in the relationship between dock workers and their employers.[7] Insofar
as the Big Strike also led to a new departure in race relations, it was
mainly—indeed, overwhelmingly—because of the growing influence of
Harry Bridges and the Left. Bridges began working as a longshoreman in

1922. In the early thirties, he was among the leaders of a caucus of longshore unionists in the key port of San Francisco that included a number of Communists. He and his allies argued that building a strong union necessitated the recruiting of black longshoremen into its ranks and ending the pattern of racial and ethnic segregation that prevailed in waterfront work gangs. During the 1934 strike, Bridges spoke at black churches and "implored blacks to join him on the picket line." Nearly a decade later he recalled, "I went directly to them. I said: 'Our union means a new deal for Negroes. Stick with us and we'll stand for your inclusion in [the] industry.'" And, he declared, "Almost without exception, they stuck with us. They helped us. The employers were frustrated in their attempt to use them for scabs."[8]

With the formation of the ILWU in 1937, and its affiliation with the CIO, San Francisco's Longshore Local 10 quickly distinguished itself as a "haven of racial equality." The substantial presence of Communist Party members and—even more so—of their "progressive" allies in Local 10 was vitally important to this achievement, as was the fact that Bridges and other leaders of the international union were based in San Francisco and played an active role in the local's deliberations. A third factor was the in-migration of thousands of black workers during World War II, when the port boomed and, according to some estimates, provided employment for as many as nine thousand longshoremen. More than two thousand of these workers were African American. Many of them became full members of the union and eventually constituted a critical mass that, in alliance with the Left, would have a significant impact on the local's internal life. Although the union did not use race as a category in counting its members, informed contemporaries estimated that blacks made up about 25 percent of Local 10's membership in 1946, and about 45 percent by the mid-1960s.[9]

Within the black community, especially in San Francisco, the ILWU's record on race received high praise, and Bridges was given much of the credit. The president of the Baptist Ministers' Union called him "a Godsend among men." The *Sun-Reporter* declared that "minority people have fared better in the ILWU under Bridges . . . than they have in any other labor union in the United States." Dr. Carleton Goodlett, a physician and civil rights activist, characterized the ILWU and the Marine Cooks and Stewards, another Left-led maritime union with a large black membership, as "the guardians of the Negro community and its economic backbone." Even the staunchly anti-Communist Wilson Record conceded in the pages of an NAACP publication that "whatever one may think of the left-wing tendencies of the Bridges-controlled [ILWU], the fact remains that through it Negroes have obtained a fair break in job opportunities and union participation."[10]

Although Bridges and the San Francisco longshore local were often the focal point of attention, the ILWU's achievements in the realm of race relations reached far beyond Local 10. By 1946, the union's research director concluded, "approximately 22% of our longshore and warehouse membership consists of Negroes. This amounts to about 11,000 Negroes out of approximately 50,000 members in these two categories." Beyond these two categories, there was the union's extraordinary breakthrough in organizing sugar and pineapple workers in the fields of Hawaii. Here virtually the entire labor force was made up of "minority peoples." In 1946, Filipino and Japanese workers constituted nearly 90 percent of the ILWU members in the Islands, and the emergence of Hawaii as the union's greatest source of growth meant that people of color would soon account for nearly half of the ILWU's total membership.[11]

Given the increasing importance of this multiracial constituency, the union moved aggressively in 1945 to suspend the charter of the Stockton Unit of Warehouse Local 6 because its members refused to work with a Japanese American who had recently been released from a wartime relocation camp. Bridges told the press that "the position of the ILWU on the question of equality for all, regardless of race, creed, color, or national origin, is clear and unequivocal. We cannot and will not compromise on it for one moment, for to do so would be to pick up the banner of fascism where Hitler dropped it." When the vast majority of the Stockton rank and file refused to sign pledge cards affirming their willingness to abide by the union's racially egalitarian principles, the suspension went into effect and, according to historian Harvey Schwartz, "an angry Harry Bridges . . . tore the Stockton Unit charter off the wall and drove back to San Francisco."[12]

There is little in Bridges's background that would explain his strong commitment to racial equality. He was born in Australia, which at that time was an openly white supremacist society. When he migrated to the United States, he lived and worked mainly among whites in a country that was also permeated by racist assumptions and practices. His dissent from American society's prevailing racial mores probably stemmed, in large measure, from the influence of the Communists and party sympathizers whom he met on the San Francisco waterfront. Whatever else one can— and must—say in criticism of the Communist Party, it's important to acknowledge that it was almost unique among predominantly white organizations in its close identification with the struggle for black equality. Recent scholarly studies have made it abundantly clear that, especially during the 1940s, the combination of Communist leadership and mass mobilization within the black community led to some remarkable achievements in the fight against racial discrimination. Although Bridges steadfastly denied being a Communist Party member, he readily acknowledged his respect for the party and some of its ideas and programs. Moreover, he was instrumental in opening the door to Communist influence in the ILWU. Over the years, the union developed a reputation as Left-led, or "Communist-dominated," and one of the sure signs of this relationship was the ILWU's unusually strong commitment to racial equality. Summing up its history in 1955, the union declared proudly that "the ILWU banned racial discrimination and segregation twenty years before the United States Supreme Court found the courage to do so."[13]

This statement may be an accurate indicator of the leadership's intent, but as a summation of the union's history it can obscure as much as it reveals. Bridges's own commitment to racial equality must be seen in relation to other principles he embraced—especially seniority, local autonomy, and a belief in rank-and-file democracy. When the practical application of these principles clashed with the ideal of racial equality, as it often did, the ILWU president was compelled to negotiate a course that, perhaps necessarily, compromised one principle while upholding another. In relation to the recurring fluctuations in the waterfront labor market, and the consequent ebb and flow of job opportunities, Bridges's clearest commitment was to seniority, which he called a "fair and honest trade union principle" that "no fair-minded, honest union member can oppose." He was convinced, moreover, that dock workers should be sharing abundance rather than scarcity. "We readily admit that . . . the peaks and valleys of demand for longshoremen will present problems," he told a congressional committee in 1955. "But we are not prepared to return to the jungle of the New York waterfront and the west coast of pre-1934 in order to have a permanent surplus of men available at each dock gate. That way is the way of sharing starvation."[14]

His strong opposition to "sharing starvation" led Bridges to propose on one occasion that a thousand longshoremen from his own Local 10 be laid off, even though he knew full well that black workers, because of their low seniority, would be disproportionately affected. He made this proposal in 1949, after San Francisco longshoremen had been working "short" weeks for well over a year and had, additionally, lost substantial income during a ninety-eight-day strike in 1948. According to the *Local 10 Longshore Bulletin*, Bridges declared that "many men on the front" had asked him to do something to "remedy the situation, as they could no longer make a living." But in this instance Bridges's allies on the Left deserted him, and so did the black longshoremen, who immediately recognized the serious problem layoffs would cause for them at a time when black unemployment in the Bay Area was very high. In fact, among the membership as a whole the solidaristic spirit that had prevailed during the 1948 strike reasserted itself, and Bridges's proposal was overwhelmingly defeated.[15]

As this incident suggests, Bridges and other union leaders were frequently constrained by the fact that they operated within the framework of a democratic organization whose members had minds of their own and a strong commitment to local autonomy. More often than not, the membership also demonstrated a strong tendency to favor "son, brother, neighbor, or friend" when jobs became available on the waterfront. The ILWU could, and did, incorporate the principle of racial equality into its constitution and insist that all of its affiliated locals abide by this ideal. But in practice the principles of local autonomy and seniority, and the "brother-in-law" system of allocating new jobs, often took precedence over the goal of racial equality. Moreover, when conflict arose over racial issues, the union was compelled to seek resolution in a larger context that became increasingly precarious. The glory days of maritime unity in the mid-1930s soon gave way to intercraft friction that was rendered more complex and bitter by the jurisdictional warfare between the AFL and the CIO. And when the ILWU was expelled from the CIO in 1950 on the charge of "Communist domination," it became even more vulnerable to raiding by hostile unions. The ILA and the Teamsters were waiting in the wings; and local unionists hostile to Bridges's agenda could use the threat of secession to keep the international union at bay.[16]

The classic example of this dynamic was Portland's Local 8, which along with its counterparts in Seattle, San Francisco, and San Pedro was one of four major longshore locals on the West Coast. For several decades, Local 8 remained an acute embarrassment to the ILWU and a blot on its reputation for racial egalitarianism. ("The ultra-liberal union directed by flaming liberal Harry Bridges has not admitted Negroes to its Portland local," the *Oregonian* reported in 1959.) According to an Oregon Bureau of Labor study, Local 8 had "an unwritten policy and system that kept Negroes from being employed as longshoremen." During World War II, when about fifteen thousand African Americans came to the city seeking employment, and the local took in 557 newcomers in a one-year period, Local 8 remained "lily white." As late as 1961, when there were about twelve hundred regular and probationary union members on the Portland waterfront, the local continued to exclude blacks. This situation would improve slightly in the 1960s, but even Bridges was unable to persuade the members of Local 8 to change their ways. Several times, when he addressed local union meetings and raised the issue of race, he was "unceremoniously booed out of the hall."[17]

As early as 1952, the ILWU's Northwest regional director expressed the leadership's growing frustration—and sense of powerlessness—in regard to Portland's exclusion of African Americans. "Sure, we talked about [the Portland situation]," said Bill Gettings. "I talked about it with Harry lots of times. The ILWU Executive Board talked about it. It worried the hell out of the whole International. We didn't like it one damn bit. But what could we do? We got sores from scratching our head about it." Gettings believed that "kick[ing] the Portland local out of the International because they discriminated" would drive its members into the arms of the ILA, which would weaken the ILWU and thereby "hurt the Negro longshoremen . . . as well as the whites. So we decided to live with the situation, bad as it was."[18]

Clearly, the ILWU leadership's commitment to racial equality was not, by itself, sufficient to shape the practice of the Portland longshore local. And the Portland example raises a broader question about the racial attitudes and practices of the union's white rank and file, including the famed "generation of the 1930s." The men who fought the 1934 strike and built the foundations of the ILWU have been justly celebrated by scholars—above all, perhaps, by this author—for their courage, their militancy, and their unusual commitment to a progressive political agenda.[19] Their behavior during the Big Strike is the stuff of legend; and in the aftermath of the strike, they achieved an extraordinary degree of control of the work process, so much so, an employer spokesman complained, that union stewards "establish the manner in which, and the speed at which, work is to be performed on the waterfronts of the Pacific Coast." What the employers lamented the longshoremen themselves could only celebrate. An "Admiral Line Stevie" was convinced that he and his fellow workers had achieved "the finest conditions in the world." An "Oldtimer," who had first joined the ILA in 1915, exulted that "we are the most militant and organized body of men the world has ever seen." Another longshoreman was moved to express his newfound sense of pride in poetic terms:

I'm called dock-walloper and wharf rat
With many laughs and many knocks.
In spite of that, I glory in my element
I'm one of the Lords of the Docks.[20]

To be sure, there was plenty of job-related militancy among industrial workers in the 1930s, highlighted by the sit-down strikes that helped spearhead the organization of the auto and rubber industries in Flint, Detroit, and Akron. But the West Coast maritime unionists, and first and foremost the longshoremen, were practically unique among American workers in the way they extended their militancy from the realm of "porkchops" to the world of "politics." They protested, and even engaged in symbolic strikes, over political issues such as the Italian invasion of Ethiopia, Japanese aggression against China, and Republican Spain's desperate fight for survival against a counterrevolution supported by Hitler and Mussolini. Longshoreman Henry Schrimpf declared that the goal of the maritime workers was not just to win better wages and conditions for themselves but to "generally advance the human cause." Schrimpf, who was closely identified with the Communists at the time, may not have spoken for all of his fellow workers, but his statement conveys an essential ingredient of the spirit and vision that animated many of them during the Turbulent Thirties.[21]

As the case of the Portland longshoremen suggests, however, the record may look quite different when viewed from the standpoint of race. During the thirties the issue of racial equality remained more rhetorical than substantive, because in the context of the Great Depression there was hardly any influx of new workers of any race or nationality on the waterfront. Race began to have a dramatic impact on the development of the union with the coming of World War II, when the vast expansion of production on the "home front" required the hiring of many new workers on the waterfront, for the first time in a generation. Many of the new workers on the docks were African Americans. This was especially true in San Pedro and San Francisco, where the pace of black migration far exceeded that in the Pacific Northwest. A closer look at the experience of the generation of the 1930s in the port of Los Angeles should enhance our understanding of the complexity of the ILWU's record on race and provide a revealing angle of vision on the consciousness of the union's white rank and file.

* * *

When World War II began, Longshore Local 13, in San Pedro, had about twenty-five hundred members. Although its ranks had always included Mexican Americans, no African Americans found regular—or even irregular—employment on the waterfront before the war. Al Langley, who began working intermittently on the docks in 1934 and became a full member of the union in 1938, recalled that "prior to the war there wasn't one black on the [Los Angeles] waterfront." According to Langley, there were only two black families in San Pedro during the 1930s, and the men of both households worked as janitors in downtown commercial establishments. Tony Salcido, a longshoreman who grew up in Wilmington (which together with San Pedro constitutes the port of Los Angeles), remembered only two or three black families in his community during the thirties. Since Local 13 had a strong tendency to favor local residents and, above all, the family members of working longshoremen in allocating new jobs, blacks were at a great disadvantage. But their absence from the longshore workforce was not merely the product of these apparently "natural" circumstances. For Langley recalled that Local 13 included in its ranks "a kind of a vigilante group of ultra-conservative[s]"—men who "had never been around blacks, or else they were southerners," and who were determined to exclude African Americans from the waterfront. On the rare occasions when black longshoremen from San Francisco sought to exercise their right as union members to visit San Pedro and work there temporarily, the local "vigilantes" made it clear that the newcomers were unwelcome. "The [black] guys" got the message, said Langley, "and they [left.]"[22]

In the first six months after Pearl Harbor, there was very little work for longshoremen in San Pedro, as the almost complete elimination of commercial shipping and the breathtakingly rapid development of San Francisco as the West Coast's principal military port of embarkation left the port of Los Angeles virtually defunct. Some members of Local 13 went into the armed forces; many others went to work in the shipyards or to San Francisco, where they worked on the docks under the auspices of Local 10. To Langley, who spent fourteen months in "Frisco," it seemed that "every second man up there was a Pedro man." But gradually shipping returned to Los Angeles, most of its longshoremen came home, and the demand for labor soon outstripped the capacity of Local 13 to provide experienced men. In these circumstances, the first two black longshoremen since the founding of the local were registered in November 1942. Both were experienced dock workers from Galveston, Texas. They were followed, in the next two years, by hundreds of other African Americans. In January 1945, according to a "rough estimate" by the local union president, the "number of Negro members in Local 13" was "between 400 and 500"—or less than 10 percent of a workforce that had more than doubled since the war began.[23]

In important respects, the presence of African Americans altered the working relationships among the men on the waterfront. Arthur Kaunisto shipped out on a Liberty ship in 1942 and came back to San Pedro in 1944. He recalled that when he returned to the hiring hall, "I didn't recognize many people. They was mostly strangers to me"—"a lot of colored people" and "a mixture that I'd never seen before." Corky Wilson, who also shipped out in the merchant marine in 1942 and returned to the docks in 1944, made the same point, although much more crudely: "I walked in[to the hiring hall]," he recalled, "and I didn't see a white guy anywhere—all niggers, all niggers. . . . We had never had a colored guy up until then, and then . . . the place was packed with colored guys."[24]

Although Kaunisto's and Wilson's recollections overestimate the percentage of blacks among the newcomers to the waterfront, they correctly imply that the transition to a multiracial work force was not an easy one. Longshoring had always required close cooperation in the work process, and therefore a sense of affinity among the men on the job. Some work gangs had been organized on an ethnic basis, and some—in part at least—on a family basis. Thus, for many whites the sudden presence of African Americans on the docks represented an unprecedented challenge to the sense of camaraderie and mutual respect that undergirded their working relationships. Langley recalled that "most of the whites were scared of the blacks, because we never had any around here and we never associated with them. . . . When they started to come in, the whites didn't want to work with them," and the blacks themselves were "more or less clannish."[25]

The way the hiring hall operated made it easy to maintain, or establish, a pattern of racial separation on the job, especially during the war, when work was plentiful and labor was relatively scarce. A man who was dissatisfied with his partner or his gang, for any reason, could simply "replace" himself—that is, return to the hall, from which a "replacement" would be dispatched, and then wait for the next available job. Joe Stahl recalled that "a lot of [oldtimers] wouldn't work with a black guy. [They'd] turn around and call a replacement." And black longshoreman Walter Williams remembered that "some of the regular 'longies' . . . would say, 'I'm going to call me a damn replacement,' if they saw a black guy coming down into the hold. And they would call a replacement rather than work with us."[26]

Williams first went to work on the docks in September 1943. Before that he had been an organizer for the CIO Industrial Union Council in Los Angeles and a welder at the California Shipbuilding Company, where he served as a leader of the opposition to the flagrantly racist practices of the AFL-affiliated International Brotherhood of Boilermakers. He recalled hearing about longshoring from fellow workers, who told him it was "great work"; besides, the pay was more than he was making as a welder; and he had been attracted to the CIO in the first place because of its progressive reputation on matters of race. So he eagerly sought employment on the waterfront. But forty-five years later, he still remembered with bitterness the reception he received there.

> I wasn't on any job [long] before I was reminded that I was a temp worker. [The white longshoremen would say,] "You guys are only here temporarily. What are you gonna do when the war's over?" And I promptly told them, "I intend to be here when the war's over. I'm gonna do everything I can to stay here."
>
>   It's a strain on a person to have to work in an atmosphere where he knows that people have these racist feelings. From time to time you have to listen to racist remarks and control yourself, or try to control yourself anyway. . . . You had a lot of brawls. You had a lot of fights down there . . . over name calling [that] involved racism.

When Williams finally got into a fight with a white worker who had called him a "black something," he remembered the experience—above all the release of accumulated tension—as downright exhilarating. "It was like letting off a lot of steam. . . . I mean, it was just like somebody had lifted an elephant off my shoulders," he recalled.[27]

The extraordinary tension that accompanied the expansion of the workforce in San Pedro was by no means unique to that community or to the waterfront. Rather, it occurred across much of the industrial landscape, as World War II precipitated an earthquake in the labor market. Millions of white men left the workplace to serve in the armed forces overseas. In their place came whites from the rural South; women who had hitherto been denied access to higher-paying blue-collar employment; and more than a million African Americans, many of them also migrants from the rural South. Their presence in factory, mine, and mill—and on the waterfront—placed enormous strains on social relationships in the workplace. Class-conscious veterans of the CIO's organizing wars chafed at the presence of class-unconscious "hillbillies" from the South; men were often ambivalent about—and sometimes actively hostile to—the presence of women. Above all, whites resented—and resisted—the influx of blacks.[28]

On the West Coast waterfront, according to an employer spokesman, "many old-timers in regular gangs [objected to working with] colored boys, not because of their color, but because most of them are shiftless and lazy, folding up after a few hours . . . [and] leaving most of the work . . . to the old-timers." Even Harry Bridges, in an article that attacked "discrimination against Negroes" as "anti-labor, anti-American and anti-white," complained that "in some cases Negro workers, lacking experience and discipline and nursing past wounds, have needlessly antagonized some older members of the union." During one confrontation that turned especially nasty, a white military policeman from Texas backed up a gang boss by forcing a group of black workers off a ship at gunpoint, and warning that "back where I come from, we shoot you."[29]

Over time, the interaction among black, white, and Mexican American workers bred friendship and respect as well as tension. But it would appear that among many, perhaps most, of San Pedro's "'34 men," there was considerable resistance to working side by side with black newcomers, letting them become full union members, and promoting those who did become full members to head a gang. The issue came to a head in 1945. After a group of temporary longshoremen refused to work under the direction of a black union member who had been dispatched as a gang boss, representatives of Local 13 and the employers reached an agreement that henceforth no man could be a gang boss until he had worked in the industry on the Pacific Coast for five years. The pact also applied to winch drivers, jitney drivers, and carpenters—in other words, to the most desirable jobs on the waterfront. Since no blacks had been members of Local 13 before November 1942, the agreement effectively placed a ceiling on their job mobility, and, according to Langley, "every one of them had to come back in and work in the hold or on the dock. . . . [Matters] had come to a head because the blacks had begun to get acclimated, and they knew their stuff. . . . They wanted to be part of the industry too. But the whites weren't ready for it."[30]

In 1946, another change of policy shifted the issue, insofar as blacks were concerned, from containment to exclusion. In April, Bill Lawrence, who had just completed a term as president of Local 13, reported that "work in this Port has dropped to the extent that we have approximately 700 or 800 men too many for the industry." Lawrence estimated that if the waterfront's war-inflated labor force was not reduced, the union would face a situation where some low-seniority men would be dispatched only about once a week; and others, once every two or three weeks at best. Thus, the local decided that its five hundred lowest-seniority members should be "deregistered" and "placed on an unemployed list." This decision was implemented on April 22, 1946, with the understanding that "no new men [would] be taken into the industry until the above 500 men were called back." (The group would become known, in the folklore of the union, as the "Unemployed 500.")[31]

The initial call for a reduction in the workforce had come from the employer representatives on the joint Labor Relations Committee in the port of Los Angeles. But the local union leadership had readily agreed with this proposal, and so had the international union. Lawrence and other Local 13 officers discussed the matter with ILWU Secretary-Treasurer Louis Goldblatt and Northwest Regional Director Bill Gettings, and reported that "[we] acted right along the lines that [Goldblatt] suggested." Bridges himself expressed the belief that the decision was not only "clearly legal, but founded on good trade union principles."[32]

When he penned these words in September 1947, Bridges could hardly have anticipated that the decision to deregister five hundred men in San Pedro would haunt the ILWU for the next twenty-five years. The problem was that nearly half of the deregistered men were black; and, even more so, that the deregistration served to eliminate about 90 percent of Local 13's black members. Since the union followed the principle of seniority in determining who would be laid off, Lawrence believed that there were no grounds for complaint; apparently, the international union agreed. But for black workers, the decision rankled, not only because so many of them were laid off but because, as Walter Williams recalled, some of Local 13's white members openly boasted that "'this union was lily-white before you guys came down here, and [now] it's going to be lily-white again.' They were just arrogant about it." In the immediate aftermath of the decision, Lawrence reported that "a few disgruntled colored brothers" had discussed the matter with Rev. Clayton D. Russell, a prominent civil rights activist who had led a campaign during World War II to expand job opportunities for African Americans in Los Angeles. Lawrence complained that Russell was "attempting to make a 'Big To Do' about the entire situation," and was, moreover, "inferring that there might have been some [racial] discrimination . . . involved." Under Williams's leadership, the ranks of the "disgruntled colored brothers" expanded dramatically. They built an informal group which they called the Afro-American Labor Protective Society; and in the summer of 1947, about sixty members of the group approached an attorney and began discussing the possibility of achieving legal redress outside the channels of the union.[33]

What served to swell the ranks of the grievants was the increasingly obvious fact that Local 13 was violating its promise that "no new men [would] be taken into the industry until the . . . 500 . . . were called back." In fact,

the union had never intended to apply the terms of this resolution literally. For the question of access was complicated by a number of earlier resolutions that gave priority to longshoremen who had left the docks to join
the armed forces or serve in the merchant marine during the war. As these
men returned, they were automatically reregistered. Moreover, the union's
membership committee decided that other former members should also
be reregistered ahead of the Unemployed 500. Thus, Local 13 members who
had transferred to other ILWU locals during the war, or who had taken
jobs in the shipyards, were given the same priority as military and merchant marine veterans when they returned to San Pedro. In addition, the
local continued to follow a policy of making jobs, and union membership,
available to sons and other male relatives of longshoremen, even if these
family members had never worked on the docks before. Here, perhaps, was
the most flagrant violation of the rights of the men on the unemployed
list, for Local 13 had voted "That no man be initiated into this Union"
before its unemployed members were "called back."[34]

What all of this meant in practice was that between the end of April
1946 and December 31, 1949, 613 returnees were reregistered and 60 new
men were registered on the Los Angeles waterfront. During the same
period, as a result of death, retirement, and other factors, 901 men were
eliminated from the registration list. And yet, during much of this time,
work on the waterfront was increasing and the need for men was growing accordingly. In fact, the employers suggested as early as January 1947
that all of the Unemployed 500 be reregistered. But Local 13 refused. From
the time of the original deregistration through the end of 1949, only fifty-
eight of the laid-off men were reregistered.[35]

The final ingredient that cemented the black workers' conviction that
racial discrimination was at the heart of the union's practice was the fact
that even when men from the unemployed list were called back for
reregistration, Local 13 ignored seniority and privileged whites over blacks.
The first man reregistered was a white worker who had been registered
on January 8, 1946, and initiated into the union on April 4, only eighteen
days before his deregistration! Overall, from April 1946 until July 30, 1947,
only ten men were reregistered; all of them were white; and all had less
seniority than many of the black longshoremen on the unemployed list.[36]

Facing the possibility of a lawsuit, the international union pressured
Local 13 to follow seniority in reregistering men from the unemployed list,
and this was done beginning in October 1947. Bridges advised the local
that men who had left the waterfront and were now seeking reregistration
should not be given "any priority" simply because they possessed a with-

drawal card. Rather, the ILWU president proposed a formula for reregistering all men in accordance with their *real* seniority (i.e., actual amount of time spent on the Los Angeles waterfront) that would, he believed, win the acceptance of "any fair-minded working stiff." But the local ignored his advice and continued favoring virtually anyone who had withdrawn from the union before April 1946 over men from the unemployed list. It was not until the coming of the Korean War, and the consequent expansion of work on the docks, that most of the deregistrants had their active union status restored. When 138 men were reregistered in December 1950, it appeared that the saga of the Unemployed 500 was finally at an end.[37]

But it wasn't. In May 1965, during the heyday of the struggle for black equality in the United States, twenty-four veterans of the Unemployed 500 filed a grievance against the shipowners, demanding the restoration of their full seniority. This time the international union threw its entire weight on the side of the grievants. The brief filed by ILWU attorney Ben Margolis acknowledged that "when the deregistration took place in April 1946, the virtual lily-white character of the Los Angeles–Long Beach . . . waterfront was restored." While this factor alone was not sufficient to establish racial discrimination, the union argued that "it does not stand alone," because events thereafter underscored "the discriminatory character of the entire process of deregistration and reregistration."[38]

But given a set of circumstances in which more than half of the deregistered men were whites, most of whom suffered the same fate as their black fellow workers, how could the union prove *racial* discrimination? The fact is that it couldn't, at least not to the satisfaction of the arbitrators who in at least two successive decisions ruled against the union's claim. In arguing its case, however, the union offered a telling—although indirect—acknowledgment of the mindset of the membership of Local 13 in the 1940s which suggests that racial discrimination was indeed at the heart of the entire process. "Examined in the total context," said the union, "the deregistration of April 1946 was discriminatory despite the short-lived economic justification therefor. It is true that the majority of the white deregistrees were treated in the same manner as the Negro members of that group." But this could be explained only by the fact that these whites "were unfortunate enough to be integrated with the first substantial number of Negroes to enter longshore employment in Southern California." In other words, representatives of Local 13 had reregistered whites from the unemployed list without regard to seniority, and in doing so had flagrantly violated the seniority rights of blacks. When faced with the threat of a legal challenge, they chose thereafter to ignore the seniority rights of whites as well as blacks among the Unemployed 500, with the apparent goal of limiting the number of African Americans in the ranks of Local 13. In the meantime, they continued to reregister virtually all former members who had voluntarily left the Los Angeles waterfront before April 1946 and who now sought the restoration of their union status, and even to register new men on the front, most of whom were the relatives of the existing membership. Among the 673 men in these categories, there were fourteen blacks who met the union's criteria and therefore were reregistered along with the others. But the net effect—and surely the unstated purpose—of this policy was to restore, and then to maintain, "the virtual lily-white character of the Los Angeles–Long Beach . . . waterfront."[39]

Understandably, perhaps, given the nature of the grievance procedure, the union tried to pin the entire blame for the discriminatory treatment of the Unemployed 500 on the employers. But this argument was simply untenable, for the decision to deregister five hundred men was a joint one, made by the union and the employers together. Moreover, in practice the union exercised nearly full control of hiring (including the registration of new longshoremen); and in reregistering men after April 1946 the employers simply followed their usual policy of "rubber stamping" the choices made by Local 13's membership committee. With regard to the laid-off men, as arbitrator Sam Kagel pointed out, "the Union was required to be the moving party . . . and it did not move." (Or, more accurately, when it did "move," it was in the wrong direction.) The conclusion seems inescapable that insofar as there was a pattern of discrimination, the principal responsibility in this case lay with the union rather than the employers.[40]

The fate of the Unemployed 500 tells us much about the character of Local 13, which seems in some respects to have functioned like an AFL craft union in the building trades. In these unions, there was a long history of reserving new jobs for the family and friends of the current members. By this mechanism, and more formal ones such as the unions' control of apprenticeships and the dispatching of work, blacks and other people of color were relentlessly excluded from various trades, and local unions retained a high degree of racial and, sometimes, ethnic homogeneity. Local 13 had its own mechanism, "sponsorship," that served to maintain and reinforce patterns of racial exclusion. To be a successful candidate for employment on the Los Angeles waterfront, one had to be sponsored by a member of Local 13. The membership voted that priority in this regard should be given to the sons of deceased members, and then to the sons and brothers of active members. Generally, the right to sponsor was based upon seniority, with the first choice given to men whose membership dated back to 1933. Since the union assumed that a member would be likely to sponsor a "son, brother, neighbor, or friend," this practice "naturally" served to reinforce Local 13's pattern of racial exclusion. For with the exception of a small number of Mexican Americans, all of the local's most senior members were white; and in the residentially segregated and racially polarized environment of Los Angeles, a Local 13 member's "son, brother, neighbor, or friend" was likely to be white as well.[41]

In an apparent attempt to further solidify this pattern, the membership voted in July 1951 that an applicant for employment on the docks had to have been "a resident of Los Angeles County for ten years." In the short run at least, the implementation of this resolution automatically excluded African Americans who had migrated to Los Angeles during World War II, along with those who continued the flow of black migration after the war. And this exclusion occurred at a time when the port of Los Angeles was booming and the longshore labor force was expanding. George Love, who served several terms as local union president in the fifties, recalled "beat[ing] the bushes" to find prospective longshoremen in 1955, because "the work was so damn good!" "We got everybody we could get our hands on," Love said. But "everybody" included very few African Americans. Prospective members of Local 13 still required a sponsor; high-seniority whites continued to favor their "sons and brothers" and, in any case, showed no interest in sponsoring blacks; and most of the African Americans in the local did not have enough seniority to be able to sponsor anyone. Thus, Tony Salcido and John Pandora, both of whom were the sons of charter members of the local, recalled few if any blacks among the men with whom they were registered. According to imprecise estimates compiled by the ILWU's international and regional staff, there were about 250 black members of Local 13 at the end of 1946 (which must have included the blacks on the unemployed list), and "over 300 Negroes" in 1964, when the Los Angeles area's black population exceeded half a million. In a southern California variation on a common pattern of ethnic succession, Mexican Americans, who had accounted for a very small percentage of the local's membership in 1934, would gradually become the majority within Local 13. But African Americans were unable to make anything like the same inroads.[42]

The African American wartime pioneers who continued working on the waterfront remained—in essence—outsiders who found it difficult to move up the occupational ladder and achieve acceptance as full members of the longshore community. There were, to be sure, black workers who simply tried to "get along," and virtually all of them were grateful for the superior wages, conditions, and benefits that waterfront employment provided. Tony Salcido recalled, however, that when blacks finally accumulated enough seniority to become gang bosses, they were "invariably . . . assigned to the worst hatches on the ship"; and that when men practiced driving winches during their lunch hour, in the hope of moving up to a better job, "it was easier for the Anglos and the Mexicans [to do this] than it was for the blacks. I actually saw the blacks get run off the [winch] handles," he said, "whereas they would tolerate myself or somebody else." He also remembered occasions when men went out on a job, and if there was a "lone black" in the gang, "it was very, very out in the open that nobody wanted to work with him." Inevitably, the accumulation of indignities took their toll. "It's a wonder," said Walter Williams, "that I haven't died of a stroke."[43]

The AFL defended its racially discriminatory practices by pointing to the autonomy of its affiliated unions. The ILWU leadership also respected the right of its local unions to make autonomous choices on many issues, including the question of layoffs. In 1946, Bridges had informed an "old-time member of the ILWU" that "every Local has complete autonomy in these matters unless there [are] clear . . . violations of the International Constitution." In the case of the Unemployed 500, the international believed that Local 13 had made a decision that fell within its proper jurisdiction, and asked only that it be implemented in accordance with the principle of seniority. It was not until nearly twenty years after the original deregistration that the international came to recognize how blatantly the rights of its black members, and the union's own principles, had been violated.[44]

* * *

How, finally, does one explain the behavior of Local 13's white rank and file toward the Unemployed 500 and toward black workers in general? Was it pure-and-simple racism? Black workers certainly saw it in those terms, and with much justification. But for the historian, it is necessary to place racism in a specific historical context and to see it in relation to a larger pattern of habits and beliefs. In summing up the character of race relations on the Los Angeles waterfront, we need to explore the ways in which class and race intersected, and to re-create the rival systems of meaning that undergirded the collective experience of white and black workers.[45]

Local 13's white rank and file shared a common history of exploitation and powerlessness in the twenties and early thirties, of triumph in the Big

Strike and its volatile aftermath, of increasing pride and cohesion throughout the remainder of the decade. For them, "solidarity" became the watchword; and their slogan, "An injury to one is an injury to all." In their relations with other unions, they would learn the limits of that slogan. But within their own ranks, it continued to resonate powerfully, as they demonstrated in 1939, when an arbitrator ruled that sixty-one San Pedro longshoremen who had refused to load scrap iron bound for Japan were in violation of the collective bargaining agreement and would thus be suspended without pay for a week. The ILWU refused to accept this ruling, which came at a time when the union was aggressively seeking to mobilize public opinion and its own membership in active opposition to fascism, and to Japanese aggression against China in particular. Bridges argued that commitment to the union's principles could not be subordinated to "the technical wording of an agreement," and the leadership of Local 13 distributed the suspended men among a large number of work gangs. When employer representatives prevented the penalized longshoremen from working, their fellow workers walked off the job, and a partial shutdown of Los Angeles harbor ensued.[46]

By the time World War II came, then, the San Pedro longshoremen had accumulated a common experience of suffering, struggle, and triumph that marked them as the generation of the 1930s. The Big Strike, in particular, became the foundation of their identity as union men. All potential newcomers to ILWU locals were interrogated as to their whereabouts in 1934. If there was any possibility that they had served as strikebreakers during this epic confrontation, they were simply unwelcome. Mickey Mahon, who joined the union during World War II, recalled: "I filled out the papers and went before [the Local 13] membership committee. They were all '34 guys, good, solid men. . . . They wanted to know where I was in the '34 strike. . . . Well, I was out here, all through it. But I was living off the land—bumming water, food, panhandling, you name it, washing dishes, whatever, just to make a buck. . . . You had to prove it to [the committee]. So I had to get verification."[47]

It was easy for Mahon to win acceptance as a member of the waterfront fraternity. He readily found a sponsor in Pat Hagerty, a fellow Irish American with whom he had worked from the time he came on the docks as a casual. ("We Irish got to stick together, you know," Mahon recalled good-naturedly.) But when the war economy brought large numbers of African Americans to the waterfront, the members of Local 13 responded in ways that revealed not only a specific identity as "'34 men" but a *racialized* class consciousness. Blacks were not only newcomers to the docks; they were, in some basic sense, "Other." They had not been on the picket lines in 1934; they had not worked side by side with the '34 men thereafter to transform conditions on the waterfront. Nor had they lived, as neighbors and friends, in the working-class communities of San Pedro and Wilmington. None of this was mere coincidence, of course. African Americans had been excluded from work on the docks for a generation or more, and at the same time white Angelenos had been ruthlessly vigilant in protecting the racial homogeneity of their neighborhoods, by means of restrictive covenants, the organization of aggressively exclusionist homeowners' associations, and—when necessary—vigilante violence. Whites accepted this pattern of exclusion and enforced inequality as natural, and necessary. In the longshoremen's experience of life and work, "whiteness" merged with class; and in spite of all the changes that had occurred in the thirties, the specific group identity of the "Lords of the Docks" remained a racialized identity.[48]

When blacks arrived on the waterfront in large numbers, they came not only as racial "Other" but as cultural "Other" as well. Most of the newcomers were from the South. Some of them were experienced longshoremen from port cities on the Gulf Coast; but many came from agricultural labor and other marginalized occupations in small towns and rural areas. In the Jim Crow South, generations of alienated labor—in the hottest, heaviest, dirtiest, most dangerous, and lowest-paying jobs—had perhaps convinced many blacks that the Protestant ethic was a fraud, that there was no hope of mobility for them no matter how hard they worked, and that therefore their goal should be "to minimize labor with as little economic loss as possible."[49]

Of course, whites also took advantage of wartime conditions—the exceptionally tight labor market, the "cost-plus" government contracts that encouraged employers to pad their payrolls, the lack of close scrutiny or intense pressure from supervisors on the waterfront—to slow down or avoid work altogether when the spirit so moved them. Arthur Kaunisto remembered it as commonplace during the war that "some guys would be working and the rest of them would be laying around." And John Mitchell, who served several terms as president of Local 13, recalled an occasion when he was showing a Navy "goldbraid" around waterfront work areas, and "half of [the longshoremen] were laying down on the goddamn [dock]." Indeed, the enviable waterfront tradition of "four on and four off"—of four men working while four rested—in the port of Los Angeles had its origins in the wartime experience of whites far more than blacks. But for whites, whether one worked hard or not was seen as a matter of individual characteristics, whereas in the case of blacks there was the perception that *as a race* they were "lazy," "shiftless," and "just wouldn't work."[50]

Whites resented the presence of black newcomers and often called a replacement rather than work with them. But at the same time they accused blacks of being "clannish." No doubt many of them were, in large measure because the experience of segregation had served to convince them that only in autonomy and self-organization could there be dignity and strength. Since interaction with whites had so often occurred in conditions of subordination and humiliation, it was better, they may well have reasoned, that blacks should stick together. The average white longshoreman no doubt regarded such a preference with relief. It saved him the necessity of working with "them"; but it also reinforced his sense that blacks were different, that they were beyond the boundaries of the waterfront's accustomed way of life and networks of camaraderie. For union officials, however, the tendency toward self-segregation was perplexing, especially in San Francisco, where Local 10 officials had waged a successful campaign to integrate work gangs. "There is a tendency . . . for the Negro worker to ask for separate working gangs," said one union official. He was confused, he admitted, that "the initiative for segregated [gangs] has come from Negro workers," and he called it "a pretty serious trend."[51]

The same union official made another observation which demonstrates that while "race" and "culture" were closely intertwined, it was in complex ways. For in confronting the presence of African American migrants from the South, even black workers from the generation of the 1930s perceived difference and often withheld the hand of solidarity. "Older Negro union men resent the newcomers and won't have anything to do with them," said the ILWU official. Black warehouseman Eugene Lasartemay, a veteran of the Big Strike, explained that "the influx of new people really made a great difference and it amazed us. Because their culture was different. . . . It was a while before we became accustomed to . . . [the] loud talking on the bus, eating on the bus, loud talking on the streets; [and] in the churches it was really loud." This was a common theme in the encounter between southern blacks and their northern counterparts. Even before the wartime migration, the *California Eagle,* an African American newspaper in Los Angeles, had referred to "unseemly loudness in public places by Negroes fresh from the lower strata of Southern life," and had declared that "veteran black citizens of California must take an active part in training incoming Negroes from the South in basic rules of culture."[52]

When World War II ended, and employment opportunities on the docks declined significantly, many whites wondered how they could restore the comfortable working environment that the war had disrupted, how—in other words—they could make their union "lily white" again. Black workers' low seniority, together with the conscious policies of the union leadership, led to a dramatic reduction in the number of African Americans in Local 13; and the use of sponsorship as the means of entry to the union when jobs did become available only reinforced this pattern of racial exclusion. For blacks, it was further evidence of racism. To whites, however, it was entirely natural that they would want their family and friends—men who were readily identifiable as "us"—to inherit the wages and conditions the union had won. Thus, George Love remembered the Unemployed 500 controversy not as a conflict between blacks and whites but as an issue of "people who live close" versus "out-of-towners." "I never considered it racial," he said in 1989. Rather, "it was a move . . . to go back to what [Local 13 had] always done. That to be a longshoreman, . . . number one, you [had to] be local and usually a relative." From Love's perspective, "you were some kind of guy if you *didn't* go to bat for your own family. And if you didn't have any sons or brothers, then [you'd] go for [your] fellow member's sons and brothers. That's what made it a good union."[53]

The way black workers responded to their deregistration and subsequent exclusion from Local 13 only reinforced whites' sense that African Americans operated outside the moral code that prevailed in the ILWU. For in 1947, a sizable number of blacks—nearly a hundred—turned to the legal system for restitution. They did so, apparently, after exhausting all avenues open to them within the local union. Initially, they sought assistance from an attorney in filing an appeal to the international executive board; and at this stage, their lawyer hastened to assure Harry Bridges that the men who had sought his assistance were "not in any sense belligerent, but rather . . . their conduct in every respect and at all times has represented the highest type loyalty toward Local No. 13."[54]

But eventually the members of the Unemployed 500 sought to resolve an intra-union dispute by going outside the channels of the ILWU altogether. Some filed a complaint with the National Labor Relations Board; others sued the union for damages. They did so at a time when the passage and implementation of the Taft-Hartley Act called into question the legitimacy of the very institutional mechanisms that the '34 men had fought so tenaciously to win. Decasualization, union control of hiring, and the equalization of earnings among "regular" longshoremen—this was the legacy of the Big Strike. The hiring hall, in particular, had become the "cornerstone" of the union. Without it, said one observer, "the ILWU would cease to exist." But in outlawing the "closed shop," Taft-Hartley made the legal status of the hiring hall tenuous at best and, in general, placed the union on the defensive. Especially after the onset of a Republican presidential administration in 1953, the NLRB appeared willing to embrace the notion that any man who had worked as a casual for a day or two could claim an "employment right in the industry," thereby undermining union control of hiring. Bridges complained in 1955, "There isn't a waterfront local union today which isn't up to its ears in sessions with its . . . lawyers, . . . seeking out a formula which will meet port manpower needs without saddling us with Taft-Hartley charges and damage suits." "Over the past years," union attorney Norman Leonard added, "dozens of charges of discrimination have been filed against both the union and the employers," because of openings in this direction created by Taft-Hartley. The union "aimed at being fair to all concerned," said Leonard, but could not permit "a few casuals, 'free riders,' or disgruntled individuals to take advantage of the situation."[55]

The case of the Unemployed 500 had arisen before the passage of the Taft-Hartley Act, but those who went to "the law" did so afterwards. In the minds of Local 13's overwhelmingly white membership, the blacks who sued the ILWU were "disgruntled individuals," and worse. Not only were they refusing to accept the union's authority, but they appeared to be aligning themselves with an array of external forces that threatened the survival of the very instruments that the '34 men had won through blood sacrifice. Thus, a Portland longshoreman expressed a sentiment that must have been shared by many of his fellow unionists in San Pedro when he declared that "anyone who is taken into this union and then sues it is an enemy of mine."[56]

* * *

Although white and black workers defined themselves, and each other, in racial terms, the saga of Local 13 was not merely a story in black and white. For from the very beginning of the union's resurgence on the Los Angeles waterfront, Mexican Americans were a part of the dock labor force; at least some of them were charter members of the San Pedro longshore local and active participants in the 1934 strike. After the strike, 2,049 men were declared eligible for registration as regular longshoremen; about eighty of them—or more than 4 percent—were Mexican Americans. Most, but not all, of these men worked in lumber gangs, partly because they preferred working with their *compadres,* partly because labor in the lumber mills and yards adjacent to the harbor was considered the province of "Mexicans." Mexican Americans were excluded from key jobs such as driving lifts and winches in the thirties, and the existence of "segregated" gangs also suggests an element of discrimination. But Tony Salcido, who joined his father, five brothers, and several cousins on the waterfront, recalled that even after gangs became "mixed," Mexican Americans preferred to work not only with family members but with neighbors, and friends of the same race or ethnicity. "The normal tendency, at least . . . for me," he said, "was to seek out another Mexican-American fella, because in the first place you grew up with him, and those were your friends."[57]

As the example of the Salcido family suggests, Mexican Americans gradually became a formidable presence in Local 13. They faced, and overcame, discrimination; in fact, numerically and politically, they would eventually dominate the local—which makes it all the more remarkable that in the reflections of white and black longshoremen, and in discussions of the union's internal life well into the 1960s, Mexican Americans were rarely part of the frame of reference. "Race relations" meant the relations between blacks and whites; and the Los Angeles waterfront was, allegedly, "lily white" until the appearance of African Americans during World War II.[58]

As the competition for place and preferment on the docks became a three-way affair, the dominant white majority saw "Mexicans" as far less threatening than blacks. For many whites, blacks represented the negation of the status and self-image they cherished. But Mexican Americans increasingly were regarded as an *ethnic* group—akin to Scandinavians, Italians, and even, perhaps, "hay shakers" from the Midwest—and hence as a legitimate presence on the docks and in the union's internal life. In such circumstances, Mexican Americans apparently saw no advantage for themselves in uniting with blacks to challenge the power of the white majority. On the contrary, such an alliance may well have appeared to be a path toward marginalization and exclusion. And relative to blacks, Mexican Americans had a number of distinct advantages. In 1940, they outnumbered blacks by about three to one in the city, and their margin would increase over the years. Their community base was not only larger but much more cohesive. Indeed, despite the persistence of segregation and discrimination, Los Angeles was becoming the "Mexican capital of the United States."[59]

Above all, Mexican American longshoremen were on a mission to establish an "ethnic niche" on the waterfront, as a means to enhance the economic security of their families and *compadres*. In what became a de facto competition with blacks, they mixed more easily with whites and in many cases shared some of their prejudice toward African Americans. Moreover, they used their greater seniority, and greater access to the levers of power within the union, to take care of their own. In the process, their very success contributed to the continued marginalization of blacks.[60]

* * *

Finally, there is the case of Walter Williams. The conspicuous failure of white rank-and-filers and the Local 13 leadership to accord him the recognition as a fellow worker that he deserved suggests that the containment and exclusion of African Americans was at the heart of their agenda. When he went to work on the docks, Williams was not an "out-of-towner"; and he had already distinguished himself as a union activist, and as a spokesman for a cause with which the ILWU as an institution was closely associated. Although born in Atlanta, Georgia, he had come to Los Angeles with his mother and brother as a one-year-old, and had lived in the city ever since. He graduated from Thomas Jefferson High School and even attended junior college for a semester before economic necessity forced him into the job market. Eventually, he worked in a foundry, where he encountered the CIO and became an organizer for its Industrial Union Council in Los Angeles. When he went to work at Calship, he was a leader in the fight against the Jim Crow auxiliaries to which the Boilermakers' union consigned its black members. In fact, he served as chairman of the Ship Yard Workers Committee for Equal Participation. In that capacity he addressed the President's Committee on Fair Employment Practice, and denounced the "auxiliary policy of the Boilermakers [a]s a contradiction to the principles which we are fighting for."[61]

Here, then, was a man with obvious leadership qualities and experience in the trade union movement. So why not welcome him into the ILWU? Bridges himself recommended that "record and background," in the union and beyond, should be a factor in deciding when to reinstate men who had withdrawn from Local 13. Indeed, the ILWU would become famous as a "haven for heretics," and would often apply political criteria in selecting registrants from among the enormous number of applicants for employment on the docks. But from the very beginning Williams identified with the aspirations and grievances of the black workers who came to the waterfront with him. He was, in other words, one of "them." In fact, he quickly became their leading spokesman. He took the initiative in organizing members of the Unemployed 500 to protest their treatment, and eventually filed an NLRB complaint against the union. But as one who had a strong commitment to unionism, he refused to sue the ILWU for damages; and he sought to persuade others to join him in that refusal. "The black fellas were split on the matter," he recalled. "I influenced quite a few of . . . the guys—in fact, most of [them]—not to sue for damages. Because the union had to survive. The idea was to get back into the industry and to help build the union."[62]

But within Local 13 Williams remained an outsider, a spokesman for black longshoremen but not—in any formal or widely accepted sense—for the union itself. Finally, he and two other African Americans from San Pedro journeyed north to San Francisco to present their grievances to Harry Bridges, and to ask for the ILWU president's assistance in fighting racial discrimination in Local 13. He recalled that during the discussion he had said to Bridges,

> "We want to know . . . what your position is going to be. . . . If you're opposed to [discrimination], we would like some assurance that you're going to help us fight it."
>
> He looked at us, had his legs crossed at his big desk there. And he says, "I'm not going to upset Local 13 over the race question."
>
> . . . Boy, that was a shock to me. . . . So I blinked and said, "Well," I said, "We're not asking you to upset the local over anything! We're expecting support from you, that's all, if the [contract] language means anything. . . . You're obliged to join with the employers to enforce the no discrimination language in the contract! That's what the contract says and that's what it means!"
>
> And he says, "Well, I'm not about to join the employers to force Local 13 to do anything." So that just about knocked the wind out of our sails. We knew what the score was. So I said, "Come on, let's get the hell out of here!"
>
> [And] Harry says, "Well, . . . I guess you guys will go to the courts now." He says, "That's what you usually do."[63]

Was this the same Harry Bridges who was lionized in the San Francisco civil rights community, and whom a black minister had called a "Godsend among men"? As Bridges himself would have put it, "of course." But for his seemingly contradictory stance to make sense, it must be understood in the context of the ILWU's internal politics. In San Francisco, principle, practical necessity, and political expediency merged in a way that reinforced Bridges's commitment to the union's black members. He was, of course, an outspoken advocate of the goal of racial equality. Moreover, as the war in the Pacific theater heated to the boiling point, the frenetic expansion of the San Francisco labor market meant that thousands of blacks, and many whites as well, found employment on the docks. As a result, the relatively homogeneous membership of Local 10 gave way to a more diverse and ideologically fragmented body politic. In 1947, a "right-wing" slate won control of the local and immediately developed a program that, in some respects, was sharply at odds with that of Bridges and his allies on the Left. Under the new regime, the *Local 10 Longshore Bulletin* began displaying an American flag on the front page, with the words "God Bless America" emblazoned underneath it. In an implicit rebuke to Bridges, who was becoming increasingly critical of United States foreign policy in the escalating cold war, the bulletin's editor announced that he had no interest in "Saudi Arabia, Karachi, Pakistan or Moscow," but was concerned only with "seeing that the brothers make a few more coconuts." Since the new leadership had the support of many whites, old-timers and newcomers alike, Bridges looked for political allies, and a solid base of support, among the black segment of the membership. Black long-shoremen would become his loyal allies in the union's internal battles, and their substantial presence in Local 10 served to reinforce its progressive reputation.[64]

In San Pedro, however, the political situation was dramatically different, and it elicited a different response from Bridges. Al Langley believed that many of San Pedro's '34 men became "rather conservative, after they [got] what they wanted." But he also acknowledged their continuing militancy on the job, to the point where "we just said, 'This is the way it is.' And that's the way it was." Moreover, the *official* culture of Local 13 remained progressive during World War II and the immediate postwar years. Even as the local's white majority was seeking to contain and marginalize African American newcomers to the waterfront, the Local 13 *Bulletin* noted with pride that "our organization . . . has always been in the forefront of every labor battle and progressive movement." It reaffirmed the local's support for the *People's World,* the Communist Party newspaper on the West Coast. It even denounced race hatred and declared that "we Trade Unionists must be the vanguard in fighting against discrimination." Indeed, only a week after the deregistration of the Unemployed 500, President L. B. Thomas informed Bridges that the Local 13 leadership had been "very successful" in encouraging members to take a day off from work on May 1 in order to participate in Los Angeles's May Day parade.[65]

Compared to Local 10, though, Local 13 had always been notoriously independent and was, by reputation, "very rebellious" and "anti-Bridges." In June 1934, it had been the only major longshore local to vote in favor of a compromise proposal that would have ended the Big Strike prematurely, with many of the longshoremen's key demands unmet; and in 1960, it was the only major local that voted against the Mechanization and Modernization Agreement (M & M), this time by a substantial margin. Bridges may have had "a chip on his shoulder" in regard to Local 13, as some of its members believed, but he also recognized the necessity of maintaining lines of communication with a local that remained vital to the ILWU and its identity.[66]

Bridges's willingness to accommodate himself to the political realities in Local 13 was no doubt strengthened by the fact that the San Pedro leadership was made up of veteran longshoremen who in many cases had fought the good fight in 1934, and certainly had done so in subsequent conflicts with the employers. However much the ILWU president objected to policies that marginalized African Americans in Local 13, he regarded the leadership and white rank and file as fellow workers with whom he had shared much travail and triumph in building the union. But the blacks in Local 13 were not only newcomers, they were a politically insignificant force; and many of them had violated the ILWU's moral code by going to "the law" and suing the union. This pattern—of blacks as an alienated and marginal element who looked for allies outside the union to resolve their grievances—would continue for many years in Local 13, and there was no political payoff for Bridges in aligning himself with such a force. Thus, at the same time he was aiding and abetting the empowerment of black longshoremen in Local 10, he turned his back on Walter Williams and the legitimate grievances of black workers in Local 13. Fortunately for him, his union's reputation as an ally of the cause of black freedom was forged in the San Francisco Bay Area's longshore and warehouse locals, and in Hawaii. From the vantage point of San Pedro, however, there was good reason to question the ILWU's claim to be "known far and wide for its progressive outlook on civil rights."[67]

In the final analysis, then, the ILWU's record on race was a contradictory one, and in this regard it had much in common with other CIO unions. At the leadership level, the organization was aggressively committed to the cause of racial equality; its widely articulated stance and many resolute actions earned the ILWU much praise for its civil rights record. But the leadership was not entirely free to impose its will upon a sometimes resistant, and famously unruly, rank and file. On the contrary, Bridges and other union leaders were constrained not only by their principled commitment to local autonomy and their belief in rank-and-file democracy but also by practical considerations that mandated the choice of institutional self-preservation over what may have appeared at times to be a quixotic attachment to principle. In the case of San Pedro (and, even more so, Portland), the "Lords of the Docks" fought to hang on to the privileges that accrued to "whiteness" and sought to use the instruments they had forged in the heroic class combat of 1934 to protect themselves and those they defined as "our kind" from the demands of African Americans for equal access to the society's resources. It is only a part of the ILWU's history, but it's a story that is very much in the American grain.

Notes

I am deeply indebted to Nancy Quam-Wickham and, especially, to Antonio (Tony) Salcido. Thanks also to Eric Arnesen, Bob Cherny, Howard Kimeldorf, Robert Marshall, David Olson, Harvey Schwartz, Jordy Urstadt, Gene Vrana, Walter Williams, and Cal Winslow.

1. CIO resolutions quoted in Michael K. Honey, *Southern Labor and Black Civil Rights: Organizing Memphis Workers* (Urbana, 1993), 120.

2. Lizabeth Cohen, *Making a New Deal: Industrial Workers in Chicago, 1919–1939* (New York, 1991), 337; Herbert Hill, "Race, Ethnicity and Organized Labor: The Opposition to Affirmative Action," *New Politics* n.s. 1 (1987): 33. Other recent contributions to this debate, focusing on CIO unions during the CIO era, include Kevin Boyle, "'There Are No Union Sorrows That the Union Can't Heal': The Struggle for Racial Equality in the United Automobile Workers, 1940–1960," *Labor History* 36 (1995): 5–23; Michael Goldfield, "Race and the CIO: The Possibilities for Racial Egalitarianism during the 1930s and 1940s," *International Labor and Working-Class History* 44 (1993): 1–32; Rick Halpern, "Interracial Unionism in the Southwest: Fort Worth's Packinghouse Workers, 1937–1954," in *Organized Labor in the Twentieth-Century South,* ed. Robert H. Zieger (Knoxville, 1991), 158–82; Honey, *Southern Labor and Black Civil Rights;* Karl Korstad, "Black and White Together: Organizing in the South with the Food, Tobacco, Agricultural & Allied Workers Union (FTA-CIO), 1946–1952," in *The CIO's Left-Led Unions,* ed. Steve Rosswurm (New Brunswick, 1992), 69–94; Robert Korstad and Nelson Lichtenstein, "Opportunities Found and Lost: Labor, Radicals, and the Early Civil Rights Movement," *Journal of American History* 75 (1988): 786–811; Nelson Lichtenstein, "Life at the Rouge: A Cycle of Workers' Control," in *Life and Labor: Dimensions of American Working-Class History,* ed. Charles Stephenson and Robert Asher (Albany, 1986), 237–59; Bruce Nelson, "Organized Labor and the Struggle for Black Equality in Mobile during World War II," *Journal of American History* 80 (1993): 952–88; Bruce Nelson, "Class, Race, and Democracy in the CIO: The 'New' Labor History Meets the 'Wages of Whiteness,'" *International Review of Social History* 41 (1996): 351–74; Robert J. Norrell, "Caste in Steel: Jim Crow Careers in Birmingham, Alabama," *Journal of American History.* 73 (1986): 669–94; Nancy Quam-Wickham, "Who Controls the Hiring Hall? The Struggle for Job Control in

the ILWU during World War II," in *CIO's Left-Led Unions,* ed. Rosswurm, 47–67; Judith Stein, "Southern Workers in National Unions: Birmingham Steelworkers, 1936–1951," in *Organized Labor in the Twentieth-Century South,* ed. Zieger, 183–22; Thomas J. Sugrue, "Crabgrass-Roots Politics: Race, Rights, and the Reaction against Liberalism in the Urban North, 1940–1964," *Journal of American History* 82 (1995): 551–78.

3. In 1961, and again in 1966, the ILWU and West Coast employers represented by the Pacific Maritime Association signed Mechanization and Modernization Agreements (M & M) that offered the guarantee of lifetime employment to the "regular" (as opposed to the "casual") longshore labor force. The dramatic relaxation of restrictive work rules (modernization), in combination with the introduction of new technology (mechanization), reduced the number of "regular" longshoremen by 40 percent in the next twenty years. On M & M and its effects, see William Finlay, *Work on the Waterfront: Worker Power and Technological Change in a West Coast Port* (Philadelphia, 1988), 6, 60–67.

4. In framing and addressing this question, I am especially indebted to David R. Roediger, *The Wages of Whiteness: Race and the Making of the American Working Class* (London, 1991); and Robin D. G. Kelley, "'We Are Not What We Seem': Rethinking Black Working-Class Opposition in the Jim Crow South," *Journal of American History* 80 (1993): 75–112.

5. Bruce Nelson, "Class and Race in the Crescent City: The ILWU, from San Francisco to New Orleans," in *CIO's Left-Led Unions,* ed. Rosswurm, 24; Sterling D. Spero and Abram L. Harris, *The Black Worker: The Negro and the Labor Movement* (New York, 1931), 182–205, quoted on 183, 199; A. Philip Randolph to George Meany, Oct. 9, 1961, A. Philip Randolph Papers, box 23, folder on Labor, Civil Rights, and the AFL-CIO, General, 1960–68, Manuscript Division, Library of Congress, Washington, D.C. See also Herbert Hill, "Labor and Segregation," *New Leader,* Oct. 19, 1959, 3–4. Hill described an "unmistakable pattern of blatant discrimination in the New York harbor."

6. Bruce Nelson, *Workers on the Waterfront: Seamen, Longshoremen, and Unionism in the 1930s* (Urbana, 1988), 133; Lester Rubin, *The Negro in the Longshore Industry,* The Racial Policies of American Industry, report no. 29 (Philadelphia, 1974), 136–41; Herbert R. Northrup, *Organized Labor and the Negro* (New York, 1944), 152–53.

7. On the Big Strike, see Irving Bernstein, *Turbulent Years: A History of the American Worker, 1933–1941* (Boston, 1970), 252–98; Howard Kimeldorf, *Reds or Rackets? The Making of Radical and Conservative Unions on the Waterfront* (Berkeley, 1988), 99–110; Charles P. Larrowe, *Harry Bridges: The Rise and Fall of Radical Labor in the United States* (New York, 1972), 32–93; Nelson, *Workers on the Waterfront,* 127–55; Mike Quin, *The Big Strike* (Olema, Calif., 1949); David Selvin, *A Terrible Anger: The 1934 Waterfront and General Strike in San Francisco* (Detroit, 1996).

8. Nelson, *Workers on the Waterfront,* 114–16, 123–25; *Waterfront Worker,* Oct. 3, 1933; Robert W. Cherny, "Harry Bridges, Labor Radicalism, and the State" (paper delivered at a conference on "Harry Bridges and the Tradition of Dissent among Waterfront Workers," University of Washington, Seattle, Jan. 29, 1994), 5; *Dispatcher,* Dec. 18, 1942, 7.

9. Kimeldorf, *Reds or Rackets?* 146–51, quoted on 146; "Note for File," Dec. 5, 1946, ILWU History Files, folder on Membership Statistics-Negroes; Lincoln Fairley to

David Mitchell, Jan. 3, 1951, ibid.; [Lincoln Fairley], "Memorandum, Subject: Estimate of Negro Membership in ILWU as of January 1, 1964," Mar. 17, 1964, ibid., folder on Minorities-Longshore, International Longshoremen's and Warehousemen's Union Archives, Anne Rand Research Library, International Longshoremen's and Warehousemen's Union, San Francisco (hereafter, ILWUA).

10. "American Minorities and the Case of Harry Bridges" (pamphlet, n.d.), ILWU History Files, folder on Minorities-Blacks, 1960, ILWUA; *San Francisco Sun-Reporter,* Sept. 29, 1951, 10; Cy W. Record, "Willie Stokes at the Golden Gate," *Crisis* 56 (1949): 188. See also Albert S. Broussard, *Black San Francisco: The Struggle for Racial Equality in the West, 1900–1954* (Lawrence, 1993), 156. Broussard states that "as far as blacks were concerned, the ILWU stood head and shoulders above other Bay Area locals in virtually every respect."

11. Lincoln Fairley to David Mitchell, Jan. 3, 1951; "Per Cent Distribution of Hawaiian Sugar and Pineapple Workers by Race; ILWU Members, 10/46," Dec. 5, 1946, ILWU History Files, folder on Membership Statistics-Negroes, ILWUA; Steve Rosswurm, "Introduction: An Overview and Preliminary Assessment of the CIO's Expelled Unions," in *CIO's Left-Led Unions,* ed. Rosswurm, 3–4.

12. Harvey Schwartz, "A Union Combats Racism: The ILWU's Japanese-American 'Stockton Incident' of 1945," *Southern California Quarterly* 62 (1980): 161–76, quoted on 166, 169.

13. Robert W. Cherny, "The Making of a Labor Radical: Harry Bridges, 1901–1934," *Pacific Historical Review* 64 (1995): 363–88; International Longshoremen's and Warehousemen's Union, *The ILWU Story: Two Decades of Militant Unionism* (San Francisco, 1955), 62–63. Important studies that illuminate the Communists' role in the struggles of African Americans include Nell Irvin Painter, *The Narrative of Hosea Hudson: His Life as a Negro Communist in the South* (Cambridge, Mass., 1979); Mark Naison, *Communists in Harlem during the Depression* (Urbana, 1983); Korstad and Lichtenstein, "Opportunities Found and Lost"; Robin D. G. Kelley, *Hammer and Hoe: Alabama Communists during the Great Depression* (Chapel Hill, 1990); and Honey, *Southern Labor and Black Civil Rights.*

14. Harry Bridges to Officers and Executive Board Members, Local 10, ILWU, Oct. 9, 1947, ILWU, Officers' Correspondence, 1934–1977, box 18A, folder on Local 10 Correspondence, 1944–50, ILWUA; U.S. Congress, House of Representatives, Committee on Merchant Marine and Fisheries, *Study of Harbor Conditions in Los Angeles and Long Beach,* Hearings, Oct. 19, 20, and 21, 1955 (Washington, D.C., 1955), 325.

15. *Local 10 Longshore Bulletin,* Feb. 19, 1948; U.S. Congress, House of Representatives, Committee on Merchant Marine and Fisheries, *Study of Harbor Conditions in Los Angeles and Long Beach,* 328–29; Record, "Willie Stokes at the Golden Gate," 175; Davis McEntire and Julia R. Tarnopol, "Postwar Status of Negro Workers in San Francisco Area," *Monthly Labor Review* 70 (1950): 616. Bridges's proposal in this instance makes it clear that, contrary to Howard Kimeldorf's suggestion in *Reds or Rackets?* he did not advocate a system of "superseniority" for black workers. See Kimeldorf, *Reds or Rackets?* 147–48.

16. *Local 13 Bulletin,* n. d. [July 1951]; William W. Pilcher, *The Portland Longshoremen: A Dispersed Urban Community* (New York, 1972), 69; Larrowe, *Harry Bridges,*

368; Ralph Freedman, "The Attitudes of West Coast Maritime Unions in Seattle toward Negroes in the Maritime Industry" (M.A. thesis, State College of Washington, 1952), 47; "Walter E. Williams Oral History Interview," conducted by Tony Salcido, Nov. 10, 1988, and by Tony Salcido and Robert G. Marshall, Oct. 4, 1990, International Longshoremen's and Warehousemen's Union, Local 13, Oral History Project (hereafter, ILWU Local 13 OHP), Urban Archives Center, California State University, Northridge, 84–86. (Since the two interviews are combined in one transcript, I will not make separate reference by date hereafter, but will simply identify the "Walter E. Williams Oral History Interview.") "Oral History Interview of George W. Love," conducted by Tony Salcido, May 16, 19, 30, 1989, ibid., 100.

17. *Portland Oregonian*, Sept. 16, 1959, clipping in ILWU History Files, folder on Minorities-Blacks, 1960, ILWUA; Rubin, *Negro in the Longshore Industry*, 145, 148; Gerald D. Nash, *The American West Transformed: The Impact of the Second World War* (Bloomington, 1985), 99; Edward Balloch Debra, "An Injury to One: The Politics of Racial Exclusion in the Portland Local of the International Longshoremen's and Warehousemen's Union" (B.A. honors thesis, University of Oregon, 1992), 24, 58 (quoted). See also Larrowe, *Harry Bridges*, 366–68; Pilcher, *Portland Longshoremen*, 67–76.

18. Freedman, "Attitudes of West Coast Maritime Unions in Seattle toward Negroes in the Maritime Industry," 47.

19. See, especially, Nelson, *Workers on the Waterfront;* and Kimeldorf, *Reds or Rackets?* Quam-Wickham, "Who Controls the Hiring Hall?" is an important step toward a more balanced view. She recognizes the extent of the ILWU's achievements but, drawing on oral history interviews with black, white, and Mexican American ILWU veterans, is sharply critical of the union's record on race.

20. Nelson, *Workers on the Waterfront*, 157–63; Gregory Harrison, *Maritime Strikes on the Pacific Coast: A Factual Account of Events Leading to the 1936 Strike of Marine and Longshore Unions,* Statement before the United States Maritime Commission, San Francisco, Nov. 2, 1936 (San Francisco, 1936), 21; *Waterfront Worker*, June 24, 1935, 7; *Voice of the Federation*, July 5, 1935, 4, Feb. 6, 1936, 4. See also Herb Mills and David Wellman, "Contractually Sanctioned Job Action and Workers' Control: The Case of the San Francisco Longshoremen," *Labor History* 28 (1987): 167–95.

21. Nelson, *Workers on the Waterfront*, 156–88; *Voice of the Federation*, July 12, 1935, 2.

22. Kimeldorf, *Reds or Rackets?* 141; Al Langley, interviewed by Howard Kimeldorf, Feb. 4, 1982 (hereafter, Langley, interviewed by HK); "Alfred E. Langley Oral History Interview," conducted by Tom W. Brown, Apr. 3, 1984, and by Tony Salcido, May 13, 1986, ILWU Local 13 OHP, 39, 62. Tony Salcido, interviewed by author (via telephone), June 2, 1994. According to the Bureau of the Census, there was one African American longshoreman in Los Angeles in 1940 (down from two in 1930). Walter Williams, who went to work on the waterfront in 1943, recalled that several black dock workers had been "passing" for "white" in the thirties; and this may well explain the discrepancy between the census data and the recollections of veteran longshoremen such as Al Langley and Tony Salcido (United States Department of Commerce, Bureau of the Census, *Fifteenth Census of the United States* [Washington, D.C., 1943], 3:245); Walter Williams, interviewed by author (via telephone), July 15, 1994.

An analysis published in 1967, after extensive investigation by the international union, concluded that "prior to 1943, . . . there was not a single Negro longshoreman employed" on the Los Angeles–Long Beach waterfront. Ben Margolis, "Brief on Behalf of International Longshoremen's and Warehousemen's Union, Local 13," Apr. 4, 1967, 34, ILWUA. Assuming the accuracy of Langley's assertion that two black longshoremen were registered in November 1942, the international union's statement should be modified accordingly.

23. Kimeldorf, *Reds or Rackets?* 142–44; *Local 13 Bulletin,* May 1, 1942, July 9, 1942; Langley, interviewed by HK; "Alfred E. Langley Oral History Interview," 43–45; Margolis, "Brief on Behalf of International Longshoremen's and Warehousemen's Union, Local 13," 35; Bill Lawrence to Agnes Quave, Jan. 5, 1945, ILWU History Files, folder on membership Statistics-Negroes, ILWUA.

24. Arthur Kaunisto, interviewed by Harvey Schwartz, Sept. 23, 1982; Corky Wilson, interviewed by Harvey Schwartz, Dec. 7, 1983, ILWU-National Endowment for the Humanities (NEH) Oral History Project (OHP), ILWUA.

25. Henry Schmidt, *Secondary Leadership in the ILWU, 1933–1966* (Berkeley, 1983), 40–41; Victor Silverman, "Left-Led Unions and Racism: A History of ILWU Local 10, 1940–1960" (undergraduate seminar paper, University of California, Berkeley, 1983), 4–5; Wilson interview; Al Langley, interviewed by Harvey Schwartz, Nov. 19, 1981, ILWU-NEH OHP.

26. Joe Stahl, interviewed by Harvey Schwartz, Dec. 7, 1983; Walter Williams, interviewed by Harvey Schwartz, Mar. 30, 1984, ILWU-NEH OHP.

27. "Walter E. Williams Oral History Interview," 28–30 (on his background), quoted on 20, 30, 61.

28. On the "social ecology of shop-floor conflict" during World War II, the best introduction remains Nelson Lichtenstein, *Labor's War at Home: The CIO during World War II* (New York, 1982), 110–35.

29. Quam-Wickham, "Who Controls the Hiring Hall?" 63; *Dispatcher,* Dec. 18, 1942, 7; John Martinez, interviewed by Harvey Schwartz, Mar. 29, 1984, ILWU-NEH OHP.

30. Quam-Wickham, "Who Controls the Hiring Hall?" 66; "Alfred E. Langley Oral History Interview," 38–40; Langley interview, ILWU-NEH OHP. See also Frank Sunstedt, interviewed by Harvey Schwartz, Mar. 26, 1984, ILWU-NEH OHP. Sunstedt maintained that "any time a black man was about ready to get a gang, the promotions committee members would go around and entice anyone else to get a gang, just to keep a black man out."

31. Bill Lawrence to Harry Bridges, Apr. 24, 1946, ILWU, Officers' Correspondence, 1934–1977, box 18D, folder on Local 13 Correspondence, General, 1945–50, ILWUA.

32. Margolis, "Brief on Behalf of International Longshoremen's and Warehousemen's Union, Local 13," 6; Lawrence to Bridges, Apr. 24, 1946; Harry Bridges to L. B. Thomas, Sept. 8, 1947, ILWU, Officers' Correspondence, 1934–1977, box 18D, folder on Local 13 Correspondence, General, 1945–50, ILWUA.

33. Walter Williams interview, ILWU-NEH OHP; Lawrence to Bridges, Apr. 24, 1946; Arthur D. Guy, Jr. to Harry Bridges, Aug. 28, 1947, ILWU, Officers' Correspondence, 1934–1977, box 18D, folder on Local 13 Correspondence, General, 1945–50, ILWUA; Nash, *American West Transformed,* 96.

34. Lawrence to Bridges, Apr. 24, 1946; Margolis, "Brief on Behalf of International Longshoremen's and Warehousemen's Union, Local 13," 16–20, 25, 28; *Local 13 Bulletin*, July 9, 1942; L. B. Thomas to Harry Bridges, Aug. 9, 1947, ILWU, Officers' Correspondence, 1934–1977, box 18D, folder on Local 13 Correspondence, General, 1945–50, ILWUA.

35. Margolis, "Brief on Behalf of International Longshoremen's and Warehousemen's Union, Local 13," 10; Guy to Bridges, Aug. 28, 1947; Arthur D. Guy, Jr. to International Longshoremen's and Warehousemen's Union, Executive Board, Sept. 16, 1947, ILWU, Officers' Correspondence, 1934–1977, box 18D, folder on Local 13 Correspondence, General, 1945–50, ILWUA.

36. Margolis, "Brief on Behalf of International Longshoremen's and Warehousemen's Union, Local 13," 31–33, 35–36.

37. Ibid., 32; Bridges to Thomas, Sept. 8, 1947; *Local 13 Bulletin*, Dec. 8, 1950; *Dispatcher*, Dec. 22. 1950, 7.

38. Margolis, "Brief on Behalf of International Longshoremen's and Warehousemen's Union, Local 13," 35.

39. Adolph M. Koven, "Arbitrator's Opinion and Award, In the Matter of a Controversy between International Longshoremen's and Warehousemen's Union, Local 13, and Pacific Maritime Association, Involving Walter Williams et al.," June 5, 1970, ILWUA; "Opinion and Decision of Sam Kagel, Coast Arbitrator, In the Matter of an Arbitration between International Longshoremen's and Warehousemen's Union, Local No. 13, Complainant, and Pacific Maritime Association, Respondent, Involving Walter E. Williams et al.," Mar. 11, 1971, ibid.; Margolis, "Brief on Behalf of International Longshoremen's and Warehousemen's Union, Local 13," 36–37.

40. Langley, interviewed by HK; "Opinion and Decision of Sam Kagel," 10.

41. *Local 13 Bulletin*, n.d. [July 1951].

42. Ibid.; "George W. Love Oral History Interview," 38–39, 49; Tony Salcido interview; John Pandora, interviewed by author (via telephone), Jan. 26, 1994. Salcido was registered as part of a group of 1,000 "limited registrants," or "B" men, in 1949; Pandora, as part of a group of 450 "B" men in 1955. Pandora did not recall "a single black" in his group; and after recalling none in his, Salcido checked the list of "B" registrants in 1949 and identified about a dozen men whom he knew to be black, plus a few men of "mixed parentage" who spoke with a "hint of a Cajun twang" and "passed" for white (Tony Salcido to author, June 4, 1994). "Note for File," Dec. 5, 1946; Bill Piercy, Jr. to Lincoln Fairley, Feb. 19, 1964, ILWU History Files, folder on Membership Statistics-Negroes, ILWUA; [Fairley], "Memorandum, Subject: Estimate of Negro Membership in ILWU as of January 1, 1964," Mar. 17, 1964; Langley, interviewed by HK. I am grateful to Tony Salcido for confirming, on the basis of his own research in the records of Local 13, that the local voted in July 1951 to impose the ten-year residency rule for prospective members.

43. "Walter E. Williams Oral History Interview," 117; Tony Salcido to author, June 3, 1994; Tony Salcido interview; Walter Williams, interviewed by author.

44. H. R. Bridges to John H. Williams, Mar. 26, 1946, ILWU, Officers' Correspondence, 1934–1977, box 18D, folder on Local 13 Correspondence, General, 1945–50, ILWUA; Bridges to Thomas, Sept. 8, 1947.

45. On coexistence and conflict among rival systems of meaning, I have learned much from Padraig O'Malley, *Biting at the Grave: The Irish Hunger Strikes and the Politics of Despair* (Boston, 1990); and Kelley, "'We Are Not What We Seem.'"

46. Richard Alan Liebes, "Longshore Labor Relations on the Pacific Coast, 1934–1942" (Ph.D. dissertation, University of California, Berkeley, 1942), 186a-90; Nelson, *Workers on the Waterfront*, 262.

47. Mickey Mahon, interviewed by Harvey Schwartz, Apr. 20, 1983, ILWU-NEH OHP.

48. Ibid.; Mike Davis, *City of Quartz: Excavating the Future in Los Angeles* (London, 1990), 160–64, 398, 401; Kelley, "'We Are Not What We Seem,'" 96–97; Earl Lewis, *In Their Own Interests: Race, Class, and Power in Twentieth-Century Norfolk, Virginia* (Berkeley, 1991), 58. In his study of black migration, Lawrence de Graaf concluded that by the end of the 1930s "Negroes had become much more concentrated in a small section of Los Angeles and were almost totally excluded from large sections of the city and most suburban areas" (Lawrence Brooks de Graaf, "Negro Migration to Los Angeles, 1930 to 1950" [Ph. D. dissertation, University of California, Los Angeles, 1962], 130).

49. Kelley, "'We Are Not What We Seem,'" 93. Kelley, an African American historian, argues that blacks had good reason *not* to work hard. See also Robin D. G. Kelley, "The Riddle of the Zoot: Malcolm X and Black Cultural Politics during World War II," in *Malcolm X in Our Own Image*, ed. Joe Wood (New York, 1992), 155–82.

50. Kaunisto interview; John Mitchell, interviewed by Harvey Schwartz, May 23, 1984, ILWU-NEH OHP; Quam-Wickham, "Who Controls the Hiring Hall?" 63; Stahl interview. On the tradition of "four on and four off," see Finlay, *Work on the Waterfront*, 53–54, 94–95. Finlay found that this practice, which he calls "a form of work rotation or work sharing," still prevailed on the Los Angeles waterfront in the 1980s, even though it was—and had long been—a violation of the collective bargaining agreement. "By accepting this deal," Finlay explains, "employers pay workers . . . a full day's pay for a half day's work. What employers get in return is greater intensity of work from longshoremen during their four hours on while restraining workers as a whole from asserting their interests through the official grievance resolution machinery" (ibid., 94–95).

51. Langley interview, ILWU-NEH OHP; Charles S. Johnson, *The Negro War Worker in San Francisco: A Local Self-Survey* (San Francisco, 1944), 70.

52. Johnson, *Negro War Worker in San Francisco*, 70; Eugene Lasartemay, interviewed by Daniel Beagle and Jan Gilbrecht, May 20, 1981, ILWU-NEH OHP; *California Eagle*, Oct. 12, 1939, quoted in de Graaf, "Negro Migration to Los Angeles," 132.

53. "George W. Love Oral History Interview," 95, 96, 114, 115 (emphasis added). The conception of "turf" that Love articulated in 1989 had by then become a staple ingredient of the "backlash" that political and social analysts wrongly saw as new among northern whites in the mid- and late 1960s. Politicians such as George Wallace, Richard Nixon, and Ronald Reagan would broaden the basis of their electoral appeal by endowing whites' determination to defend their turf with an aura of moral high ground. As Nixon declared in 1972, "There is no reason to feel guilty about wanting to enjoy what you get and what you earn. . . . Those are not values to be

ashamed of; those are values to be proud of. Those are values that I shall always stand up for when they come under attack" (quoted in Thomas Byrne Edsall with Mary D. Edsall, *Chain Reaction: The Impact of Race, Rights, and Taxes on American Politics* [New York, 1991], 97).

54. Guy to Bridges, Aug. 28, 1947; Guy to International Longshoremen's and Warehousemen's Union, Executive Board, Sept. 16, 1947; Walter Williams interview, ILWU-NEH OHP. In his letter to the ILWU Executive Board, attorney Arthur Guy stated that "certain members of the group [had] proceeded to employ the various remedial processes available within the Union to obtain reinstatement." When they failed in that endeavor, "I was employed as legal counsel for the unemployed group on or about the 15th day of July, 1947." By mid-September, ninety-nine members had formally requested that Guy represent them.

55. Walter Williams, interviewed by author; Harold Irving Roth to Local Executive Board, ILWU Local 13, Oct. 28, 1950 (document courtesy of Tony Salcido); U.S. Congress, House of Representatives, Committee on Merchant Marine and Fisheries, *Study of Harbor Conditions in Los Angeles and Long Beach,* 324–25, 345.

56. Debra, "Injury to One," 66. This issue continues to drive a wedge between blacks and whites. In his investigation of the Los Angeles waterfront during the 1980s, Finlay found that a group of black longshoremen sued the Pacific Maritime Association (PMA), charging that access to the much-coveted position of steady crane operator was racially discriminatory. As a result, the PMA and Local 13 "were required to add an affirmative action criterion" in selecting candidates for crane operator training. This challenge to seniority was, says Finlay, "another blow to union solidarity," because "the senior men regard the black workers as interlopers arrogating their job opportunities" (Finlay, *Work on the Waterfront,* 171). See also "Willie McGee Oral History Interview," conducted by Tony Salcido, Feb. 25, 1991, ILWU Local 13 OHP, 21–33.

57. Langley, interviewed by HK; "Men Who Are Eligible for Registration," n.d. [Nov. 1934] (document courtesy of Tony Salcido); Tony Salcido to author, Apr. 15, 1994; Max Chavez, interviewed by Tony Salcido, Dec. 28, 1983, ILWU Local 13 OHP; Henry Gaitan, interviewed by Daniel Beagle and David Wellman, May 14, 1983, ILWU-NEH OHP; Tony Salcido interview.

58. This is true of many of the oral history interviews cited throughout this essay when they discuss matters of race and racial conflict. See also Margolis, "Brief on Behalf of International Longshoremen's and Warehousemen's Union, Local 13," Apr. 4, 1967.

59. Walter Williams, interviewed by author; "Alfred E. Langley Oral History Interview," 87; Nash, *American West Transformed,* 108; Ricardo Romo, *East Los Angeles: History of a Barrio* (Austin, 1983), 170.

60. On the development of a labor market "niche" as a means to further the economic status and security of an ethnic group, see Suzanne Modell, "The Ethnic Niche and the Structure of Opportunity: Immigrants and Minorities in New York," in *The "Underclass" Debate: Views from History,* ed. Michael B. Katz (Princeton, 1993), 161–93; Gaitan interview; Tony Salcido interview; Walter Williams, interviewed by author.

61. "Walter E. Williams Oral History Interview," 22–30; Alonzo Smith and Quintard Taylor, "Racial Discrimination in the Workplace: A Study of Two West Coast

Cities during the 1940s," *Journal of Ethnic Studies* 8 (1980): 42–44; Herbert Hill, *Black Labor and the American Legal System: Race, Work, and the Law* (1977; rpt., Madison, 1985), 185–208, quoted on 200.

62. Bridges to Thomas, Sept. 8, 1947; Larrowe, *Harry Bridges,* 369 (quoted); Walter Williams, interviewed by author; Walter Williams interview, ILWU-NEH OHP.

63. "Walter E. Williams Oral History Interview," 34–35.

64. "American Minorities and the Case of Harry Bridges"; Bruce Minton and John Stuart, *Men Who Lead Labor* (New York, 1937), 179–80; Kimeldorf, *Reds or Rackets?* 143–51; *Local 10 Longshore Bulletin,* Aug. 21, 1947, Feb. 17, 1948; *San Francisco Chronicle,* Jan. 14, 1948, 12; Larrowe, *Harry Bridges,* 366.

65. Langley, interviewed by HK; *Local 13 Bulletin,* Mar. 5, 1942, June 27, 1944, June 28, 1945; L. B. Thomas to Harry Bridges, Apr. 29, 1946, ILWU, Officers' Correspondence, 1934–1977, box 18D, folder on Local 13 Correspondence, General, 1945–50, ILWUA.

66. "Walter E. Williams Oral History Interview," 84; "George W. Love Oral History Interview," 68, 69; Finlay, *Work on the Waterfront,* 60, 86.

67. Finlay, *Work on the Waterfront,* 171; *Dispatcher,* May 5, 1961, 12.

Contributors

Eric Arnesen teaches history and African-American studies at the University of Illinois at Chicago. He is the author of *Waterfront Workers of New Orleans: Race, Class and Politics, 1863–1923* (1991; rpt. Urbana: University of Illinois Press, 1994). He has published on race and labor in the *American Historical Review, Radical History Review, Labor History,* and *International Labor and Working-Class History.*

Colin Davis is an associate professor in the Department of History, University of Alabama at Birmingham. He received his Ph.D. from the State University of New York at Binghamton. His most recent publication is *Power at Odds: The 1922 National Railway Shopmen's Strike* (Urbana: University of Illinois Press, 1997).

Howard Kimeldorf is an associate professor of sociology at the University of Michigan. His research focuses on twentieth-century class formation in the United States, with a particular emphasis on unionization, politics, and worker consciousness. He is currently completing a manuscript on the role of syndicalism in the formation of the American labor movement.

Bruce Nelson teaches history at Dartmouth College. He is the author of *Workers on the Waterfront: Seamen, Longshoremen, and Unionism in the 1930s* (Urbana: University of Illinois Press, 1988) and of a forthcoming study of class, race, and organized labor in twentieth-century America.

Calvin Winslow teaches history at the Center for Worker Education, City College, City University of New York. He has published essays on English and American social history, including "On the Waterfront: Black, Italian and Irish Longshoremen in the New York Harbor Strike of 1919," in *Protest and Survival: Essays for E. P. Thompson* (New York: New Press, 1993).

Index

Books in the Series
The Working Class in American History